Sustainable Wealth

Sustainable Wealth

ACHIEVE FINANCIAL SECURITY IN A VOLATILE WORLD OF DEBT AND CONSUMPTION

Axel Merk

Foreword by
William Poole

WILEY

John Wiley & Sons, Inc.

Published by John Wiley & Sons, Inc., Hoboken, New Jersey.
Published simultaneously in Canada.

For general information on our other products and services or for technical support,
please contact our Customer Care Department within the United States at (800)
762-2974, outside the United States at (317) 572-3993, or via fax (317) 572-4002.

Wiley also publishes its books in a variety of electronic formats. Some content that
appears in print may not be available in electronic books. For more information
about Wiley products, visit our Web site at www.wiley.com.

Library of Congress Cataloging-in-Publication Data:
   Merk, Axel.
      Sustainable wealth : achieve financial security in a volatile world of debt and
consumption / Axel Merk.
         p. cm.
      Includes index.
      ISBN 978-0-470-49658-9 (cloth)
   1. Finance, Personal—United States.   2. Financial security—United
States.   I. Title.
      HG179.M4318   2010
      332.024–dc22
                                                      2009023151

Printed in the United States of America
10 9 8 7 6 5 4 3 2 1

To my children:
Felix, Helena, Katarina, and Lina

Contents

Foreword

Sustainable Wealth is a timely guide for investors, full of common sense and packed with useful information. There is financial heartbreak today. Few of us have come through the financial crisis completely intact. Many have lost their homes, their retirement savings, and their jobs.

We need to remind ourselves how we have managed to lose so much so quickly. Too many of us yielded to the temptation to consume too much and to borrow too much. Some may still have their flat panel televisions and fancy cars but no house and no garage to put them in. It did not have to happen this way. Sensible investing, creating sustainable wealth, would have protected investors even in the face of the financial crisis. And if many more had followed sustainable investment policies, the boom and subsequent bust would never have occurred.

We are, however, where we are. The same practices that would have protected investors from getting carried away during the boom can help us to prosper as the economy recovers from the bust. Consuming and investing wisely now can build sustainable wealth for the future.

The investment climate today is difficult and full of uncertainty. Merk emphasizes that the Federal Reserve's massive credit creation and the federal government's massive debt creation risk an unhappy future of inflation and dollar depreciation. Whether these problems will occur is not yet clear, but the risk is there. Merk explains these risks and how investors can track the likelihood that they will dominate economic outcomes in coming years.

One thing is clear. Investors who believe that the near future will be like the present may make terrible mistakes. Booms aren't sustainable; but busts do not last forever, either. The natural state of the U.S. economy is growth, and growth will come. The entrepreneurial environment in the United States is unparalleled in the world.

Be cautious, diversify across asset classes and regions of the world, but do not bet against the ability of the U.S. economy to adjust and thrive. Axel Merk's book will help you.

April 2009   WILLIAM POOLE
                                                Former Chief Executive,
                                                Federal Reserve Bank of St. Louis

Preface

In a world where the rules of the game seem to change every day; in a world where policymakers throw trillions at problems; in a world that may become increasingly more volatile—how do you save? How do you invest? How do you plan for retirement? And how do you sleep at night without worrying what may happen tomorrow to your investment portfolio? To your *wealth*?

Sustainable Wealth seeks to empower you to achieve your financial goals, no matter how uncertain the future may be. In the first part of the book, I discuss the world we live in, the dynamics that drive this world, and the ways they may affect your finances. I focus on the temptations of our society: *credit, consumption, policy change,* and *complacency.* Once you have read the first part, you will no longer be at the mercy of pundits when interpreting the news, but will be able to put your financial decisions in both a personal and a global context.

In the second part of the book, you will apply these lessons to your personal finances. I start out by *challenging conventional wisdom* before illustrating how to *save and spend in a volatile world. Sustainable Wealth* goes beyond that and shows you *how to invest* when either you or the economy at large is *faced with a crisis;* are you prepared to stick to your college savings or retirement plan?

Sustainable Wealth is about learning a lifestyle. Once you are equipped with an understanding of what drives this world and know how to position yourself in times of turmoil, you are in good shape to reap the benefits of *sustainable investing, sustainable wealth,* and—as pointed out in the final chapter—the *pursuit of happiness.*

Sustainable Wealth is *not* a get-rich-quick guide; call it a "get-rich-slowly" guide, if you will. If you like to see the forest rather than be overwhelmed by the trees, *Sustainable Wealth* is for you. Once you look through the turmoil of the day, focus on your priorities, and take one step at a time, you have everything you need to get to where you want to be. When you have finished reading, *Sustainable Wealth* should become second nature to you. Indeed, if you get the feeling that many of the values discussed are values your grandmother abided by, that's no coincidence; it's because achieving financial security isn't rocket science. You can do it, but you need the courage to tackle your challenges and untangle a confusing and confused world.

Join me and become a wealth sustainer. It's an adventure like no other you've pursued. You and your loved ones are worth it.

INTRODUCTION

Financial stocks led a broad move down in the market on the heels of Geithner's unveiling of the Treasury's bank-rescue plan and Senate passage of the stimulus measure. The Dow Jones Industrial Average dropped by roughly 350 points, or 4.2%, reaching its worst levels of the day in mid-afternoon trading. Bank of America and Citigroup experienced double-digit percentage losses.
—*The Wall Street Journal* market alert, February 10, 2009

I bet that if you had heard this on the radio today, it would have raised your heart rate, however briefly. Thoughts would probably flash through your mind about your money, your financial security, your long-term financial future. Uncomfortable thoughts. What should I do next? Should I do anything at all?

"Fly the airplane!" is what pilots are trained to do in times of crisis. You may remember "Miracle on the Hudson" pilot Chesley Sullenberger, who saved the lives of 154 people when he made an emergency landing on the Hudson River in New York City when both engines lost thrust after hitting a flock of geese. Decades of training helped him prepare to make this appear as a safe landing.

What does flying an airplane have to do with financial headlines? A lot, actually. In today's financial world, the smooth air has virtually disappeared. As we exit the first decade of the 21st century, financial turbulence is everywhere. When turbulence hits, investor preparation should start months, if not years, earlier than the day the markets plunge. And when an unexpected crisis hits out of the blue, keeping one's priorities straight is key.

"Staying the course," as many in the financial community preach, is not the answer—neither is a hyperactive re-juggling of investments. Sustainable wealth is about earning, keeping, growing your nest egg; it's about reaching your goals and being able to leave a legacy. Building and achieving sustainable wealth is a steady lifestyle that will test your endurance from time to time; it is not a trade. I am speaking as a professional investor and active private pilot.

Whether or not you fly airplanes, you're looking for smooth air, too—that is, financial smooth air. How do you find smooth air, altitude, and airspeed for your finances? For your wealth? How do you ensure your retirement, your kids' college tuition, your flexibility to start a business, quit a job, or enjoy the fruits of your labor as you please? How do you leave a legacy of financial security and wealth—rather than debt—to your loved ones, when Wall Street is bouncing your economic Cessna?

That's what this book is about. It's about achieving *sustainable wealth*—that is, financial well-being in a turbulent, debt-ridden, temptation-ridden world so that you can sleep well at night.

Achieving Excellence as a Financial Pilot

A good pilot responds calmly yet effectively to any change in flying conditions. A better pilot anticipates them and adjusts in advance. In that spirit, I'm going to brag a little, and tell you that I predicted the 1999–2000 tech bubble and the 2008–2009 credit crisis early.

Now, my point isn't really to brag. It's to tell you that if you keep a close eye on the conditions and airspace ahead of you, you can predict the turbulence, too. You can avoid it or adjust to it, and as a result, you, too, can achieve sustainable wealth.

Why is it important to achieve and maintain sustainable wealth? Well, you're the manager, leader, chaperone, director, steward—as well as the pilot—of your own finances. You are—and I'll say this over and over—in charge of your own financial destiny; you are the pilot in command; the buck stops with you. You make a lot of financial decisions—what to buy, what to save, what to invest, what you leave as a legacy to your loved ones. Financial decisions are not made all the time, nor every day; in some cases, they are made only once a year. By all means, you may enlist the help of a trusted financial adviser, but *you must* be involved; you cannot outsource your financial well-being and hope for the best. Hope won't prepare you for the rough realities of inflation, taxes, bubbles, and crises; only understanding the world in which we live and preparing for your needs will hold you in good stead.

Very few individuals or professional money managers saw the credit crisis coming. While some predicted a slowdown and others predicted a correction, few foresaw a 40 percent drop in stock prices in 2008, the loss of almost half of the dollar's value against the euro from 2000 to the spring of 2008, the collapse in real estate prices, a threefold swing in oil prices, a freeze of the credit markets, and an unquantifiable drop in the mood and outlook of almost every living and breathing soul with any sort of investible worth. The more you had invested, the more you lost.

So what went wrong?

Somewhere along the way, we lost touch with the reality that we invest and put capital at risk because we see opportunity and value. Here's the problem: People took an overly myopic, hubristic view of each egg in their nest. In other words, once investors owned something, they tended to believe it would appreciate in value even if that belief was not rational. Pundits proclaimed a Goldilocks economy, and we all enjoyed the ride. In a bull market, we tend to feel very smart. Investors assumed the big picture was okay, that real estate prices would go on forever, that inflation would stay steady, that the money made by lending into the real estate and corporate markets was "good" money and would produce the desired economic results, and that everyone would continue to buy U.S. debt to make this all happen.

Few people challenged the conventional wisdom. However, the big picture was not okay, and few looked closely enough to realize that. It's sort of like an astronomer trying to explain the universe by looking only at the stars or planets, while ignoring gravitational and other forces governing their movements. They do get a good look at the star or planet, but they can't explain the universe or predict that a comet may hit the earth sometime in the future. Note, however, you neither need to be an astronomer nor a rocket scientist to make sense of this world.

What do I mean? Bringing this discussion back to Earth, I mean that people lost sight of the larger forces that make economies run. They lost sight of the system. More precisely, they failed to take into account larger forces such as credit, interest rates, consumption, trade, and government policy, as well as even more abstract forces like perceptions and complacencies that shape boom/bust cycles and, more generally, how the economic planets align.

That's where *Sustainable Wealth: Achieve Financial Security in a Volatile World of Debt and Consumption* comes in.

What Is Sustainable Wealth?

First, let's talk about wealth for a moment. You've probably seen a definition similar to the following: *Wealth is what you own, less what you owe.* It's what you have, less your debts. It's your *net worth.* It is cash or other assets that you can use, as you please, now or later.

And that "later" part is important. Many people have high incomes and can afford a lot, so they spend a lot. But are they prepared for the next unexpected expense? College education? Health crisis? The next chance to buy some shares, or some real estate, or a car, cheap? Are they prepared for retirement? In a surprising number of cases—no. They haven't built *wealth*—that is, the untapped potential to purchase what they want, when they want it. Conversely, there are those with modest incomes who seem to be able to afford all they need, have no or little or no debt, and have ample savings to retire on.

However, many Americans have gone the other way. If you own a house with a large mortgage, you don't *actually* own the house; the bank does. You have debt, not wealth. In fact, with real estate prices down and high mortgages, many people have negative net worth. And it's not just Americans as individuals. Indeed, one of my biggest concerns is that the finances of the country are on the road to financial peril; we'll get into that, too. However, I don't just lament the ills of society. This book aims to provide a path to build sustainable wealth in the world we live in.

Sustainable Wealth is hardly the first book on this subject of wealth; it is a favorite topic for book authors and publishers. The bookshelves are lined with titles about building wealth, either by earning more income, spending more wisely, or investing successfully, or some combination of all of the above. They offer relatively simple formulas—build a budget, manage your debt, invest your 401(k), find the best stocks or real estate or funds or, lately, fixed income investments to buy.

Pick up one of these books and you'll come across great ideas from time to time. But those ideas tend to work only until the next economic crisis is upon us. We've seen it before—in the late 1990s, we saw book after book about day trading and buying technology stocks—then came the dot.com bust. Then, in 2005–2006, out came the books about "flipping" houses—then came the real estate bust. Not surprisingly, today's real estate shelf is filling with titles about buying foreclosures and profiting from the credit crisis.

So what's missing? Two things, really. First, most of these books take aim at quick fixes—how to get ahead and make more money now. *Sustainable Wealth* is about lifestyle choices, how to have more wealth 10, 20, or 30 years down the road. Second, these books live in the *micro* world; they deal with specific asset classes, or "planets"—stocks, real estate assets; and how to blend these assets into a portfolio. Little to nothing is made of the global economic "universe" in which these investments exist. Who cares if an investment earns 5 percent if the economic universe is poised to bring a 6 percent inflation rate that will sap the value from your investment, not to mention the taxes one has to pay on the "gains"?

So, then, what is sustainable wealth? I didn't invent the term; it is attributed to Elizabeth M. Parker, who defined sustainable wealth as "meeting the individual's personal, social, and environmental needs without compromising the ability of future generations to meet their own needs." The "meeting needs" part is clear and straightforward, and is in fact the subject addressed in most other books on the financial bookshelf.

What's often overlooked is the second part of the definition, the "without compromising" part. This is very interesting, for it implies that sustainable wealth is not only about us being able to meet our own future needs, but those of our loved ones and of future generations as a whole. In short, I believe we can do better than parting this world with a reverse mortgage, leaving zero equity in a home.

My purpose is not just to coin a term; instead it's to give you a recipe for creating, maintaining, and *sustaining* your financial well-being and, ultimately, your peace of mind. Any recipe that does this should endure even in a difficult economic environment.

Sustainable wealth is about understanding how the greater economic universe works, how it will affect your finances, and how to manage those finances to provide a sustained, comfortable future. It is about managing your financial "planets" within the known forces of the economic universe—the little picture inside the big picture. This "space" is where few personal finance books have gone before.

Ultimately, too many have become slaves of their finances rather than masters of them. There's a saying that those who understand interest earn it; those who don't pay it. I will show you that with good common sense and some insights into what makes the world tick the way it does, you, too, can achieve sustainable wealth.

Many individuals have gone down the wrong path, sacrificing too much of the future for the present or disregarding their future altogether. But there's a greater issue here, one you've probably already heard about: As a nation we're mortgaging our future, one printed dollar at a time, to give ourselves a comfortable present. That's a problem, because it compromises *all our* abilities to provide for our own future needs. So here's an important part of sustainable wealth management: As economic forces and remedies combine to compromise our futures, we need to learn to play "economic defense" to achieve peace of mind in the long term. In times of crisis, we must be particularly prudent with our finances, not be lured into spending with refund checks. The best long-term "economic stimulus" is one that fosters long-term savings and investment—politicians would rather have you spend now to allow them to win the election that's around the corner.

With the sustainable wealth concept in mind, let's look at some of the reasons why the present is proving to be a particularly challenging time to achieve it.

A Volatile World of Debt, Consumption, and Temptation

As we near the end of the first decade of the 21st century, deficits have soared, unemployment has reached levels unseen in almost 30 years, wage growth is elusive, energy prices have led to the first real inflation scare in decades, and real estate prices have plummeted, leading to a credit crisis of proportions not seen since the Great Depression. Worse still, the Federal Reserve and other policymakers scramble to patch up a broken system rather than instill confidence. We cannot rely on the government to fix our personal finances; we must find ways to achieve sustainable wealth independent of what the next government decision may be.

Yet calls for government help are omnipresent; citizens are willing to give up just about anything for another bailout. These calls for help are rooted in deep fear about the uncertainty ahead, about the volatility of the markets that has shattered their investment portfolios, about the volatility of policy decisions that at times makes the government appear rudderless.

A key to understanding the world is to understand what volatility is and how it impacts investors. In a capitalist world, we strive to maximize our profits. We have all heard that as we seek higher returns, the risks also increase. It requires a serious bear market, however, for investors to take the risk part seriously. In essence, volatility is nothing but a metric for expressing risk. As such, volatility is not to be feared, but it must be an integral part of an investor's expectations.

Think of volatility as your pulse: When you go jogging, your pulse will be elevated, but you welcome the cardiovascular exercise as it strengthens your heart. Athletes have a lower resting pulse rate than sedentary people. However, an out-of-shape person who ran a marathon would jeopardize his or her life. One can experience an irregular heartbeat for a variety of reasons. Just as with your personal health, it is imperative that you recognize the warning signs of unreasonable risks and thus volatility early. When you experience an irregular heartbeat, stop the exercise immediately and call for help.

But whereas an elevated pulse is something that's easily recognized—anyone can see their portfolio swinging widely during turbulent times; more dangerous and more difficult to detect early is the unhealthy drop in blood pressure that may be the precursor to a heat stroke. Translated to the markets: The absence of volatility, a perception that the world is risk free, may be the single best warning system for predicting a bubble. The difference between a bull market and a bubble is that a bull market maintains a healthy dose of risk. In contrast, the tech bubble was marked by first tech stocks, then all stocks moving up more or less in tandem; in the ramp up to the credit crisis stocks, bonds, commodities, real estate again all rose together—in a healthy market, in contrast, money typically flows from one asset class to another, or from one sector in the market to another.

Why So Much Volatility Today?

Volatility—as a measure and as an economic experience—has clearly been on the increase lately. Why? To find answers, one must look at the recent boom/bubble/bust cycles—and the response to those cycles. Short answer: Volatility is bound to return to any market as bubbles burst. That's the point when those affected cry for help. What many fail to acknowledge is that the boom sows the seeds for the trouble down the road; the bust is a healthy cleansing of the system. The real trouble starts when individuals remain in denial as the bubble bursts or when policymakers try to stand in the way of market forces. With the best of intentions, unintended consequences tend to make the cure worse than the disease. As we saw in 2008–2009, the temptation to "fix" the housing bust and its impact on the financial industry is simply too great. The problems and their aligned policy temptations have led to unprecedented volatility, which has made it more difficult for us as individuals to achieve financial peace of mind.

To be sure, some of that volatility is a natural outcome of the increased speed of business, enabled by technology, which allows billions of dollars to change direction in a second with the stroke of a keyboard. That volatility is systemic and will not go away. But some of that volatility is brought on by the strong medicines handed down from Washington, D.C., the Federal Reserve, and other places. In this book we'll explain those sources of volatility and what you need to understand about them.

Unintended Consequences

We will go beyond this and discuss the implications of policymakers' attempts to tame this volatility. When one administers strong medicine or tries to change the forces of the universe, inevitably there are unintended consequences that can stand in the way of sustainable wealth, especially if the consequences are not well understood. I will highlight the unintended consequences of good intentions gone wrong throughout the book and help you learn to recognize them. Let me introduce some of them here:

- *We have become serfs to debt.* Our debt, both as individuals and as a nation, has grown out of control. Like a strong medicine, debt is okay, even good when used properly. But too much debt is expensive, it reduces our flexibility, and of course, it has to be paid off someday. Increasing debt brings uncertainty that undermines our economic strength, just as too much medicine can kill the patient.
- *We are pushing the problem farther and farther into the future.* The bow wave out in front is getting bigger. Again as individuals and as a nation, our debt loads are growing and our key industries are getting weaker. Debt is okay if you have a way to pay it back someday, but we have reached the point where

we have to grow our economy at any cost just to service the debt. I liken the present situation to that of a hamster on an ever-faster moving wheel—unless the wheel slows at some point we may simply not be able to keep up. Our kids and grandkids will have to pay the price—a clear violation of the sustainable wealth concept.

- *We are destroying the middle class.* Transitioning to a credit-driven society over the past two decades was great for those who knew how to deal with credit. But an ever-larger number who didn't know how to handle debt fall through the cracks, as they were also much less "shock-resistant" to job losses and other financial surprises. Low interest rates, while designed to give a broader number of people access to credit, actually increased the wealth gap. Worse, as printing money and inflation may be the answer to many of the government's fiscal problems, savers and those financially less sophisticated will suffer the most. Policies, despite their best intentions, risk destroying the social fabric of the country; in the process, resentful voters may increasingly vote populist politicians into office.

- *We threaten the essential premise of capitalism.* Capitalism is a universe that uses natural forces to properly allocate capital to the places where it achieves the best return, creating the greatest benefit both for the individual owners of capital and the society at large. We've been messing with that a lot lately—throwing dollars at overpriced real estate, keeping bad banks and businesses afloat, taking equity stakes in this and that, guaranteeing low-quality investments and loans. The government is playing God in place of the natural forces of the universe; if that keeps happening at the present frenetic pace, the government will eventually own everything and run everything! That's socialism, not capitalism.

The Flight You're About to Embark On . . .

The purpose of *Sustainable Wealth* is to help you make the lifestyle choices necessary to sleep well at night with your financial and investment decisions. This book is about understanding the major trends in a volatile world of debt and consumption that affect your personal finances. At first, the right choices in life may appear to be some of the hardest; but once you focus on what is important to you and understand the dynamics of the world we live in, you will have the confidence to succeed. You won't find hot stock tips to brag about at cocktail parties, but you will earn the respect and admiration of your friends once they realize you are on a sustainable path.

You must be willing to be alert, to learn, and to take action. I predicted both the tech bubble and the credit crisis, but the best prediction doesn't help if you fly into the thunderstorm anyway—that is, if you don't change your behavior. For instance, I fared okay during the tech bubble, but decided to be more assertive "the next time" a major crisis would hit. In anticipation of the credit crisis, I not only changed the way I invested, but re-engineered my business, the way I save for my kids' college education, and the way I save for retirement. I started the process as early as 2003, years before the crisis fully developed and blew out in the open. You, too, can learn how to predict major crises by reading this book.

In the first part of the book, I will discuss today's economic universe by explaining current problems and what has and hasn't worked to address them. Through those explanations you'll gain a better understanding of how all the "moving parts" work together, and you'll learn to recognize the unintended consequences that get in the way of sustainable wealth. You'll learn how it affects you and your finances.

The global economy is explained as a series of "temptations." These temptations—credit, consumption, policy change, and complacency—are areas that both investors and governments can "fall" for, leading to adverse consequences—including a temptation to fall for *more* of that temptation later on. When we take on too much consumer debt, we're taking a bite from the apple of credit temptation. These temptations are described in Part I.

In Part II, I explain how to achieve financial peace of mind and security by guarding against these temptations, and how to insulate yourself from the temptations of others. I cover the basic principles of personal finance and investing, with an emphasis on being in the right place to survive a financial crisis and to ensure long-term—not just temporary—prosperity. If you follow my advice, you'll be calm rather than tense and worried the next time a global or personal financial calamity hits, and you'll have the resources and flexibility to do what you want to do in life. Like a pilot, you'll be able to plan ahead when bad weather approaches, diverting as needed or landing to take cover—it is okay to let an opportunity pass if the risks involved are unclear or outweigh the potential benefits. Like a marathon runner, you may endure some pain along the way, but long-term preparation and conditioning will get you to the finish line with a true sense of accomplishment and an eye forward to the next race.

When it comes to your finances, you are in control—prepare and be ready. *Sustainable Wealth* will tell you how to do that.

PART I

A WORLD OF TEMPTATIONS

In ancient Biblical lore, the world of temptation started with the bite of the apple—and as the familiar story goes, nothing has been the same since. As you'll see in the next four chapters, we as economic individuals and a society have sunk into a dangerous world of economic and policy temptations. Federal budget deficits in the trillions are but one result.

Arguably, these temptations—the temptations of credit, consumption, policy change and complacency—have not only created and perpetuated bad financial habits, but have led to still greater temptations. The temptation of credit has led to a temptation of consumption, which has in turn led us into financial difficulties as individuals and as a nation. To deal with those issues, we've succumbed to the temptation of policy and policy change. Policy change fosters yet another dangerous temptation of complacency—complacency toward risk and the seriousness of our economic problems—and shakes the very foundation of the free market system responsible for our prosperity from the beginning. The cycle may become more vicious, and unintended consequences along the way may create still more economic turmoil.

We've bitten into several bad apples, all of which create volatility, all of which will make it more difficult to create and sustain wealth in the future. Understanding and dealing with these temptations to create a secure financial future is the central challenge of sustainable wealth.

Part I, *A World of Temptations*, puts the four temptations and their consequences on your radar. After reading Part I of this book, you will have a much better understanding of the dynamics driving the economy and, ultimately, your finances.

1

The Temptation of Credit

A pig bought on credit is forever grunting.

—Spanish proverb

Over the past 20 years, the United States has increasingly become a credit-driven society with a credit-driven economy. As recently as 1990, while some consumers ran up their credit cards and many had a mortgage to finance their home, leasing a car or obtaining a loan to buy a car was only starting to become popular. Nowadays, we buy everything on credit, including a mattress or exercise machine; to buy a car, we are lured with zero percent, six-year loans.

Is that a good thing or a bad thing? In the 4th century B.C., Aristotle wrote in his book *Politics*, "the most hated sort [to make money], and with the greatest reason, is usury, which makes a gain out of money itself, and not from the natural use of it. For money was intended to be used in exchange, but not to increase at interest." Christianity, Judaism, and Islam have all tried in vain to prevent the spread of credit. Christians were banned from charging interest through much of history; in the 12th century, Christians were banned from receiving sacraments or a Christian burial if they charged interest. Jews were also banned from charging interest, but the restriction only extended to fellow Jews; as they were also banned from owning land, Jews became merchants and the first bankers, giving loans to Christians. Muslims, to date, are not allowed to charge interest; as a result, Islamic loans are typically structured as profit-sharing agreements. The traditional dislike for credit also extended to ancient China, where usury was prohibited. It wasn't until the Industrial Revolution that interest-bearing loans to facilitate trade became common and accepted practice.

As a result of credit, the economy as a whole gets money to spend now in addition to money it already has. The same goes for your own personal "economy"—credit represents more money to spend in addition to the money you already have. At both levels, it represents an expansion of purchasing power. That has good consequences, but too much of a good thing can mean big problems. Too much money in circulation reduces the value of each unit of that money—that's *inflation*. And when more money is created by credit than can be paid back with current incomes, that leads to (or should lead to) reduction in spending and an economic contraction.

During the credit crisis, or credit "bubble," we saw some of both problems. The access to easy and cheap credit, which has become the standard dose of medicine for economic slowdowns, created—more accurately, amplified—a rise in asset prices. During the early part of 2008, we saw levels of inflation in commodities and asset prices that had not been seen for 30 years. As prices rose, lenders began to see less risk in their lending, and so lent more easily to more borrowers who might not have otherwise qualified. As with most bubbles, everything reversed almost at once, leaving those borrowers who had too much debt and not enough income unable to make their payments. The boom became a bust as more debt went sour, and that cycle fed upon itself. The modern Federal Reserve (or "Fed") uses consumer price inflation expectations as its sole measure on whether to pop a bubble or not; the Fed stood by idle during the boom, because the asset inflation did not translate into an expectation of higher consumer prices. This focus has its shortfalls, as it allowed an unprecedented bubble to build; in the next chapter, on consumer temptations, I will discuss in more detail what held back consumer inflation.

Other forces in the universe were also out of alignment, including consumer spending, asset prices, and risk appraisal. The fact that the United States had already become the largest debtor nation in the world, and the fact that consumer debt was already at record levels helped to accelerate an increase in insolvency and an accompanying deterioration in confidence, hence the downturn in the economy.

In short, credit is a strong economic force; it has tremendous power to expand or contract an economy—the 2008–2009 experience could hardly serve as a better example. Just as credit amplifies U.S. and global economies, it also amplifies your own personal economy. Used wisely, it's a good thing. But if you fall to the temptation of credit and spend too much, it can throw your own economic universe out of balance and lead to far greater problems later.

The Relationship Between Credit and Debt

Credit, in its purest sense, represents a potential, an ability, to borrow money to pay for something. A *credit card* is simply a device for doing that—by buying something on a credit card, you're exercising a promise to pay that amount later. "Later" can be any time; you can pay off the balance at the end of the subsequent billing cycle, with no interest, or you can let the balance roll into the future, incurring interest charges along the way. The "later" may become "never" in case of bankruptcy or death.

Essentially, when credit is used, it becomes debt; credit is a future opportunity, whereas debt becomes a present reality. Credit can be a good thing, for it enables you to buy more goods at a time in the future. But when too much credit is used, it becomes too much debt. The buildup of onerous amounts of debt can naturally get you into economic trouble.

On a global or national scale, *credit* is simply the ability to borrow—or print—more money for governments to spend directly (*fiscal stimulus*) or to put into the banking system so banks can spend it (*monetary stimulus*). Just as for consumers, credit used and spent or placed into the economy becomes debt.

Good Credit, Bad Debt

Imagine, for a moment, a world without credit.

Now, as a consumer, you might be able to get by. You earn money doing whatever you do, and you take that money and buy food and clothing and other basic necessities of life. You rent shelter, so the amount you have to pay is current to the amount used or consumed. Before the days where everyone everywhere had credit, this is how people lived. In fact, you probably lived this way through college, assuming your tuition bills were taken care of elsewhere through savings or scholarships. You didn't have income, so—at least in the pre-1990s "old days"—you probably didn't have credit, because no one figured that you could pay it back once it turned into debt.

As soon as you need something that you can't pay for right away, credit assumes a center-stage role in your economic life. That could be college tuition, if you, your parents, or your grandparents didn't save for it. Or, through the course of life it could be a car or a home or furniture for a home. Credit enables you to purchase those things when you need them and pay them off over time. You can have them and use them, and if you earn enough to pay for them plus the interest accrued, you'll come out okay. If they are things you really need, it makes sense to use credit to buy them. However, if they aren't really needed, then credit is simply enabling you to buy things that you can't afford. Do that enough, and you'll create a debt, which has a rather persistent tendency to grow once it gets started—it's too easy!

Credit can make your own personal economy work better if used to buy things that you need, or things like college tuition that have a greater payoff down the road. But do you really "need" all the things many take out credit for? One can make an argument for college tuition; however, college tuition may be the one bubble yet to burst, as there has been a popular mindset for too long that thinks that the more expensive a college is, the better it must be. At some point, when we cannot afford the tuition anymore, even with the help of loans, college tuition should come down. There's certainly an argument to be made that you don't "need" most of the things you consume. You don't need that TiVo, you don't need that vacation in a five-star resort, you don't need that new pair of sneakers or that pedicure.

As the U.S. economy digests the "credit crisis" of 2008–2009, many are wondering just what the proper role of credit is. It is an important question to ask, as there are pros and cons to credit. There's a saying that those who understand interest charge it; those who don't understand interest pay it. In my humble opinion, a society that embraces credit had better *understand* it—as that society otherwise will pay dearly. If you buy everything on credit, your monthly paycheck may get you much further: you pay $200 for your car and $13 for your mattress every month, rather than waiting until you can pay for them in full. Former Federal Reserve Chairman Alan Greenspan (who was Fed chair from August 1987 through January 2006, and largely oversaw the transition to using credit in every facet of our lives) praised this trend, as it made the U.S. economy more "efficient"—money sitting idle in your bank account is money that does not contribute to economic activity; conversely, when you make a down payment on a loan, you are leveraging the usefulness of that down payment.

But it's a two-edged sword—borrow too much, and the burden of paying back the debt, plus the cost of the interest, can get you in trouble. Too much debt makes a consumer—or a business or a society—more vulnerable to shocks and surprises. A job loss, big medical bill, or car repair is a lot harder to accommodate with a debt burden to service in addition to ordinary, current expenses. If you know how to deal with credit, you may thrive; if you don't, you become a slave of your debt. As a result, easy access to credit without the proper training for those who receive it increases the wealth gap.

The Debt Spiral

So credit, used to fund the right things, can help both a consumer and a business. But used too much, or used for the wrong things, it can lead to trouble. Consumers, businesses, even responsible governments can run out of steam.

Credit excesses create a downward spiral. When consumers or businesses have too much debt, there's a tendency to borrow more, either as a perpetuation of bad habits, or to "clean up" the debt—to consolidate it and make it more current. Remember the push to get you to sign up for a home equity loan during the boom phase of the credit bubble, to "pay off all those bills?" That's an excellent example of the so-called debt spiral. Essentially, the message is "borrow your way out of debt." That sounds like a pretty strange idea, right? I'll come back in Part II of this book to give more pointers on managing personal debt.

Access to credit has major implications for the social fabric of a nation. As a result, it is high time that a public debate be held addressing how much credit we deem is healthy for society as a whole and for the government. Most would quite likely agree that credit plays an important role, provides opportunity, and has contributed to our standard of living; returning to a society based on barter alone is something most would not favor. Conversely, however, the credit bubble has shown that extreme credit may lead to catastrophe. The level of credit in a society is not simply decided by bankers, but influenced by tax and interest rate policies, among others.

To a great extent, it is a political choice. Every citizen should have a view as to whether we want to move further toward a Latin American society, with a thin class of the very wealthy, but the masses living in poverty, or foster a strong middle class. While most have views about how tax policies influence wealth distribution, few are aware that interest rate policies play at least as significant a role: Higher interest rates tend to make for a more robust middle class, as they encourage saving by discouraging borrowing and paying higher returns on the savings; conversely, extended periods of low interest rates lead to a growing wealth gap, with a select few who thrive, but a great many who can't cope with the easy credit.

Credit as Money

What is credit then? Credit, simply defined, is the creation of money to be paid back in the future. Let's look at what we commonly understand as credit. The most basic form of credit is currency in circulation—the dollar bills in your pocket. It's credit because currency represents a loan issued by the Federal Reserve to you. The money printed by the Fed is credit; a dollar bill is a Federal Reserve Note, the most basic form of "money supply." The only peculiar thing about this most basic form of credit is that it is not redeemable unless the Fed chooses to retire the bills. If you were to take your dollar bill to a bank or the Fed itself, all you would get in return would be a sheet of paper stating that you may exchange it back for a dollar bill. I'll talk more about the Fed's ability to print money further below.

How Banks Create Credit

Most of us think of credit as what happens when a bank issues a loan. Banks take deposits and use them as a base to extend loans. Banks lend out a multiple of what they have as deposits. That bank lending is money creation, too; money is not physically printed, but created nonetheless. And indeed, the person receiving the loan will buy something with it; let's say the borrower took out a loan to buy a car. The car dealer may then deposit the proceeds from the car sale with his bank. As that is a deposit, the bank can make fresh loans. While an initial deposit may be leveraged about 10 to 1, by the time every loan has made it through the system as new deposits, an initial $1 deposit may increase to serve about $100 in loans. Healthy banks are crucial to a credit-driven society, as they are a key engine for creating credit.

How the Fed Creates Credit

The Fed influences the amount of credit available, not only by printing currency but by other means. The Fed also sets the reserve ratio, the amount banks must keep as collateral when making loans. The Fed is a membership-based organization, and member banks are required to keep a deposit at the Fed.

But Fed money creation goes a step further. Whenever the Fed buys something, it creates the money—it's merely a bookkeeping entry, done with the stroke of a keyboard. When the Fed buys a typewriter or a car for a staff member, the Fed provides a stimulus to the economy. To stimulate economic growth, the Fed is better known for buying securities, traditionally Treasury securities, from banks. When the Fed buys a Treasury bill from a bank, the Fed receives the T-bill and the bank receives cash; this is all done electronically through bookkeeping entries—no physical cash changes hands. With the cash received, the banks can make fresh loans. This activity is commonly referred to as "adding liquidity" to the banking system. Conversely, if the Fed wants to reduce the credit available in the economy, it can sell securities to banks, typically Treasury securities. By selling securities to banks, the Fed "drains liquidity"—it removes cash from the banks, reducing the banks' ability to extend loans. This adding to and draining of liquidity is what is referred to as the Fed's *open market operations*; typically, the goal of these operations is to get short-term interest rates to where the Fed targets them to be.

How Credit Is Created (and Taken Away) by Everyone Else

After the tech bubble burst in 2000, the Fed lowered target interest rates from 6 ½ percent over three years to as low as 1 percent to stimulate the economy. In 2004, the Fed started raising interest rates again. Money supply, however, continued to grow. That's because credit creation is not limited to banks. Homeowners, too, create money when they borrow against equity in their homes. So do hedge funds when they leverage their investments. In a world where homeowners thought the value of their homes always went up; where banks thought their clients were creditworthy; where hedge funds thought that the more leverage they applied to a trade, the more profitable that trade would be—in such a world, *everyone* created money. What a great world, right? Not so, in fact. Indeed, I like to argue that the Fed lost control of money supply as it allowed the private sector to unleash a credit bubble.

When everyone creates money, the money has to flow some-where; and it did: into real estate, stocks, bonds, commodities, art, and antiques, to name a few areas. Indeed, the best way to spot a bubble is when asset prices go up uniformly across asset classes. Such bull markets make for seemingly very smart investors, but when such moves are not accompanied by an increase in real wages of similar proportions, you may want to be cautious. In a healthy market, money flows from one type of asset—or *asset class*—to another, rather than into all asset classes at once.

Partially because interest rates were so low, banks, hedge funds, pension fund managers—everyone—looked for ways to increase their returns: Pension funds, for example, needed to ramp up their returns to achieve their target returns to pay obligations in the future. The obvious answer was to apply leverage, which seemed like a good idea. How else can you get a 20 percent return when interest rates are in the low single digits? At the peak of the credit bubble, no project seemed too exotic to finance. Banks cre-ated off-balance sheet vehicles—structured investment vehicles (SIVs)—to circumvent reserve requirements and apply even greater leverage than banks take as part of their normal course of business. Characteristically, the risk recorded on the books was merely any accrued losses, rather than the bank's full exposure.

The amount of credit created by the private sector during the boom that recently ended in 2006 creates another problem: While the private sector creates credit, it is also the private sector that takes it away. When former Fed Chairman Greenspan said that cen-tral banks in today's world are "less relevant," that's precisely what he was referring to: If you allow the private sector to create money, the private sector can also destroy money through a process known as *deleveraging*. It's money that simply vaporizes as risk takers from banks to hedge funds to homeowners pare down their risk profile, reduce their debt, and deleverage.

The Power (and Un-Power) of Central Banks

Without going into too much further detail on how money creation works, one should note that when the Fed creates money it can be considered *super money*. What makes it super is this: When the Fed provides capital to the banking system, the banks can then use it to make loans comprised of a multiple of that money. Similarly, when the Fed removes liquidity, it has an amplified effect. That poses a challenge in a highly geared economy. In an economy with highly leveraged consumers and businesses, these borrowers are very interest rate–sensitive. Small increases in interest rates may push consumers "over the cliff"—giving the Fed much less room to maneuver.

Conversely, however, central banks also have a challenge: They can create all the credit—money—they want, but they cannot force the private sector to take it. In an environment where consumers, businesses, and/or banks are scared, they may not want to take on another loan. Financial institutions concerned about their own health may be reluctant to lend; and even if they are healthy, they may not want to provide loans if they are concerned about the health of their clients.

This happened in 2008, and it's part of the reason why the Fed decided to introduce an array of facilities offering funding directly to industry and bypassing banks, ranging from providing funding for consumer loans, automotive loans, home financing, or working capital for major enterprises. But when the Fed provides money

The Fed Plays Favorites

Recently, the Fed has changed course and has begun to pick specific sectors and industries to support. This action goes bluntly against the design of the Fed: Rather than providing "wholesale" money, where the Fed influences the amount of credit in the economy, the Fed is engaged in credit allocation to specific industries. That's traditionally in the realm of Congress to decide where and whether to provide subsidies. Such an encroachment on fiscal policy—not to mention micromanagement—is also fraught with risks. If, say, the Fed provides funding to GMAC, the finance arm of General Motors, GMAC will stay afloat, but the Fed will not encourage private sector participation—no rational person would provide funding to GMAC or any of its competitors at the same terms. So in doing this, the Fed doesn't encourage private sector participation—it replaces it.

directly without using banks as conduits, the Fed's money loses its *super money* effect. That makes the Fed policies extremely inefficient; indeed, even the almighty Fed with its printing press is not powerful enough to provide funding for all economic activity.

A Debtor Nation

The government, too, uses credit extensively; in fact, as of 2008, we have almost $11 *trillion* in national debt. To get a better idea of the size of that figure, it's $35,189 per U.S. resident—and growing, as we'll see in Exhibit 1.2. This number does not include the tens of trillions in unfunded liabilities of Medicare, Medicaid, and Social Security. If these obligations are included, the total debt load has been estimated in the neighborhood of $65 trillion. Relevant to the credit crisis is that the government guarantees, expenditures, and cash injections to recover the economy from the great credit bust of 2007 and 2008 have amounted to over $9 trillion, as of early 2009. To the extent that no money is actually spent, but only guarantees are provided, the money will not show up in national debt statistics.

The gross domestic product (GDP), a measure of all output in an economy, in the United States is around $14 trillion. According to estimates of the Treasury Department in early 2009, total borrowing in 2009 could be as high as 18 percent of GDP. To put this into context, states that are members of the Eurozone have committed themselves to a stability and growth pact that prevents them from raising their debt levels by more than 3 percent of GDP in any one year, although the treaty does allow for exceptions if such increased expenditures are considered temporary.

For you and me and for businesses to borrow money, somebody must lend it. And that requires a lender confident enough in our ability to repay to make the loan. The interest rate reflects the price of the loan, and that goes up or down according to how risky the borrower is and how long the money is borrowed—the loan period. Longer loan periods typically, but not always, bring higher interest rates; it all depends on the market—supply and demand—for short- or long-term loans.

The United States has run budget deficits for all but two years in the last forty. Those deficits are funded by borrowing money, and that money is usually borrowed from lenders who have money. In recent years, China and Japan have topped the list of countries with money to lend, and they've gladly absorbed U.S. debt, because that keeps the

United States buying their goods and services, which keeps their economies strong.

Some of that deficit is covered by simply printing money. But printing money is inflationary; that is, the new money dilutes the value of the existing money. Another way of saying it: more dollars are out there chasing the same amount of goods and services in the economy, so each dollar must be worth less, right?

Printing money is easier today than it once was; the United States was once on a *gold standard,* meaning every dollar in circulation had to be backed by an appropriate amount of physical gold in a vault. The United States officially abandoned that standard in 1971; while President Roosevelt substantially weakened the gold standard back in 1933, it was entirely abandoned less than 40 years ago. But the United States still relies on its reputation as a strong economy, with good resources and minds to manage it, so the U.S. dollar is still considered a *reserve currency,* that is, a solid way to hold and keep money in the world. Relative to, say, holding Kenyan shillings, the dollar may still be a pretty good bet. But if you consider Swiss francs or Chinese yuan, that bet may be getting a bit tenuous as the United States goes further into debt. No one—no individual, no business, no county, no state, no country—can rely on past achievements for too long, but must continuously earn the trust of others to attract investment capital.

Bottom line: The U.S. consumer and the U.S. government have been spending too much and saving too little, and relying on credit to make up the difference. That habit has gone on for a while and may have severe long-term consequences on the U.S. economy and your own personal economic health if it continues unchecked. Unfortunately, the policy measures enacted thus far have only served to perpetuate those habits instead of dealing with the real problems. And that causes a growing threat to sustainable wealth for all of us.

Sizing the Debt Problem

For effect, if nothing else, it makes sense to take a short glimpse at the size of the debt burden from several perspectives. Debt figures are quite remarkable for their absolute size. Many researchers and authors choose to show these figures as charts, but I prefer the raw numbers—it's easier to comprehend just how big they are. I've attempted to put them into perspective by showing change over the last approximately 60 years and by comparing debt to the population and the size of the economy.

Exhibit 1.1   U.S. consumer debt, 1950-2008.

Year	Consumer Debt, Total $ (1)	Population	Per Capita Consumer Debt	Number of Households	Consumer Debt per Household
1950	$ 23,229,160,000	151,325,799	$ 153.50	49,615,016	$ 468.19
1960	$ 60,025,310,000	179,323,175	$ 334.73	52,742,110	$ 1,138.09
1970	$ 131,551,550,000	203,302,031	$ 647.07	63,531,885	$ 2,070.64
1980	$ 351,920,050,000	226,542,203	$ 1,553.44	75,514,068	$ 4,660.32
1990	$ 808,230,570,000	248,708,873	$ 3,249.69	85,762,025	$ 9,424.11
2000	$ 1,717,652,400,000	281,421,906	$ 6,103.48	103,245,963	$ 16,636.51
2008	$ 2,562,286,380,000	304,059,724	$ 8,426.92	112,362,848	$ 22,803.68

(1) defined as revolving (example: credit cards) and nonrevolving, or installment, debt. Mortgage debt is not included.
Source: Federal Reserve, Bureau of Public Debt, Bureau of Economic Analysis

Exhibit 1.1 shows the absolute dollar size of combined revolving and installment consumer debt. Revolving debt is best exemplified by credit cards, where the amount isn't fixed and consumers can add purchases as they please and pay off, with some constraints, as they please. Installment loans have a fixed amount, a fixed payment, and a fixed period; car loans are a good example. These figures do not include mortgage debt, debt used to buy securities (margin), or other forms of debt that may be incurred in a consumer household.

As evidenced in Exhibit 1.1, consumer debt has grown from $23 billion to some $2.5 *trillion*—a hundredfold increase—in 58 years, compared to a twofold increase in population growth. The debt burden has grown to an average of $8,427 per person and, more strikingly, $22,804 per household. While it's dangerous to compare averages—which can be skewed by a small number of individuals with very large debts—to medians, it's striking to note that the median household income in 2007 was $50,233, so it would take nearly six months of income, on average, just to pay off the debt burden. And again, that's just the *consumer* debt—no mention of mortgage or other forms of debt here.

Exhibit 1.2 switches gears to show national debt statistics and trends. The first column shows *nominal GDP*—the sum total of economic activity in goods and services in the dollars of the time. So the $231 billion produced in 1950 grew to $14.27 trillion in 2008; some of that represents economic growth, some reflects inflation. That's not so important here; what is important is to observe the

Exhibit 1.2   U.S. national debt and GDP, 1950-2008.

Year	Nominal GDP ($M)	National Debt ($M)	National Debt as % of Nominal GDP	Per Capita National Debt	Consumer Debt as a % of GDP
1950	$ 231,010	$ 256,100	110.9%	$ 1,692.38	1.3%
1960	$ 425,340	$ 284,100	66.8%	$ 1,584.29	2.4%
1970	$ 867,560	$ 370,100	42.7%	$ 1,820.44	3.5%
1980	$ 2,280,080	$ 907,700	39.8%	$ 4,006.76	6.8%
1990	$ 4,765,710	$ 3,233,300	67.8%	$ 13,000.29	11.4%
2000	$ 8,049,940	$ 5,674,200	70.5%	$ 20,162.61	17.5%
2008	$ 14,264,600	$ 10,699,844	75.0%	$ 35,189.94	18.0%

2008 GDP figures are from estimates.
Source: Federal Reserve, Bureau of Public Debt, Bureau of Economic Analysis

relative amounts of public debt and consumer debt required to make this growth happen.

As the exhibits show (maybe surprisingly to some), national debt was actually larger than GDP in 1950, due to large debt-financed government outlays to finance World War II, with some leftover debt from the Great Depression. Debt actually declined as a percent of GDP for the next 30 years, then started rising again rather dramatically in the 1980s, as tax cuts and "trickle-down" economics took hold as central economic philosophies. But from 1980 to 2008, a twelvefold increase in national debt brought only a six-fold increase in GDP (inflation is in both figures, but affects them equally)—suggesting the debt increase was out of proportion to the increase in economic activity it supported.

At the same time, per capita national debt and the consumer debt as a percent of GDP have grown by more than an order of magnitude. The only reasonable conclusion is that we have, collectively, financed a great deal of our expansion—and our increase in standard of living—with debt.

A Crisis in Confidence

Because of the tangled web of upside-down mortgages (also referred to as "underwater" mortgages), in which the value of the home is less than the value of the mortgage, defaulting buyers, and the securities represented by their loans, investors who once flocked to lend money are turning around and hoarding cash to avoid losing money. The contagion spreads, and soon any investor who has lent money to anybody gets nervous. The result is deleveraging, in which the entire corporate and financial sector tries to shed debt all at once. With everyone trying to sell at once, the value drops further and becomes harder to quantify, and the process continues.

In 2005–2009, we went from a cycle of rampant leveraging and expansion of credit and debt to one of deleveraging. Government bailouts and artificial stimulus might provide temporary comfort and confidence to create short-term benefits, but rational risk seekers are likely to remain on the sidelines until the ills of the bubble have been corrected. Those risk seekers, in the meantime, have lost a lot of their capital, and it will take a while before they put their capital back to work. Deploying a continued credit temptation to solve systemic financial problems only creates greater problems down the road; instead, policymakers would be well advised to address the disease, debt, not the symptom, a lack of spending.

Credit Crisis Consequences

Beyond the triggering of a nasty recession marked by a large and persistent GDP decline, a substantial rise in unemployment, and an enormous erosion of consumer confidence, the bursting of the credit bubble has had outsized consequences, the breadth and depth of which haven't been seen since the Great Depression.

Zombies

The banking system simply froze, like a deer in headlights. Banks wouldn't lend to customers and wouldn't lend to each other; they hoarded capital, afraid to make a move. They looked for more capital, but for the most part couldn't raise it because of fear of their asset quality and a greater, prevailing fear that continued deterioration would lead to nationalization, wiping out private equity. They worried about runs on their assets, which happened and led to some of the early failures. The banks became *zombies*—a term first applied to Japanese banks in the early 1990s after that real estate and credit bubble burst. They were still big—too big to fail—but too hogtied by their problems to move forward.

Unlike Japan, where the government didn't do much, the U.S. government did try to help the zombie banks by extending yet

The End of the Financial Services Industry—As We Know It

The "golden age" of finance, as we know it, might be over. For a long time, finance was the glamour profession, consuming the best and brightest from business schools and industry. But now the industry appears poised for a major contraction. According to figures from *The Economist*, the industry share of corporate profits climbed from 10 percent of all corporate profits in the early 1980s to a stunning 40 percent in 2007—all from moving money around, with little real value created. The financial industry's share of market capitalization went from 6 percent to 23 percent during the same period. As fast as this rocket rose, it appears poised to fall farther than the 1980s "ground" levels. Beyond that, some estimate that as many as 50 percent of hedge funds will close. Some of those funds will restart, as the compensation structure favors new funds with growth over old funds with losses. But that industry in total will contract, too. And the last straw may be the threats, or even necessity, of bank nationalization. Bank nationalization does not mean that the government should run the banks in the long run; call it receivership, if you prefer. The FDIC has an established mechanism to seize failed banks, then sell off the good pieces. This approach minimizes the cost to taxpayers. In the end we need good banks, not bad banks.

more credit, but it wasn't enough to overcome the underlying problems of asset valuation and risk.

Businesses Gone Bust

When banks stop lending, businesses that have sound business models during good times can fail. Unless they have budgeted conservatively, they run out of working capital to spend on vital parts of their business, such as inventory. They can't pay for projects or even make their payrolls. They can't refinance the debt used to buy long-term assets.

Some big corporate flags went down: Circuit City, Charter Communications, and Smurfit-Stone. At the time of this writing, others, such as Sirius Satellite Communications and Borders Group, hang on the precipice, hit by the double whammy of lower consumer spending and a dearth of funding for working capital and to refinance debt. Still others, some big blue-chip names like General

Electric, have been hurt by the asset deterioration and credit squeeze to an extent most didn't think possible. And these are the big names—this contagion has affected many, many other small businesses beneath the radar.

The solution for these businesses, however, is not to cry for help to the government, but to align their assets and liabilities. Why should an enterprise finance long-term investments with short-term funding? Sustainable businesses do not rely on the commercial paper markets for such projects, but use long-term debt to pay for long-term projects (commercial papers are unsecured, short-term debt instruments issued to finance working capital of a corporation). If they don't, they cannot be assured that funding is available the day they need to refinance. The Fed stepping in to provide short-term funding only helps to prop up a broken system. Some firms, such as GE, have since taken steps to rely less on the commercial paper market. However, other firms, such as GMAC, have intensified their reliance on government-sponsored funding.

The principles of sustainable wealth apply to businesses, too.

Possible Deflation?

As the deleveraging and the recession gained steam, suddenly the worry became *deflation*, not inflation. While deflation—a persistent decline in the price of goods and services—may sound attractive, it is a reflection of an economy in protracted decline.

In a deflationary spiral, people hoard cash, because the longer they hold it, the cheaper the goods they buy with it become. But businesses get caught in a bind; they must buy resources at today's prices to sell goods and services at tomorrow's lower prices. The loss inherent in doing that makes them reluctant to buy resources at all—exacerbating the spiral. The economic effects can be devastating, and have only been seen in consequence in the United States in the early part of the Great Depression.

There is only one positive consequence of deflation. While inflation is a tax on savers, who must watch their savings lose value, deflation is a tax on borrowers, who must pay back with dollars that are worth more later. That, however, is precisely the reason why deflation is poison to a credit-driven society—the relative value of your debt increases when deflation is present, making it all the more difficult to service. There are two solutions to this: reduce the level of your debt, or hope for the government to create inflation to bail you out.

In fact, it's the latter that the government is planning to do. In the fall of 2008, when the collapse of the financial system was in debate, deflation was a possible outcome. Since then, the U.S. government has made it abundantly clear that it will try to prevent a deflationary spiral at just about any cost. However, the government had two choices: after stabilizing the financial system, policymakers could have allowed for an orderly price adjustment to weed out the excesses of the credit bubble. Instead, the government is on course to prop up the broken system and to try to infuse inflation into the system to bail out those with too much debt. If you don't want home prices to come down because too many borrowers would be upside down in their mortgage, an alternative is to raise the price level of all other goods and services, so that the relative cost of homes is less.

A Bond Market Bubble?

Credit bubbles are built on the availability of cheap credit, credit that often fails to incorporate the true risks of the underlying assets and resulting leverage. The Fed injects liquidity into the system by printing money and buying bonds, driving bond prices up. Investors see bond prices rising and figure they'd better buy their fixed-income investments while the yield is as good as it is. And in the most recent credit bubble, foreigners, looking for the safety of the dollar or to subsidize American spending and importation of their goods (notably, China), bought bonds. Large numbers of bond buyers in the market mean higher bond prices, which also mean lower yields, and the cycle continues.

While "textbook" asset bubbles occur with more tangible assets, like tulips, tract homes, or stocks, many feel we could be flirting with the dangers of a bond market bubble. If investors perceive, all at once, that bonds are a bad deal—that prices are too high for the risk involved—a bond selloff could occur, meaning higher interest rates in the future. With the government in the market borrowing to finance stimulus programs at the same time, there's a mood that interest rates, under the right (or wrong) set of circumstances, could rise dramatically. The consequences of that would be severe,

Don't Alienate Your Favorite Customers

In early 2009, the Fed made moves to drive the bond prices still higher in the interest of driving mortgage rates down, by buying so-called "agency" (Fannie Mae, Freddie Mac) securities. That move, of course, was favorable to the mortgage borrower and designed to stimulate home prices and favorable refinancing for some owners (though ironically, perhaps not the ones who really need it, because of bad credit histories). But it also drove bond prices higher, high enough that it might jeopardize the interest of Chinese buyers in U.S. bonds. That could end up triggering an end to the bubble, bringing higher interest rates.

starting with the cost of servicing the national debt and extending well into the destruction of economic growth and beyond into the destruction of the value of the U.S. dollar, as seen already in the United Kingdom.

Credit as a Threat to Sustainable Wealth

Economist Milton Friedman once said: "Inflation is just like alcoholism. In both cases, when you start drinking or when you start printing too much money, the good effects come first. The bad effects only come later . . . ." In that spirit, we now come to the conclusion of this chapter, intended to examine the temptation of credit and its consequences both on a national scale and for your own personal finances.

Make no mistake—the flood of liquidity that was handed down as the 2008–2009 crisis proceeded could end up being like gasoline on a fire. It may make many problems worse and lead to an overextension and weakening of the government and its ability to combat future problems. Whether it's you individually or us as a national entity, cheaper credit doesn't help if you're already too much in debt with insufficient income to pay it back.

Specific threats to sustainable wealth include:

- *Volatility.* An economy more overextended and more out of balance creates sharper ups and downs in the business cycle, and makes everyone more vulnerable to economic shocks like oil shortages or political events.

- *Increased risk.* Volatility is really an outward sign of the greater risk inherent in leverage and overextension of credit. When that risk isn't properly measured or appraised, resulting defaults and dislocations can bring still more instability and volatility.
- *Asset bubbles.* Excess credit—especially when used to fix problems created by excess credit—creates bubbles. We've seen it twice—perhaps three times if there's a bond bubble—in ten years. When asset prices move out of line with reality, that's a direct threat to sustainable wealth, if that wealth is tied up in those assets. There's also an indirect impact as volatility grows and credit is likely to be further extended, starting the cycle over again. Importantly, as those who needed to sell a home in 2008–2009 know, it's hard to get rid of assets bought in a bubble once on the backside of the bubble event.
- *Policy shifts.* Credit expansion and contraction creates dire results, like asset bubbles, which in turn can lead to policy shifts, like changes in lending or tax policy. One example is the proposed judicial capability to modify mortgage terms for borrowers, which while well intended could mean more risk for the investors who originally provided the funds. If you happen to be one of those investors or, more generally, count on steady contractual returns on your fixed-income investments, such changes pose a risk.
- *Currency depreciation.* Geometrically expanding debt has put us on a path toward substantial devaluation of the U.S. dollar, once the debts come due and especially if the U.S. loses its favored reserve currency status. As a major portion of U.S. goods and commodities are imported, that would indicate a decline in standard of living for all of us.

Credit as Fuel for Other Temptations

Too much credit can lead to too much debt. By itself, that might get you into trouble, but it's usually some other triggering event, like the loss of a job or a major new expense, that really causes the problem; the debt just makes it worse.

Just as debt amplifies bad outcomes, credit tempts us toward other behaviors that cause problems, both individually and in our collective public finances. The next three chapters cover the temptations of consumption, policy, and complacency. Credit can play a stimulative role in all three, that is, the availability of easy, cheap credit can lead us to make bad decisions for ourselves, and lead policymakers to make bad decisions for our economy, which can affect all of us.

The Temptation of Consumption

Too much credit makes it tempting to consume too much. Simply swipe the plastic, and you have that new backyard barbecue; that was easy, right? Credit leads to consumption, which leads to debt, and if we don't manage our finances properly, we repeat the cycle—more credit, more consumption, more debt.

Policymakers, driven by the politically correct objective of maximizing employment and sustainable growth, want us to consume as much as possible, and have in recent years been accommodating that objective through easy credit. We'll explore that temptation in the next chapter.

The Temptation of Policy Change

Likewise, the temptation of credit can lead to questionable policy decisions, both for you as an individual and for the policymakers who manage the economy. This chapter reviews the policy decisions tied to and fueled by credit, which may lead to bigger economic problems down the road.

The Temptation of Complacency

The availability of plastic in your wallet or purse makes you a more confident shopper, because you know you'll be able to buy what you want regardless of whether you have the cash in the short term—you'll be able to pay it back later. Credit works in many ways to give us a false sense of security about our finances. It also makes it easy to keep old, bad habits going. This chapter talks about some of those habits and how they are fueled by credit, including the use of credit to keep inefficient businesses going through bailouts.

Using Credit Wisely

There are many, many differences between personal credit and national credit. You can't print money or lower the interest rates!

And it's not likely that you'll receive a bailout if you make mistakes managing credit. But as a builder and manager of sustainable wealth, you need to observe the parallels, too—how, as a nation, we got drunk on easy credit, and overused it to buy, fix, and bail out lost causes. The personal and policy implications of credit and debt, and how they affect your efforts to create and manage sustainable wealth, are covered throughout this book.

2

The Temptation of Consumption

Never spend your money before you have earned it.
—Thomas Jefferson

Headline, January 2007, from the National Retail Federation:

NRF Forecasts 4.8% Growth for 2007 Retail Sales—Soft Landing Should Poise Economy for Accelerated Growth

That's a pretty rosy headline, to be sure. It came even in the face of falling home prices and rising delinquency and foreclosure rates. It came even in the face of all-time high consumer debt levels. And it came even in the face of rising energy prices, the absence of real income growth, and lackluster employment growth. Spending would continue, and the "soft landing" would take care of the evils in this land of spending temptation.

As we all know, the "accelerated growth" never happened; instead, U.S. retail sales languished for a year and a half, then fell off a cliff in late 2008, with declines not seen for 16 years. Sector-specific reports were even worse, with chain store sales in October 2008 at their lowest levels in 35 years.

The results left a lot of very smart people scratching their heads. What happened? Did consumers suddenly change their collective minds about shopping? About buying and owning things? Was it just a matter of ever-expanding "amount due" figures on credit card statements? Why was there so much spending and consumption, and why on Earth did it last for so long? Was it all the consumers' fault, or was he or she caught up in a wave of irresistible temptation that made it a natural outcome? And what are the consequences, intended and unintended, of such a temptation toward consumption, both on an individual and national level?

Here's the story in a nutshell. The idea was to spur consumption, and consumption was supposed to boost the economy, achieve full employment, and make America a better place to live for everyone, all in the name of "progress" and political expediency. However, the best of intentions went sour.

That push into consumption went into overdrive after the dot. com bust. The ample supply of credit—manifested by low interest rates and easy credit terms—fueled an asset bubble, foremost a real estate bubble, of titanic proportions. That, in turn, made consumers *feel* wealthy. That feeling of wealth, what economists refer to as the "wealth effect," combined with strong stock prices and continued easy credit, fueled a boom in consumption—a consumption bubble some now call a "standard of living" bubble.

But in the end, that consumption bubble served to mask real economic problems and prop up failing industries. At the end of the day, the temptation of credit and the temptation of consumption worked together, hand in hand, to create distortions and imbalances in the world economy that will likely cost us all for some time to come. Those distortions spread well beyond U.S. borders into other economies, notably China and other parts of Asia. They have also served to amplify the bust, making it worse and harder to recover from—but as the crisis unfolds, policies continue to support the very same activities that got us there in the first place. But this time, fearful consumers aren't responding; instead, they're hoarding what they have as savings—for the first time in years—not only because lenders have reduced the throttle of free money, but also because consumers are in total fear of what might happen to them financially. It's a prime example of Keynes' so-called *saving paradox*, where economic fear leads consumers to save, normally a good thing, but not what the policymakers intend during a financial bust. In fact, most policymakers want people to save, but want them saving on the next politician's watch, as "saving now" would cut into short-term economic growth.

It is perfectly rational for someone to consume out of an inheritance, say, drawing down wealth, or out of capital gains in general.

But we must distinguish temporary from permanent. What is not sound is to consume out of rising housing wealth under the assumption that house prices will rise at a rapid rate forever, or will never fall.

A savings-oriented economy would have been better all along; however, saving—and investment—should not have been introduced by fear, but should have been supported as a national goal all along. We embark on our journey to explore the temptation of consumption by illustrating the dynamics of consumption, saving, and investment.

The Consumption Paradigm

Suppose you were an alien making your first landing on planet Earth. By happenstance, you choose a landing spot in the United States. And you choose to land in a city, because you want to capture, in a brief visit, the nature of the social, economic, and political landscape of this strange otherworldly population.

Chances are pretty good that you would land somewhere near one of America's hundreds of retail Meccas dotting the suburbs, a commercial or shopping area punctuated by enclosed malls, strip malls, big-box stores, and clusters of little-box stores and restaurants and filling stations all geared to support the American consumer economy. If you didn't land in one of these areas, you'd soon be clued in to their existence by the steady flows of traffic to and from these commercial centers of consumption. And if you were from an alien culture familiar with telecommunication technologies, you might have already captured the vast flow of Internet-based shopping traffic that, at least for now, accompanies the activity in the retail arena.

The reality you would soon find is this: More than any other economy in the world, America's economy is tied to—and is dependent upon—consumerism. That is, consumer spending, lots of it, growing, continuing, day in, day out, come Hell or high water or possibly even a grinding recession.

Consumption in Fact

Consider the facts. American private consumption, as a percentage of GDP, is about 70 percent. That means that 70 percent of the U.S. economy is driven by consumers buying products and services—not by private business investment, not by providing goods and services for export, not by government consumption of goods and services.

Now such a figure doesn't mean much in a vacuum, until compared to other countries. For the world as a whole, the percentage is 61 percent (naturally driven upward by America's figure); for the Eurozone it is 58 percent, for Japan it is 57 percent, for China it is only 36 percent. What makes up the balance? Businesses and governments. If you desire a less consumer-oriented society, but don't want government to assume its place, the obvious choice is to encourage business investment.

America is said to have six times the retail space per capita than any other developed nation. (Sweden, driven by the "IKEA effect," is second). That retail space, of course, supports this vast consumerism, but it also makes U.S. retailers, at least without intermediation, vulnerable to spending downturns. And indeed the recent bankruptcies of Linens 'N Things, Circuit City, and a list of troubled commercial property developers bear this out.

There are numerous other indicators of America's profligate and growing consumption. One comes from the real estate sector: The average square footage for a new home in 1978 of 1,750 square feet grew to some 2,500 square feet by 2006, as America executed its love affair with McMansions in the far distant suburbs. That, of course, resulted in a dramatic increase in demand for automotive transportation, with average miles driven increasing some 151 percent from 1977 through 2001—about five times the average growth in population—and average commute times increasing some 10 percent in a three-year period (2003–2006) alone. On top of that, 53 percent of the vehicles sold were trucks or minivans. The 2007–2008 downturn did finally temper the growth to the tune of a 10 billion–mile (4 percent) reduction in annual miles driven— evidence that downturns can cut into even the most entrenched forms of consumption.

Beyond automotive transportation, the McMansion boom also fostered increased consumption of other goods and services, from energy to lawn care services to house paint. Consumption aside, the McMansion boom creates other longer-term concerns—what happens when children grow up, or future generations don't have as many children, and don't need or can't afford such large homes? The McMansion boom may create a negative overhang for a long time; it is little wonder these outsized homes have been at one of the epicenters of the real estate bust.

Consuming More Than We Produce

As we saw in the National Retail Federation headline at the outset of the chapter, consumer spending continued to grow even as the storm clouds of recession built and as income and wealth sources dried up. The next and most obvious question is—how did the consumer pull this off? How can one spend more money than they have, month after month, quarter after quarter?

There are two obvious answers: first, consumers would plunder their savings. Second, they would take advantage of all that cheap, easy credit.

Plundering the Piggybank   The gradual "plunder" of U.S. consumer savings has been going on for quite some time. The *personal saving rate* is defined, very simply, as the percent of personal income that is *not* consumed. In the 1960s, the personal saving rate ranged from 6 to 10 percent and rose gradually through the decade. It got a boost with two recessions, one mild and one fairly severe, in the early 1970s—the saving rate reached 12 percent in 1974 and peaked at almost 14 percent in 1975. "Why does recession trigger such gains?" you might rightly ask. It's because people realize they're overspent and, further, gain (or regain) an aversion to risk; they don't want to expose themselves to layoffs or income disruptions, so they save.

As individuals saw some economic stabilization, and especially as inflation "taxed" savings by depleting purchasing power, the personal saving rate faded back to the 8 to 10 percent range, still healthy by today's standards. It peaked at 12 percent again during the 1982 recession, then saw a long, slow decline, first to the 6 to 8 percent range in the late 1980s; falling off steadily to 2 percent in the late 1990s; finally going into negative territory for the first time in 2005. It has hovered near zero ever since, although as the 2009 recession unleashes its full fury, there are signs of a return to a slightly positive saving flow.

A closer look at what was really happening with savings during the real estate boom paints a still bleaker picture. When consumers took equity out of their homes, it would effectively be deducted from the saving rate. During the boom, many argued it shouldn't be, because the houses were worth more; after the real estate bust, it is clear that the saving should have been rightfully put in context of income, not assets. Conversely, however, as consumers can no longer use their homes as ATM machines, will that reflect an even stronger shift to saving than that reported by the figures?

What does this all mean? It means that Americans, stimulated and encouraged to consumption by policy, by habit, by marketing pull, and by the feeling of wealth created by asset price rises, simply threw saving responsibilities out the window. Put another way, the consumption train continued full speed, even though little to no "steam" was provided by rising incomes—as it should have been and perhaps would have been had fewer jobs been exported overseas, primarily to Asia.

Stoking the Fire   So where did the "steam" come from? It came from several sources. The first and most obvious is borrowing. A lot of that borrowing was supported by assets with rising values—specifically real estate. Policy made that easy by keeping interest rates low and by requiring little proof of creditworthiness, especially as the boom gathered momentum. The government-sponsored enterprises (GSEs)—Fannie Mae and Freddie Mac—relaxed their heretofore high standards and expanded their real estate mortgage purchases and loan guarantees. Those guarantees gave an immunity to risk to both borrower and lender, perpetuating the process and putting still more coal on the fire. Combined with low taxes and cheap Asian goods, there was enough coal in the firebox and steam in the boiler to fuel consumption and to drive up home prices in a manner not seen before. And as home prices went up, that led to more "wealth," more consumer confidence, and more borrowing; pretty soon this locomotive was headed down the track at full throttle.

Lower taxes and other fiscal stimuli are nice, but they create deficits that must be paid for. So the government borrowed, too—in huge quantities, so much so that it must now borrow more than $2 billion a day to support the current account deficit. The current account deficit is the trade deficit plus or minus some financial flows; it is exactly the amount foreigners need to invest in the United States to keep the dollar from falling. It should be noted that some of that current account deficit is funded through the sale of U.S. assets; these flows put such U.S. icons as the Pebble Beach golf resort and corporate names like Anheuser-Busch into foreign hands.

The Consumption Imperative

In fact, the consumption boom just ended in the 2008–2009 recession traces its origins to the end of the early 1990s recession. At 17 years, that boom was longer than most, considerably longer than most business cycles and indeed largely unaffected by the downdrafts in 1994, 1997–1998, and 2001–2002.

The 1990s recession was caused by a mix of global political events and a necessary transformation into the information society we have now become. The global political events included the Iraqi invasion of Kuwait and the resulting Gulf War I, and uncertainty as to the economic effects of the downfall of the Soviet Union and the Iron Curtain. The process automation—computerization—of industries had spawned a lot of investment but had not really been fully implemented; companies were still struggling to realize the return on their technology investments. Even tech stalwart IBM had to reinvent itself.

Importantly, the burst 1999–2000 tech bubble had little impact on consumer spending; it continued largely as before. The fallout of that bubble landed more squarely on the business sector and was somewhat more confined to companies and parts of the country more heavily invested in technology; the consumer at large kept up spending and drove a rather speedy recovery to that downturn, egged on by low interest rates and largely unfazed by the political and social calamity of the 2001 terrorist attacks. In fact, it seemed that "retail therapy" was an antidote to the gloom brought on by those attacks and negative headlines generated by the dot.com bust. But while businesses reacted to the downturn by improving their balance sheets and rationalizing technology investments, consumers continued to pile on short-term credit card debt.

Policy changes in the early 1980s were pivotal to triggering the 1990s consumption boom. Low tax rates originated in the Reagan administration, and Greenspan began our transformation from an income-driven society to one driven by assets and credit by lowering short-term interest rates. Both helped push the consumer along; in addition, emerging economies, especially China and the so-called "Asian tigers," got on the bandwagon, too. They saw they could propel their expansion and emergence into the economic mainstream with exports, so they did what they could, including accommodating local business, relaxing trade barriers, and keeping their currencies cheap, to encourage Americans to buy. And buy they did. As a result, not only did consumers support the U.S. economy; they also supported Asian and other world economies. In fact, it became the whole world's interest to support U.S. consumer spending.

Did the Consumer Jump, or Was He Pushed?

In Disney/Pixar's *Toy Story*, when Buzz Lightyear is accidentally bumped out the window of the bedroom, the toys gather to ponder whether Woody did it. "Murderer," exclaims Mr. Potato Head. "He didn't fall out of the window. He was *pushed.*"

So did the U.S. consumer jump on his own, or was he or she pushed?

Consumers have become conditioned, many from their early childhood, to consume. And they've received plenty of help, in the form of private solicitations, marketing, and public "funding" through cheap credit, all with a backdrop of cheap goods made available by foreign suppliers looking to boost exports. These three factors make it so a consumer would probably jump even if not pushed; the gentle shove of low interest rates only makes their trajectory out the window farther and faster.

Consumers have gotten used to a land of plenty. They are conditioned by the abundance of stores and the abundance of advertising and marketing to push product. It's easy to succumb to temptation when there's so much available. And consumers, especially those born in the 1950s and later into the "convenience generation," have been conditioned to be part of a consumption culture from day one.

Those who study the habits and preferences of Japanese culture soon learn to recognize a big difference from the American culture. Americans are conditioned from birth of a land of opportunity; that there is always *more* to be had, whether it's land, money, or goods and services. The Japanese, on the other hand, constrained and conditioned by a shortage of available land above all else, approach life to be thankful for what they have and to believe that there always could be *less.*

For the average person, "things" have become identical to wealth. Individuals crave the accumulation of "stuff" and consider it the equivalent of being "rich." Personal wealth—and worth—are measured in terms of accumulation, whether earned or accumulated through debt and spending. In short, they established a standard of living they could not afford. It's addicting—once one attains a standard of living he or she cannot afford, the short-term satisfaction takes over, pheromones are released, and the tendency is to want to repeat the experience again and again. And many of the younger folks have never experienced a significant recession; the bursting of the consumption bubble could bring some unpleasant withdrawal symptoms, as credit contraction, inflation, higher interest rates, job and income squeezes, and increased taxes come home to roost. These individuals have never had to live within their financial means, and they've been conditioned from day one, by observing the lifestyle of their parents, that this is okay.

For the individual, it's important to recognize the temptations of credit and consumption and only succumb to them to the extent one can afford, both now and later. Better yet, it's best to simply stay away from the temptation. I always say this: without debt, you can't be *forced* to work; you are *free* to work. Think about it. The difference between the two choices is enormous.

But if kids are given ice cream or candy, just exactly how much can you blame them for accepting it? That's the other side of the debate.

The U.S. government, for a variety of reasons, many of which date back to the horrors of the Great Depression, supports full employment and steady growth almost above all else. Americans tend to vote their pocketbooks, and so when there's a "chicken in every pot," why would they not support and vote for the regime and party in charge? So for the most part, until the growth becomes so strong that it kicks off inflationary pressures, government economic policy pushes consumption as a driver—and evidence of—economic success.

This side of the debate holds that Americans are simply responding to the economic stimuli they receive. They spend because it's easy. As we found out in the real estate boom, many spend for fear of being left out. The temptation of consumption becomes a self-fulfilling prophecy—people spend, the economy thrives, they're rewarded with opportunities and incentives to spend more.

But like most other meddling with the natural order of the economic universe, there are unintended consequences.

The Cost of a Consumption Economy

What should have been a natural order of producing more than we consume, living within our means, and saving the difference went into decline starting in 1990, and almost left completely during

2003–2007. Cheap imported goods, easy credit, and the wealth effect combined to move consumption along despite the absence of income and employment growth. It was built on the illusion of growth; one indication that the growth was not real was that job growth was rather lackluster.

As the 2008–2009 recession unfolded, the policies that created the bubble in the first place were kept alive. The target Fed funds rate was ratcheted down to near zero, lower tax rates were extended, and additional fiscal stimulus was put in place, all to put more money in people's pockets. But the consumer was fearful of the risks and ambiguities of the decline. Many of the consumers who would have normally benefited from lower interest rates couldn't qualify for the credit from fearful banks. Much of the stimulus was simply put into savings or favorable havens, such as gold or U.S. Treasuries. Maybe more importantly, the stimulus was inherently short-run, one-shot; it didn't have the sought-after effect of getting the economic wheels of consumption turning again. Asset prices and consumption continued to fall, increasing unemployment and further perpetuating the bust, while at the same time laying the groundwork for inflation later on with the flood of cheap money. A stimulus to longer lasting business investment would have been much better, because the effects would tend to add up, that is, to be cumulative.

It's worth taking a global look at the effects of the consumption bubble and the temporary and permanent economic dislocations it caused, and what probably *should* have been done in lieu of giving in to temptation.

No Stimulus at Home

The story of the migration of manufacturing capacity to Asia, and especially China, is well known. As a result, however, consumption-stimulating initiatives did progressively less to aid the U.S. economy and only made many of its difficulties and dislocations worse.

Consider the 2008 fiscal stimulus, ranging up to $1,800 for a tax-paying married couple. Did this money end up helping U.S. firms and ultimately, U.S. consumers? Not so much. First, this stimulus was created during scary times, so as much as half of it was saved. Ordinarily savings are a good thing, but when the government is printing money (or borrowing it from the Chinese) to make it happen, and it's just being stashed away as insurance against the future, it accomplishes little in the way of true economic relief.

Second, and worse, if that money was spent on something, in all likelihood it was spent on items made somewhere else; perhaps, a big-screen TV made in Korea. We exported the consumption. This not only does little to stimulate the U.S. economy (outside of supporting a few low-paying jobs in the supply chain and retail industry), it led to a continued production "bubble" in Asia, which eventually led to pricing pressures and distortions in that region to be ultimately exported here.

As Marc Faber, publisher of *The Gloom Boom & Doom Report*, put it in July 2008:

> The federal government is sending each of us a $600 rebate. If we spend that money at Wal-Mart, the money goes to China. If we spend it on gasoline it goes to the Arabs. If we buy a computer/software it will go to India. If we purchase fruit and vegetables it will go to Mexico, Honduras[,] and Guatemala. If we purchase a good car it will go to Germany. If we purchase useless crap it will go to Taiwan and none of it will help the American economy. The only way to keep that money here at home is to spend it on prostitutes and beer, since these are the only products still produced in US[sic]. I've been doing my part.

I would be hard pressed to express this any more clearly. While this particular quote does not reference history, what I most appreciate about Faber are the historic references he often draws in his newsletter. I am not talking about references to the past booms or busts, but about what has happened to other cultures in history that have spent too much and saved too little. As an economic historian, such references are second nature to him. Check out his newsletter at www.gloomboomdoom.com.

Long-Term Borrowing, Short-Term Stimulus

The real estate boom and bust revealed something else important in the pattern of consumption. We were borrowing long-term to create a short-term economic jolt—nice while it lasted, but hardly in the best long-term economic interest.

In the recent residential and commercial real estate construction, most construction was financed by long-term debt, up to 30 years on the residential side. In the case of a home, we, as a society, borrow for 30 years hence to get a short-term economic boost from the construction of the new home—labor, materials, managing the transaction. The boost, and taxes paid on the income generated by the boost, all occur in the current year. But long-term, we are saddled with a debt to repay; in addition, there is little new tax revenue, but instead a mortgage interest expense deduction eating into future tax revenues.

This pattern was repeated millions of times—borrow, build, boost, then service debt and pay less tax. It spread into the commercial real estate sector, for more real estate offices, construction company offices, lenders, mortgage insurers, lawyers, and escrow officers needed space as well. In many parts of suburbia, entire office communities were created to support real estate construction and sales activity—all on borrowed money.

So individuals were induced to buy real estate, at inflated prices, essentially funding original owners or new construction activity. New, borrowed money went to old owners and overextended businesses;

Federal Ponzi Schemes?

If the preceding dislocation sounded like a Ponzi scheme, that's not so far off, except that unlike a true Ponzi scheme, there is no central "schemer" pulling the strings. However, I maintain that the Federal subsidy of real estate, which started in the 1930s with the introduction of Fannie Mae, comes close. Fannie Mae was put in place to foster the housing market with subsidized loans. All any subsidy does is make it cheap for initial buyers to buy a home; they can afford more. If there was no subsidy, home prices would stay lower and be more affordable; those who worked and saved could afford homes anyway. Arguably, the Federal government, through these lending enterprises, has created a giant Ponzi scheme by inflating real estate prices in the first place; subsequent owners must pay the price for the benefit of earlier owners. I see similar effects with college tuition: The best of intentions, through government aid and lending programs, has only served to drive tuition costs higher. We may yet see a bubble burst in tuition prices; yet another similar burst may occur in Treasury bonds.

the new buyers would only be bailed out if still more buyers with still more borrowing potential showed up. Such bailouts have stopped, with drastic effects on the underlying asset prices, but more importantly, debt-wise, and tax-wise, we will live with the effects for a long time to come.

The Return of Inflation

Why were policymakers able to pursue pro-consumption policies in the face of inflation? Typically, policies designed to stimulate demand and consumption create inflation, as the supply of dollars comes to exceed the supply of goods and services available. What was different this time?

One of the biggest differences was the availability of cheap goods from overseas, which was in turn related to local policies to stimulate exports and trade. China, in particular, wished to keep its expansion going, and invested heavily (and accommodated private investment) in literally thousands of local businesses destined to succeed or fail based on export demand and cheap labor. At one point, there were some 8,000 toy manufacturers alone. They also kept their currency artificially low. The Asian goal was not only to create and sustain prosperity, but also social stability in the massive migration of rural workers to the urban areas. While some of these workers have returned to their distant homes in the wake of the recession, the hope of the government is that many remain, and sustaining export growth is the key.

This glut of manufacturers and the resulting overproduction kept the cheap goods coming and served well to stem the tide of inflation in developed countries and the United States in particular. But importantly, while global overproduction holds back inflation, it doesn't eliminate it. The overproduction led to a global surge in commodity prices, on everything from oil to nickel to scrap steel and other recycled materials. Worse, for the American consumer, was the stubborn presence of inflation on products that can't be imported—like college education, health care and local services. You can't import these from China or buy them at Wal-Mart.

China and the rest of Asia exported low prices for a long period, but at some point all good things had to come to an end. In the spring of 2007, the trend reversed: goods exported from China started increasing in price. Stories surfaced of mundane items like wire coat hangers doubling, tripling in price. What had happened? It was pretty simple: The United States had offshored—exported—all production and couldn't compete. And that wasn't about to change, for once gone, the cost differential between U.S. and Chinese or Vietnamese manufacturing could never be overcome, even if the dollar were to weaken substantially. The pattern has been repeated in many other forms of metal goods, textiles, plastics manufacturing, and a wide range of other goods.

Worse, commodity prices escalated, causing many exporters to reach a pain threshold and go out of business. Although the world's importers assumed that foreign producers could absorb the higher cost of doing business; they couldn't, and succumbed to the margin pressures of both higher prices and higher local wages, particularly those with no pricing power in the United States. The disappearance of so much production capacity, and the tendency for those remaining with pricing power to pass on cost increases like the aforementioned wire hanger manufacturers added further to the inflation fire. As many as half of the toy manufacturers—some 4,000 companies—failed, and most of the rest couldn't export profitably. Starting in the spring of 2007, the cost of imports rose in the United States; within a year, the annual cost increase reached over 20 percent—while the amount was boosted by the spike in the price of oil, there was a surge in just about all import prices. Had there not been the global bust, inflation would have taken a firm grip on the U.S. economy. The worst may be yet to come.

The High Cost of Exporting Production

The export of manufacturing capacity and the subsequent flood of overproduced cheap goods from Asia left corporate U.S. squeezed in the middle. It didn't have pricing power, because consumers can't afford to spend more as a result of high debt levels and because consumers don't have to pay more because of the influx of cheap goods from Asia; both situations are further aggravated by high commodity prices. As a result, the remaining companies with domestic facilities had to try to lower variable costs—translation: labor. So the consumption bubble, triggered initially by well-intended easy credit and accommodating tax rules, actually accelerated the offshoring trend. Make no mistake—globalization and offshoring would have

Survival of the Fittest

The export of production and the glut of overconsumption had its effects in Asia and other countries, too—some good and some bad. Asian countries had a keen interest in the employment and support of people migrating to the cities during the boom. The policies in place—low exchange rates, easy access to capital, lax environmental regulation—encouraged overproduction, a production "bubble" in today's parlance. Naturally, that turned into an oversupply of businesses, creating a cutthroat competitive environment, especially in China. Think about it from a businessperson's perspective: how on Earth can you compete when businesses are created left and right that would not be able to compete without subsidies such as an artificially low exchange rate? Subsidies aside, it also meant that firms able to compete in such an environment had to be extremely well run. It also meant that not only competing Asian firms, but also U.S. firms, had better be scared of them.

Take, for example, South Korean electronics giant LG, which entered the U.S. markets on a greater scale a couple of years ago selling cellular phones, appliances, and large-screen televisions. LG had been in China for some time, being one of the early adopters to move production from near the main industrial centers further inland to reduce costs (which helped them take advantage of the post-boom migration of workers away from the large population centers). A firm like LG learned how to operate profitably in China before expanding in the United States; many Western firms don't succeed in Asia because they cannot absorb the culture fast enough. For example, Wal-Mart withdrew from South Korea (and Germany) because it couldn't adapt to the local business models; it had too much overhead. Even Sony and Sanyo and other Japanese companies have had similar issues in offshoring their production. When a company like LG succeeds as it has, take note. Also, think about this: There are Chinese companies, currently nameless and faceless on the world stage, poised to grow into world economic powers.

happened anyway, but U.S. policies, combined with Asian encouragement, made it happen more quickly.

The acceleration of offshoring made the onset of U.S. economic problems faster and more severe. The offshoring trend had dampened job growth for years; some 4 million manufacturing jobs alone, not to mention jobs in the various supporting overhead functions, have been lost since 2000.

Many of the people who lost jobs had a problem: lots of debt. From a macroeconomic perspective, a lot of debt has its advantages: those with debt have an extra incentive to find a job, as they have become slaves of their debt. However, because of the outsourcing trends, the jobs simply weren't there. So what do they do? Many of these dislocated employees start their own shops, mostly small, home-based businesses. But as is common, nine out of ten such businesses would fail. The tenth firm may become another Google or otherwise very successful company. The good news: Because the U.S. economy is so flexible, it was—mostly—able to adjust to this rapidly changing world. The bad news: "New economy" firms that started afresh were best suited for this; not everyone would succeed, and credit woes made it difficult for many of these small firms to get started.

Protectionism Is *Not* the Answer

Over the years, one of the strongest positives of the U.S. economy is that it can adjust so quickly. Regulation and government intervention in business activity are low compared to other countries, and the entrepreneurial spirit is always alive and well. However, bad times lead to cries for more intervention; specifically, protectionist trade measures designed to secure jobs and even entire industries. Even if one doesn't like the pace or the way globalization has occurred, one ought to be extremely careful about these protectionist measures. That's because economic isolationism hurts those who have learned how to adjust. There are always new jobs that cater to a world of trade—not just traders, but jobs throughout the procurement chain; economic isolationism will destroy those jobs and prop up legacy jobs doomed to fail. And the tit-for-tat nature of resulting trade wars will only serve to weaken exports and exacerbate economic problems in other countries, further aggravating the crisis—we learned the consequences of that in the Great Depression. *Economic isolationism* is another term for *protectionism*, but is more to the point and doesn't sugarcoat the concept as something that sounds like it would "protect" you.

Long-Term Consequences

The recent consumption bubble has led us all further down the road into becoming a nation of spenders—a nation that consumes more than it produces, a nation dependent on consumption. Ironically, while consumption was king, we dismantled the production base—manufacturing—and it isn't likely to come back, as outsourced production became more competitive during the boom.

We've moved away from a balance of manufacturing, marketers, and financial facilitators to become a nation of financial engineers, except that we are now doing our best to destroy that industry, too. Once again, it isn't consumption per se that caused the destruction of U.S. manufacturing; it was the well-intended consequence of keeping growth high that accelerated outsourcing, thus turning counterproductive. As a further consequence, we've become more vulnerable to the effects of economic cycles, as there is less within our borders to influence or control.

Increased credit and the resulting debt have also made us more vulnerable as a nation to economic cycles. Not that manufacturing is immune from such cycles; quite the opposite. But when a nation keeps its own manufacturing base, a dollar of stimulus turns into a dollar of results. Further, the export of production—and consumption—has left us all mired in debt; debt makes us less flexible, and it makes us more sensitive to small changes in interest rates. If the bond market were to collapse at this point, driving up interest rates and cutting off funding sources for consumption and stimulus, we would have few switches and levers to pull.

Other countries face—or have already faced—the difficulties of an unbalanced economy. Arguably, the United Kingdom went through similar times at the end of the 19th century; as their post–Industrial Revolution manufacturing base disappeared to less expensive destinations, they became more vulnerable to economic woes and gave up much of their empire after World War I. It happened in Japan to a degree from the 1980s into the 1990s, when they saw a sizeable piece of their economic empire move to China and other Asian destinations.

This is not to say that we should dismantle the financial industry; far from it. In fact, if we had allowed it to function properly, we might not have had a lot of the systemic risks and problems we faced today. For example, if the complex collateralized debt obligation (CDO) instruments had traded on an exchange, with exchange rules, central clearing, and proper margin monitoring, speculators (and purchasing institutions) would have been wiped out before these instruments caused a threat to the system as a whole. The financial industry made some mistakes, but remains vital to the function of a balanced economy; destroying the financial industry serves no purpose. It will be interesting to see what happens as Singapore, already balanced with a strong base of trading, manufacturing, and finance, welcomes financial businesses now out of favor in New York, London, and elsewhere.

The Real Risk: Retirement

Indeed, the United States is in a struggle to avoid becoming another Japan. Japan's well-chronicled real estate bubble and subsequent banking malaise bears some resemblance to the U.S. boom/bust cycle, except that Japan's government debt is held by consumers and does not have to be funded externally.

But Japan ran into the saving paradox in a big way. Stimulus did not achieve the spending result. Japanese consumers instead saw increased risks in their pensions and retirement security in general, and hoarded their cash. That led to a deflationary cycle, which only caused them to hoard more cash (it will be worth more later). And unlike the intergenerational perpetuation of the U.S. consumer, Japan may actually have a problem in that their younger consumers may have learned not to spend.

Unwinding the Consumption Bubble

The purpose of *Sustainable Wealth* is to help you understand economic forces and how they affect your financial lifestyle and well-being. It is not to preach nor to offer policy alternatives for the policymakers and those in power. It is worth noting the potential solutions to the consumption bubble, for they not only serve to enhance your understanding of the problem but also may, in and of themselves, affect your finances. Following are some ways the addiction to consumption could be reduced:

Encourage Domestic Saving

We need a national policy to provide more incentives for saving. A higher after-tax return on investment is what we need, and reduced incentive for debt. We can increase the return on investment by allowing tax deductibility of investments (rather than long amortization periods) and by encouraging entrepreneurship.

How about a simple way to provide an incentive to save? Increase interest rates. In fact, interest rates paid on savings accounts and time deposits dropped to ridiculous levels, less than 1 percent—who would save in that environment, especially when inflation was still at 3 percent (and perhaps more—many consumers, especially in light of skyrocketing education, health, and energy costs stopped believing these figures)? As a long-term solution, a policy of free, market-based (and probably higher) rates would help, but in the short term, obviously it would bring more economic pain. "Free" rates would be higher because they would reflect true market risk and balance between short-term consumption and long-term investment. Still, if higher rates were offered as a long-term policy goal, they could, especially combined with recent retirement fears, turn us into a nation of savers. Further, higher interest rates would boost returns on pension plans and retirement accounts already in existence, helping them to rely less on risky investments and increasing retirement security overall.

All that said, simply hiking up interest rates may also cause economic harm. What we need is more prudent long-term policies, so that the Fed no longer has the urge to lower rates to rock-bottom levels.

Increase Consumption and Spending by Exporting Countries

Initially, the 2008–2009 bust was dampened a bit by strong foreign demand; U.S. companies with a strong export base, such as Hewlett-Packard and Caterpillar, flourished, jobs were created, and everything looked like it would turn out okay. But as the credit crisis spread overseas and international economies sagged, this became less the case. As seen in Japan, stimulating foreign spending is a tricky business; foreigners must feel financially safe, there must be something to buy, and the price must be right. The Chinese tried to counteract their U.S. export recession by stimulating consumption, but with only limited success as goods were relatively unavailable and their currency had been kept artificially weak. In addition, they haven't released the consumer credit mechanisms—like credit cards—so abundant in the United States. What consumption has happened hasn't resulted in buying U.S. products; they may love and buy U.S. *brands*, or Japanese for that matter, but the products are manufactured in China.

China has said that it wants to increase its standard of living through increased investments; further, it grapples with the fact that too much stimulus would have only led to local inflation. One of the best ways to increase foreign demand for U.S. goods is to offer competitive products to buy. Rather than Chrysler minivans, it would make sense, for instance, for the United States to once again assume world leadership in automotive technology—could we not become the source of choice for, say, plug-in hybrid vehicles? That is the direction U.S. policy should go, rather than artificially propping up old products and businesses or encouraging consumption of cheap goods from overseas. Having said that, the way to achieve this is not by subsidizing failed automotive companies, but by providing incentives to invest in new technologies—these technologies may come from new entrants. Right now, Tesla Motors, maker of the all-electric roadster, must compete against billions of subsidies given to Chrysler and GM.

Increase Foreign Investment in the United States

In a manner similar to increasing foreign consumption, an increase in foreign investment would also help achieve greater balance and strength in the U.S. economy. At least, if consumption remains strong, a purchased Toyota built in Georgetown, Kentucky has a greater positive effect on the U.S. economy. Such investments, however, are more likely with a more stable financial and economic base; with a weak and overspent U.S. economy, unstable asset prices, and an unstable currency, there's little to attract major foreign investments.

What This All Means for You

Through every chapter, and through the examination of every boom and bust cycle and policy decision, we need to focus on lessons learned. We've seen how the temptation of consumption leads us down the wrong path, toward more debt, less savings, and more vulnerability in our personal finances. We've also seen how the economic dislocations created by such consumption bubbles can affect our ability to prosper long term.

As a nation, improved finances will mean the tough medicine of reduced economic output and employment in favor of savings and balanced budgets, a scenario not politically expedient but necessary. Every policymaker, instead, wants the saving to start happening on the watch of their successor, as saving means less consumption in the short term.

For you as an individual, it means largely the same thing—adopting a mentality of saving, hopefully to be rewarded with higher interest rates eventually. You must keep current in your job skills to capitalize on the economy's ability to adapt to change, and not rely on old, obsolete jobs or industries to keep you going. You need to avoid the temptation to consume beyond your means, despite what the government and policymakers want you to do, and no matter what the temptations of credit and rising asset prices motivate you to do.

In the next chapter, we'll take a deeper look at how the temptations of credit and consumption originate from the temptation of policy change; and how good, bad, and ever-changing policy and regulation affect your finances.

Would Higher Interest Rates Have Saved the Auto Industry?

One wonders what, other than a complete reinvention and make-over, would have helped the various old-economy firms, like the auto industry, out of trouble. These firms have proven too rigid to adjust quickly to changing consumer tastes and global economics; they're like supertankers, hard to turn. Like an individual in too much debt, throw in a few strategic mistakes and/or a difficult economy and you end up with real trouble. Ironically, had we had higher interest rates and higher taxes, the automotive industry might have been in better shape. Why? Because people would have saved, and now, needing a new vehicle, would be able to spend. Lenders would be in better shape, as would consumer confidence. Instead, little has been right with the auto industry since the "keep America rolling" advertising campaign after the 9/11 terrorist attacks, which set the downward spiral in motion. Don't be so sure that low interest rates are what the auto industry really needs.

3

The Temptation
of Policy Change

Recovery is sound only if it does come of itself.
—Joseph Schumpeter, 1934

"The world we live in is uncertain and cyclical because the U.S. economy is dynamic, inventive, experimental, and entrepreneurial. Some ideas are carried to excess, we discover after the fact. Look at the littered landscape of dead railroads, dead auto companies, and dead airlines to illustrate the dynamic nature of the U.S. economy, illustrated just within the transportation sector." Those are the thoughts of William Poole, former President of the Federal Reserve Bank of St. Louis, a leading voice against the bailout mania to which many of our policymakers seem to be hostage.

These days, many policymakers seem to picture a financially idyllic world in which everyone has the money to buy what they need when they need it. The economy is steady and adequate to support all needs. The economy grows slightly to accommodate the natural population growth. It grows slightly more to accommodate a modest growth in our standard of living. We earn income, spend it on what we need, and perhaps in addition buy a better car, or a nicer sofa in the living room, or a better college education for our kids than the one we enjoyed.

This idyllic economy performs the mantra often associated with a socialist ideal: "From each according to his abilities; to each according to his needs." In this idyllic world, income distribution is natural and tracks economic contributions. You perform work and are compensated commensurately with the value of the work you perform. You can invest in this economy safely; your investments grow with the economy. In this idyllic world, there is no such thing as a business cycle. The economy grows, you grow, everyone prospers.

Sounds attractive, right? You would like to reap the rewards for what you do, throw economic worries aside in favor of more important things like family and how to remove the weeds from your garden, and live happily ever after, right?

But wait—such an idyllic world neither exists nor could it function. Despite what many of us may have been told during the past few decades, there *are* business cycles. The value of the work you perform is gauged by demand of the goods and services you provide, not based on what you may deem is appropriate. And human nature will guarantee that there will always be some sort of intervention in the economy. The status quo is also not a free market solution, because it is influenced by established tax codes and regulations. As we have to deal with intervention anyway, the question is: What kind of—and how much—intervention will facilitate rather than hinder our pursuit of happiness? How does it work, and how should it work?

Most importantly, do policy and regulatory efforts reduce or increase risks (and thus volatility) to our investments? Do they smooth out short-term volatility only to push problems into the future and make us all more vulnerable to long-term volatility? What signals from government and policy intervention should you take to help manage your own financial well-being? To achieve sustainable wealth?

The Boom/Bust Cycle: Can You Fool Mother Nature?

Economists have been studying the question of boom/bust cycles for years, and for the most part, as have I, they have concluded that they are natural and unavoidable. They arise out of ordinary business practices and are helped along by two dominant factors: the imperfection of information and the evolution of tastes and technology.

The imperfection of information has a benefit in the creation of markets, which thrive on the difference of opinion, but the information becomes more imperfect with the diminished foresight available during times of uncertainty—it's something of a vicious circle not always accounted for in the risk models we use. While I'm hardly a fan of the pain these two driving forces can cause in the bust portion of the cycle, I do think the bust serves a useful purpose in moving the economy and society forward and, like black ants on a forest floor, clearing out the dead economic wood of society. When not magnified by uncontrollable events and bad policy, busts serve an important and ultimately valuable purpose.

Let me elaborate a little. Business cycles arise from the natural forces of economic change and the ways that well-intentioned people react to them. Economic change can take a number of forms, from the advent and perfection of new technologies to new resource constraints to the simple fact that not every business decision maker has perfect access to information. Technology change is easiest to describe by example: In the early 1980s, the word processor was invented and sold by companies like Wang Laboratories as the hottest, latest, and greatest digital convenience. That lasted just a few years until the PC, Microsoft Windows, and word processing software made it completely obsolete. Yet those original companies made big investments, as did other companies in their supply chain. These business changes led to *malinvestments*, to the detriment of those invested in the industry.

Such industry-specific errors usually don't have much effect on the economy. The word processor "bust" was offset by gains in the PC business. Most "up" cycles—booms—are led by innovation, fueled by optimism, and capped off by rising asset prices across the board. This happens as the difference of opinion about the future subsides and people choose to underestimate or ignore risk. Imperfect decisions are made along the way, but they're industry-specific and don't attenuate the optimism. In the "down" cycle—the bust—massive mistakes, including overestimated demand, bankruptcies, and underutilized assets, take center stage. A healthy bust is characterized by a purge of inefficient businesses, a correction in job assignments that do not produce enough value, and a general movement of prices, including asset prices—closer to an acceptable, fairer value base.

Can Policy "Fix" the Business Cycle?

These cycles have occurred throughout history, and while they make news and cause angst among individuals and policymakers, they are a perfectly normal outcome of the capitalist system. Risk, too, is normal; in fact, society has created the limited liability corporate structure and the bankruptcy system to facilitate risk taking. This risk, while good for moving the economy forward as a whole, can lead to exaggerated boom/bust cycles when real risks are ignored or excessive risks are taken. What is less widely understood is that government policy, while often described as intended to smooth out business cycles and bring us closer to that "idyllic world" I described in the intro to this chapter, can in reality make the cycles worse.

Government intervention, specifically central bank intervention, has through history made the boom portion of the cycle more pronounced and extended the busts. While government policies are intended to cushion the impact of the bust, what can happen is that all the well-intended efforts only extend the day of reckoning, thereby making recovery efforts mostly expensive but ineffective. In general, any subsidy, be it for a company, an industry, or an economy as a whole, creates more problems than it solves. We saw it in the 1920s and again in every upside business cycle since. Expansionist credit policies delivered through open market operations, reduced reserve requirements, and, in the 1920s, low margin requirements all served as fuel to the decade-long boom. Predictably, it led to numerous *malinvestments*—everything from Florida land and stocks selling for 50 times earnings to the enormous Union Terminal rail passenger station in Cincinnati, Ohio, built just as the automobile was writing ominous messages on the wall for intercity rail travel. Beyond specific malinvestments, the feel-good mentality, the "revolution of rising expectations," as author/historian Frederick Lewis Allen called it, had everyone of the mindset that it would last forever.

Of course, it didn't, and the resulting crash and depression were the largest in history. That depression took the form of a typical bust, albeit a severe one, with inefficient businesses, undercapitalized banks, overpriced stocks and misguided employment quickly weeded out. The "bust mentality" made it worse and made it last longer, but arguably, government policy played a role, too. Just what the government did and what it should have done have been a subject of debate for years.

The 1920s boom was long, strong, widespread, and enhanced by the hand of government, led in part by then–Secretary of Commerce Herbert Hoover. The bust was equally so, and the government again intervened, also at the hand of then–President Herbert Hoover. But the interventions served, to a degree, to make the problem worse.

When faced with a downturn, governments and policymakers, motivated by political forces and the desire to sustain individual and business incomes (and keep tax revenues up), generally step in to try to dampen the effects of the downturn. They open the monetary spigot and try to replace the consumer and business demand that has dried up. The problem is that it is hard to turn off the spigot at exactly the right time, and it perpetuates the economic distortions and maladjustments that got us in the situation in the first place. Further, the flow of money from the spigot masks the true economic problems that lie below the surface, like the auto industry, real estate and construction, and the lending industry in the most recent bust. Those industries are brought forward as they are and perhaps when they shouldn't be. "Even turkeys fly in a high enough wind" is an old stock market adage that applies here.

In the Great Depression, there was a similar rush to prevent or delay liquidation of bad businesses. It didn't happen immediately, as the allowed failure of banks caused bank runs that hurt even the stronger banks. But ultimately, Hoover and his successor Roosevelt put policies in place, including a substantial erosion of the gold standard, to inflate the economy, preserve old businesses, artificially prop up wages, and stimulate consumption. Protectionist tariffs kept prices artificially higher and hurt overseas demand, further harming the economy. The result was a depression that lasted a lot longer than may have been necessary, and in fact was only "solved" by the arrival of World War II.

The point is that government policy and intervention actually works differently than many think. While these policies can make us all feel better during both the boom and the bust portion of the cycle, and while they're intended to smooth the business cycle, they have unintended consequences that can make the cycles and the economic events they cause actually worse. As a steward of sustainable wealth, you need to be aware of these effects, learn to recognize them, and defend your finances accordingly.

In this spirit, let's finish the Joseph Schumpeter quote from the beginning of the chapter:

> [Our] analysis leads us to believe that recovery is sound only if it does come of itself. For any revival which is merely due to artificial stimulus leaves part of the work of depressions undone and adds, to an undigested remnant of maladjustment, new maladjustment of its own which has to be liquidated in turn, thus threatening business with another [worse] crisis ahead.

The Austrian School of Economics

The *Austrian School* of economics has no physical campus or classroom, but rather is a school of thought put forth in the early 20th century by Austrian economists, most notably Ludwig von Mises. Neither the details nor the history are important here, but the basic premise of the Austrian School is that human choices are subjective and too complex to model, and thus it makes no sense for a central authority to force economic outcomes. It is a *laissez-faire* economic philosophy.

The Austrian School takes the view that most business cycles are the inevitable consequence of damaging and ineffective central bank policies. Those policies keep interest rates too low for too long, resulting in excessive credit creation, speculative economic bubbles, and reduced savings. They upset a natural balance of consumption, saving, and investment, which, if left alone, would make the consequences of business cycles far less damaging.

Here's how it works: Low interest rates tend to stimulate borrowing from the banking system. The banking system expands credit with leverage in today's *fractional reserve* banking system (the bank can lend $10 of credit or more for every $1 in capital). The resulting money supply expansion leads to an unsustainable *monetary boom*, during which the artificially stimulated borrowing seeks out diminishing or more far-fetched investment opportunities (like Florida real estate in 1925–1928 or, for that matter, in 2005–2007). This boom results in widespread mal-investments, causing capital to be misallocated into areas that would not attract investment had the money supply remained stable.

The correction happens when the credit creation cannot be sustained; the bubble bursts, asset prices fall, and we enter a recession or bust. If the economy is left to its natural path, the money supply then sharply contracts through the process of deleveraging; people change their minds and want to pay off debt and be in cash again. Once the deleveraging is over and risk is put into proper perspective, and once the market "clears," the economy can prosper again. If and when governments and policy get involved to stem the tide and mitigate the pain of the bust by creating artificial stimuli, they delay the inevitable economic adjustments, making the pain last longer and setting us up for more difficulties later—harsher cycles and more inflation.

If this sounds like what I've already described, that's not a coincidence. The most recent boom/bust cycle has the unmistakable earmarks of the Austrian scenario. While the Austrian School is comfortable with almost no government intervention at all, I see the government role more as one of referee, scorekeeper, and broadcaster than a player in the game. As a referee, it offers a consistent and proper regulatory environment to set boundaries; as scorekeeper, it collects data and measures economic activity; and as a broadcaster it provides some transparency to what is happening on the field.

As an investor and conservator of your personal finances, it's important to recognize impending economic cycles—and bad policy—when they occur. The Austrian model will help you do that. For those interested in a deeper treatment using the Great Depression as a prescient example, I refer you to Murray Rothbard's *America's Great Depression*, published by the Ludwig von Mises Institute. You'll want a rainy afternoon and a cozy fire for this one.

Goldilocks Intended

Despite the natural flow of business cycles, many believed, especially in the 1980s and 1990s, that the central bank—the Federal Reserve—had once and for all found a way to "cure" the business cycle. Better information flow in the 1980s and a confidence-boosting but laissez-faire government stance led to an attenuation of business cycles in the 1990s, most clearly illustrated by the avoidance of long-term effects of the 1987 stock market crash.

At this point, it's worth taking a moment to review the intended role and track record of the Fed.

The Fed, in addition to monitoring the banking system and avoiding panics, has two primary monetary policy objectives: to maximize employment and to stabilize prices. Those objectives are inherently in conflict—full employment will challenge stable prices. So the Fed must walk a tightrope between these objectives, and, at least traditionally, it uses monetary policy to do that.

In theory, at least, the supply of money should match the supply of goods and services available in the economy, with some left over for savings and investment in capital items necessary to produce the goods and services. If there's too much money chasing too few goods and services, that leads to inflation, for every dollar is worth relatively less. If there isn't enough money—or credit—in the system to buy the available goods and services, that leads to a recession, as those goods don't sell (at least not for the price intended), and the prosperity and employment of those who produce the goods eventually falls.

That's the theory, but it can be a lot more complicated than that. Supply shocks, like oil shortages and resulting high oil prices, can "push" inflation even if the money supply is in line—we saw that in the wake of the 1973 oil embargo and again in the early 1980s, and yet again with the oil markets in 2008.

If we rewind the story back to the late 1970s and early 1980s, we can see that the economy then had suffered large inflationary and monetary shocks. Several factors, including a full-employment policy, oil price shocks, a deficit hangover from the Vietnam War, and a lack of confidence in the system (translation: expectations of *more* inflation) drove annual inflation rates into the double digits. The Fed responded to a horse already out of the barn by raising interest rates to unprecedented levels, almost 19 percent for the Fed Funds rate and almost 16 percent for long-term Treasury bonds. This interest rate rise led to a sharp recession in 1981–1982, and from that point forward, the Fed vowed to keep inflation under control.

From 1980 on, starting with Fed Chairman Paul Volcker and continuing with Alan Greenspan, the Fed made good on its vow to stabilize prices. While doing that, the Fed also became a "best friend" of the stock markets, injecting plenty of liquidity—money— during market crises like the 1987 crash. Wall Street and Main Street investors became accustomed to the Fed stabilizing the ship in stormy seas. When inflation started to set in, the Fed took away the punch bowl to slow the party at hand, adjusting money supply downward by raising interest rates toward creating a soft landing. In fact, the Fed became known for promoting a "Goldilocks" economy—not too hot, not too cold, but just right.

This sense of stability—the sense that "they finally figured this thing out"—created an almost unprecedented era of comfort for investors to invest. Technology finally gave businesses and policymakers fast access to data and the ability to adjust quickly to changing conditions. It also boosted productivity, giving a "free" output increase without increasing cost drivers and thus inflation. The advent of self-directed retirement plans, like 401(k)s, and cheap and easy-to-use Internet brokers brought the stock markets to everyone. Many new investors came into the markets, and the stock markets enjoyed a historic bull run from 1982 through 2000.

Savings Glut Contributes to Goldilocks

But this sense of tranquility was misleading, not just to consumers, but also to the Fed. That's because a new phenomenon had entered the markets that misled many investors and policymakers alike: As Asian countries recycled their trade surplus proceeds by buying U.S. government and agency securities, long-term interest rates were kept artificially low. Officials have referred to Asia's "savings glut," pointing out that this contributed to a lower risk premium and thus contributing to the credit bubble.

These dynamics certainly also played a role, but I take exception with arguments that try to externalize problems. Asian countries recycled their savings because selling them would have provided upward pressure on their own currencies, making Asia's exports to the United States less competitive. The buying of U.S. debt doesn't happen in a vacuum, but is a result of U.S. policies and national interests being pursued in Asia.

If there is a positive that comes from the financial crisis, it is that Asian countries have learned that they must develop their domestic markets more. That doesn't mean Asian countries have to give credit cards to their consumers to spur credit growth, but that they should encourage the building of a healthy middle class as well as domestic credit markets.

When Goldilocks Met the Bears

The era of stability and "easy" investing got out of hand in the late 1990s. Increased globalization had brought economic efficiencies but had also enabled countries to more easily export economic problems. The 1997 Asian currency crisis and 1998 Russian debt defaults roiled the markets, but brought liquidity and easy credit from the Fed, and the panics were relatively short lived. Investors, who had banked earlier stock market profits and enjoyed a sense of confidence and peer pressure from other investors, chased almost any dot.com stock that moved. Stock tips were the highlight of any cocktail party. Unfortunately, it turned out to be a bubble; the frenzy evaporated, as did most of the venture capital supporting these enterprises. That and the September 11, 2001 terrorist attacks led to a short but painful downturn.

Greenspan, not liking the idea of a downturn triggered by the stock market, dropped the Fed funds rate substantially, once again injecting liquidity into the financial system. Indeed, it marked a subtle Fed shift from a role of sustaining *incomes* to one of sustaining *asset prices*, a shift that brought a lot of trouble later with real estate. But the immediate interest rate drop helped get employment and

Confidence: The Best Medicine of All

When the economy is good, everyone's an expert, nothing is risky, and everything works. But when things go bad, suddenly that ebullient can't-go-wrong mentality goes out the window. Indeed, lack of confidence becomes a vicious circle, a self-fulfilling prophecy.

So what do we need the most when the tide goes out? What do rational market participants, what do entrepreneurs, what do investors really need? Do they need bailouts? Do they need stimulus packages? Do they need low interest rates? No. The top priority for any reasonable person to put capital at risk is *confidence*. And that confidence runs deeper than simply the idea that the stock market or the value of your house won't go down. It's the confidence that the market will provide fair prices and that one has a fair chance to be fairly compensated for the risks one takes. It's a confidence based on the transparency and ability to comprehend the financial instruments (e.g., collateralized debt obligations) and firms (e.g., investment banks) in the market. Capitalism does not require low prices, low interest rates, or easy access to credit; capitalism requires fair prices, fair interest rates, fair access to credit, efficient markets, and transparency. "Fair" means *free*, not artificially manipulated or influenced by any outside force.

economic growth back on track, while the market was pretty quick to weed out the malinvestments in the dot.com world. Inflation figures in general stayed in line, but unfortunately, the extra liquidity, extra credit, and a resulting overleveraging kicked off the real estate bubble about two years later, and that created a still-bigger credit crisis.

When business cycles work as they're supposed to, the Fed will tap the brakes when prices rise, "mopping up" excess liquidity by selling bonds in open market operations and raising interest rates. If unemployment rises or growth stalls, the Fed injects more liquidity into the system to prime the pump. But too much, too soon prevents the economy from weeding out the bad players and bad investments and can perpetuate a fail-safe mentality among consumers. While tempting, these actions inevitably lead to bigger economic problems down the road.

Above and Beyond: The Fed Ventures Into Fiscal Policy

Recent policy choices during the 2008–2009 recession showed that even when policy isn't working as planned, the temptation for intervention remains a strong force—or becomes even stronger. The credit and banking crisis and the risk contraction that caused it were sharp enough to neutralize the effects of typical monetary injections used to combat the worst effects of recession and unemployment.

The Fed lowered interest rates and bought bonds from banks to inject liquidity in the system, as it has done in the past. The idea was to unlock the banking system and stimulate it to lend, getting a stronger bang for the buck through the multiplier effect (that is, banks can lend $10 for every $1 or so in capital). But these injections didn't stem the tide of falling asset prices, deleveraging, and contracting economic activity. There were two main reasons. One is the classic demand destruction, or saving paradox, where overextended and fearful consumers deleverage and go into savings mode despite the availability of cheap credit (notably, the U.S. personal savings rate increased from near zero to 5 percent in January 2009, a level not seen since 1993). The second is a similar response, also a demand destruction of sorts, where banks, fearful of the health of other banks and the companies they might lend to, hoarded the cash instead of lending it as intended in the support of commerce. In fact, many of these banks turned around and invested the new funds with the government in longer-term Treasury securities rather than lending to the private sector.

The Fed as Innovator

As a result, the Fed, determined to pull the right levers to get the economy going, tried some new ideas in the interest of providing stimulating liquidity. In 2008, the Fed stepped up its buying of many forms of debt securities, including mortgage-backed securities, car loans, and corporate commercial paper. They created a special program called the Commercial Paper Funding Facility (CPFF) in October 2008 to buy billions in short-term (three month or less) commercial paper directly from issuers (not through banks or securities firms) to unlock that market and shore up short-term corporate financing. In November they announced a program to buy $600 billion in mortgage-backed securities from the government-sponsored enterprises (GSEs), Fannie Mae and Freddie Mac. On the same day, they also announced the so-called TALF program (Term Asset-Backed Securities Loan Facility) to lend some $200 billion secured by high-grade asset-backed securities. Finally, in a first-ever move, the Fed began paying 1 percent interest on funds deposited with the Fed.

These innovations came rather easily. All the Fed has to do to create these funds is to create an entry onto its balance sheet with a stroke of a keyboard. They don't need to print money per se, and more importantly, they don't need Congressional approval to do it, as the Treasury does. In fact, Congress rather likes this path because in the end it's an "off–balance sheet" way for politicians to spend money; the Fed is not bound by any spending caps. Indeed, the Fed's balance sheet expanded to over $2.3 trillion at its peak in 2008 from less than $900 billion in the pre-credit crisis era. This explosive growth may only be an early taste of what is to come if the Fed buys government bonds to finance government spending.

Unintended Consequences

While these programs did help to stop some of the bleeding (for instance, yields on top-rated overnight U.S. commercial paper dropped 74 basis points, or 0.74 percent, to 2.94 percent the day the CPFF program was announced), the unintended consequences may cost plenty in the long run.

First, by engaging in these activities, the Fed had by implication gotten into the banking business as a commercial bank, not as a central bank. It is replacing, rather than encouraging, market activity and keeping unhealthy businesses alive. It also delayed the necessary adjustments in home prices and the value of the toxic assets held by the banks. In the longer term, the Fed creates new inflationary risks down the road, especially if the Fed doesn't go to the market at some point to "sterilize" the injections, that is, mop up the excess liquidity (cash and credit in the market) by selling bonds back to the banks. It was notable that some of the moves, like buying GSE (Fannie Mae, Freddie Mac) securities, can't be properly sterilized because of their long-term horizon; that's billions in excess cash that may remain in the economy for some time, adding to the inflationary pressure.

There may be other unintended consequences. If the Fed buys too many securities, say, GSE securities, it artificially inflates the prices. Currently, the United States is in a position where it must sell bonds to fund the budget and current account deficits, and those deficits are on a path to expand rapidly over the next few years, making us more dependent on foreign investment—especially from China—for funding. Yet if we artificially overprice these securities (that is, lower effective interest rates) they will become less attractive, especially at a time when China and other Asian countries are turning their resources inward to deal with their own economic woes.

With intervention in short-term corporate finance, as with the CPFF program, governments are effectively subsidizing some businesses and making it harder for nonsubsidized businesses to compete. Warren Buffett, for instance, has stated that he can't compete effectively with government-subsidized businesses.

Finally, by keeping unhealthy businesses alive, the Fed slows down the effective redeployment of capital and labor resources, which could be going to other areas of the economy. It risks a political backlash when people perceive too many resources going to the wrong things. Ultimately, this micromanagement of the economy could jeopardize Fed independence altogether. Additionally, too much government participation not only crowds out private activity by consuming capital and resources otherwise available to the private sector, it also adds another element of risk to "efficient" capitalists, who themselves may have to deal with government interference and who may find it harder to achieve fair, market-based rates of return.

In short, the Fed stepped out of its traditional role of stimulating or contracting economic activity through monetary policy—the setting of interest rates, regulating the banking sector, and influencing the money supply directly or indirectly through open market operations. Instead, the Fed began dealing directly with companies and guiding where the funds should go. This is fiscal policy, which ran the twin dangers of perpetuating market distortions and adding to an already significant inflationary pressure.

About the "Other" Fiscal Stimulus

In early 2009, Congress passed a stimulus package known as the American Recovery and Investment Act of 2009, projected by the Congressional Budget Office to cost $787 billion over 10 years. President Barack Obama signed it into law.

Beyond the inefficiencies pointed out about Fed fiscal stimulus, this more direct form of government stimulus is also inefficient. First, much of the spending doesn't happen for a year. While markets may have enjoyed the expectation of more spending and economic activity, they became equally—or more—nervous about the effects of additional government borrowing (higher interest rates) and possible tax increases to fund it. It's hard for private investors to invest with such an overhang. Additionally, such spending is inherently less efficient in fixing a free market than tax cuts, because the government rather than free market decides where the money is allocated. Finally, the package did not encourage business investment. Prior tax cuts implemented during both the Reagan and Kennedy years helped businesses, encouraging investments and leading to more permanent economic improvement.

Finally, such stimulus packages don't encourage a change in consumer behavior to save and invest more; they keep debt levels high instead. That sets us up for more failure later, as the Fed can't raise interest rates if inflation reappears (which is likely) without crushing the economy. Meanwhile the government crowds out private borrowing, further reducing investment.

Beyond these dangers, there's still a significant risk that these actions won't really work. The central banks can provide all the money they want, but they cannot force banks to lend, nor consumers to take loans. As a result, the Fed is skipping banks and going directly to the industry, but this is a slippery slope.

What's important is for you, as an investor and wealth sustainer, to recognize the consequences of such headlines—what may sound good in bad economic times may have severe adverse consequences later to the value of your savings and investments. It's important to take a long-term view of what's really going on.

More Bad Medicine for Boom/Bust Cycles

Although well-intended, the temptation for policy change at the Federal Reserve and within the government in general can do more harm than good. In some cases it is like medicine too strong for the illness—the cure is worse than the disease. In other cases, it's like a prescription for the wrong medicine—the disease goes on unchecked while new adverse consequences come to light.

Inflation: A Way Out?

In the long term, inflation is like a tax, making dollars we own—our savings—worth increasingly less. The Federal Reserve can control inflation over the medium term, if it has the will and if it retains the public's confidence in its ability to do so. Incidentally, the most predictive indicator of future inflation is not money supply, but inflation expectations. As long as the Fed can make people believe that it has everything under control, people and businesses will be reluctant to demand wage increases and raise prices. However, this doesn't mean policymakers should abuse the trust the market has in the Fed's ability to contain inflation. When money is printed to finance government spending, a boundary is crossed that we all may live to regret. While I agree that inflation expectations drive future inflation, a stubborn focus on inflation targeting may make one ignore the warning signs as the seeds for future inflations are placed. Once the tiger of inflation is out of the cage, the beast is very difficult to control.

Today's Federal Reserve policies may be setting the table for considerable inflation later on, as more dollars are printed to solve current financial problems. Indeed, through its actions during the financial crisis, the Fed appeared to be embarking on a strategy of deliberate inflation—that is, inflating our way out of economic difficulties.

There's a reason why the Fed wants to embark on an inflationary course. First, debtors must pay back their debts in dollars, but those dollars aren't inflation indexed, so the true worth of what's paid back later is less. Second, by inflating prices on goods compared with real estate, real estate looks relatively attractive; such action may finally stem the fall of real estate prices. Third, the actions that spark inflation also lead to a fall in the U.S. dollar, making U.S. goods more attractive. But for those with a long-term view, there are problems with all of these consequences. The biggest is the erosion of savings and the disincentive to save, which makes us all more vulnerable to economic shock and deprives the system of funds needed for investment. The second is that our dollars buy less in foreign goods, aggravating trade deficits and leading to further inflation. It's a vicious cycle that, once started, is difficult to control.

The Folly of Preserving Bad Businesses

My earlier discussions highlighted the risks of preventing necessary economic adjustments, particularly in the bust aftermath of the boom cycle. The recent troubles in the auto industry have more to hang their hat on than just a boom/bust cycle, but the cycle no doubt made it worse, so the question of whether to bail out U.S. automakers is only partly a manifestation of the business cycle.

In October 2008, there was the real threat of a disorderly collapse of the financial system. Policymakers around the world guaranteed the banking system, clearly communicating that they wouldn't let that happen if they could prevent it. However, many thought that the economy should then bounce back and called the programs a failure. That's incorrect, as we indeed did not have a collapse of the financial system. I sympathize with policies aimed at preventing a collapse.

Aside from preventing pure systemic collapse, however, subsidizing bad businesses only extends the agony, no matter whether we subsidize a steel industry, the cotton industry, or the banking sector. Old practices and processes are kept alive. Furthermore, it becomes less clear to the remaining players what the rules are and what the downside risks of any action might be. Fewer mortgages will be issued as a result, as one has to price in the risk that the government will change the terms. It may not sound like much, but such meddling in corporate affairs can disrupt the flow of capital, for we never know who will become "eligible" for help. In short, changing the rules is bad; the economy as a whole has to suffer for the sake of bailing out a group.

Nationalizing the Banks: Best Medicine?

As the credit and banking crisis unfolded in late 2008, there was considerable debate as to how to deal with it and what to do about the banks involved. Options included buying toxic assets, providing guarantees, injecting fresh capital, setting up a "bad bank" to absorb troubled assets, or outright nationalization.

There was considerable debate over the options. I have always felt that nationalization was absolutely the cleanest—and only—way out of the mess. Not a permanent nationalization through a government-run bank or bank system, but an FDIC seizure of the institutions, followed by a sale of the "good" parts to private interests. With that approach, losses to taxpayers are minimized and we can move on.

The key here is not that we would be moving toward socialism—quite the opposite, in fact. There are established ways to deal with failure, such as bankruptcy; for the banking system, there's a proven path on how to proceed. Political decisions had to be made on whether to punish *all* creditors—including depositors—or only stock and bondholders. Aside from that tricky decision, the rest, to me, was obvious: Pursuing any form of subsidy will keep bad institutions alive. We need good banks, not bad banks.

In my view, what the system really needed was to make the appropriate price adjustments to fix the valuation problem with the toxic assets—a mark-to-market approach—and to take the writeoffs necessary to make that adjustment. The system needed confidence, which means clearing out all the things that took away confidence—bad loans, mispriced assets, even the management layers so accustomed to making any loan to any customer at any cost to meet compensation targets.

The other approaches, to me, were at best treating the symptoms, not the problem, and prolonged the agony.

Fix It, or Get Out of the Way

As the first decade of the 21st century came to a close, I saw a disturbing trend toward what I call "duct-tape" fixes. Bear Stearns needs a bailout—arrange a shotgun wedding. AIG needs another bailout—write another check, buy some more preferred stock. Unemployment goes up—extend benefits. The economy sags—pass another stimulus bill. It was as though we were fixing a crumbling bridge by adding a bit of duct tape here and there. We can't take the pain of a big fix. If asset prices are inflated and certain businesses are unviable, that's too bad, but the economy simply needs to adjust, because policies to uphold bad investments, bad businesses, and inflated prices simply push the problem further into the future.

Indeed, the right path is to allow private market forces to play out. At first, the government came in and wiped out shareholders at every turn—they may have deserved it, but it provided little encouragement for private sector money to come to the rescue of other institutions. Then, the opposite happened and the government injected money at terms the private sector would not match. A key problem at this stage was that there was never enough capital provided and that private sector participation was not encouraged in whatever was done; indeed, as the programs and their rules kept changing, private sector participation was discouraged. The government applied duct tape; in the meantime, the economy continued to slide, rendering any capital injections useless. By early 2009, it had gotten to the stage where only dismembering these firms would create good banks.

But note, again, that good banks are only one ingredient in a healthy economy. Ultimately, what needed to be fixed were house prices not justified by people's incomes. That can't be fixed with price—that is, interest rate—controls; it's fixed with the market adjustment of lower home prices. Any policy against market forces playing out drags out the recovery, making all the freshly printed money flow to other places, creating inflation and bubbles in new areas while not curing the root of the problem.

Regulation and Taxes: Consistency Is the Best Policy

Policy and policy change do not just come in the form of monetary and fiscal adjustments designed to move the economy in one direction or another. They also surface as ongoing regulation of financial markets and in the taxation of income and spending to finance government and achieve economic objectives.

While the Austrian School model and many variations of laissez-faire capitalism appear to shun government intervention at all levels, I am a believer that there is a place for regulation in the markets, just as there is a place for a referee and team of officials on a football field or basketball floor. Done properly—consistently and in line with known and transparent rules—these striped shirts make the game better and more entertaining for everyone. When the referee starts throwing flags or calling fouls with no apparent reason and in favor of one side over another, that's where the trouble starts.

In my view, even extensive regulation and high taxes are better than tax or regulatory uncertainty. You can't plan a business if you don't know whether what you do is legal or illegal; or if and how much the government takes away from you. There are many examples around the world of high-tax, highly regulated environments that work in Europe and even California, which continues to attract venture capital money despite its more active stance on regulation and taxes.

Clarity is as important as consistency. Whether "pro-business" or not by nature, known and transparent regulation and taxes are always better than the unknown. Clarity is one of the reasons that Singapore has become such an important destination for international trade and capital: The rules are simple and clear and not burdened by the bureaucracy of overlapping agencies (such as, for instance, the complex state/federal/local regulatory and tax structure found here in the United States). Without clarity in rules, risk taking, vital to economic growth, may not take place.

It should be again emphasized that I'm not a proponent of high taxes and extensive regulation, any more than I'm a proponent of low prices and low interest rates. What's important is that regulation and taxes be clear, consistent, and fair, just as it is important that prices and interest rates be fair and properly tied to the underlying costs and risks involved.

When Good Regulation Goes Bad

If a referee, without explanation, exempts Team A, or even its superstar, from foul calls, he or she burdens a basketball game with uncertainty and a tainted, unsustainable outcome. Poor or unfair regulation and tax policy, and for that matter, ineffective enforcement of that regulation—we've seen a fair amount of that lately, too, with the Securities and Exchange Commission (SEC) and Bernard Madoff—can become a burden to the economy and to you as a sustainer of wealth.

We've just lived through an era of bailing out individual players and even markets in favor of a false prosperity. Despite the fact that the rules allow failure, the Fed under Alan Greenspan bailed out the markets for years—for example, during the Long-Term Capital Management (LTCM) hedge fund implosion in 1997. That sort of bailout became so predictable that many referred to it as the "Greenspan put" (translation: Free government-sponsored insurance against the failure of the investment markets). Rather than bailing out individual players like LTCM or AIG or Citigroup later on, the focus should be on mitigating systemic risks (i.e., the risk that their errors could bring the whole market down).

That could be best done by increasing market transparency, especially for the opaque financial instruments that brought on the 2007–2008 banking crisis. In stock and especially commodity markets, players can make bets and hedge positions—but these bets are "marked to market" daily (that is, their value is reassessed based on market action). When they work out poorly, there's an almost immediate margin call, and the position is closed out and settled; the loser takes the loss. But with CDOs and other instruments, there is no such market, no such transparency, and no such resolution of bad bets—hence the buildup of "financial weapons of mass destruction," as Warren Buffett described them, which detonated later, causing extensive collateral damage to the system. It is this sort of systemic risk that regulators must handle: Provide a level, clear, transparent playing field and blow the whistle or throw a flag when someone commits a foul—instead of changing the rules of the game.

The result of such rule changes, of course, is that private capital players in the game don't want to play any longer. Why would they, if rule changes might cut into their expected returns or wipe them out altogether? That's why I wasn't and still am not in favor of forced "cram-down" loan modifications for individual mortgage holders.

Like a bad officiating crew, the Fed and many regulators have effectively embarked on a course of picking winners and losers. Instead, they should let the proven bankruptcy laws work and provide transparency and resolution to "paper" losses in the financial markets. There are already processes in place through the FDIC to dismember insolvent financial institutions. In short, they should let the system work and deal with the fouls and penalties; they should let the winners win and the losers lose. The alternative is a propped-up, broken, inefficient, bordering-on-planned economy.

Long-Term Policy Consequences

As part of managing sustainable wealth, you must stay aware of the events, policies, and policy changes that might affect your finances not only today, but also for the long term. It is important to keep track of individual policies and regulations as well as the bigger picture. The big picture has two elements. First is the way policies work together—that is, tax policy and monetary policy—to achieve favorable or unfavorable outcomes. Second is how the policies work in sequence—or, in many cases, a vicious cycle, which can create a cure worse than the disease. More policy leads to more change, which leads to more doubt, which leads to more inefficiency, which leads to more unemployment, which leads—back to the beginning.

Sustainable wealth management means looking at the disease, the symptoms, the cures, and the unintended consequences of the cure all together, as a system.

Following are some of the more obvious long-term questions raised by policy.

The Debt Factor: Now More Than Ever

Temptations of credit, consumption, and policy have several effects that have been discussed in these first three chapters. But there is hardly a bigger effect than the mountain of debt left behind in their wake.

Individual and societal debt in the United States has risen to unprecedented levels. In fact, as this book is written, we may be in the midst of a bond market bubble. Bond prices have risen beyond proportion to their value, especially in the long term, because of Fed intervention and what still remains a healthy appetite among foreigners to own U.S bonds—either as a safe haven or to keep local economies going. A bubble in the bond market makes some sense when viewed as a rotational player in the sequence of stock market bubble (1999) to real estate bubble (2005–2006) to commodities bubble (2007–2008) to now, a bond market bubble.

More importantly, and more dangerously, this bubble, like other bubbles, can and will burst at some point. Foreign demand for bonds may wane for reasons we've already discussed; in addition, even the slightest puff of inflationary pressure could turn bonds into a far riskier investment. The resulting crash in bond prices would send interest rates soaring and would perhaps take away the last policy tool in place to help avoid severe economic contraction or even depression.

A sharp collapse in bond prices would indicate that the government's ability to borrow would be largely gone, and any attempt to keep interest rates low in such a scenario would be extremely inflationary. In fact, a worst-case scenario would be an inflationary depression—prices out of control while the economy was in extreme contraction—a scenario never before experienced. The government would have to spend in the place of Americans who couldn't, which would make the cycle worse.

The way to avoid this, of course, is as we've already laid out—to accept (and not meddle with) the recession, allow the adjustments, return ourselves to a nation of savers. The adjustment, hardly painless, is essentially a makeup strategy for years of excessive borrowing.

Is There an Exit Strategy?

Beyond the bond market bubble, I continually worry about the exit strategy from current policies in place. As with the principles of the universe, every action gets a reaction, and the reaction to much of the monetary and fiscal stimulus is an enormous pool of excess liquidity—too much money—in the marketplace. Too much money chasing the same amount of goods is by definition inflationary. So how will the government remove all of that liquidity—how will they sterilize and mop up the cash—without causing other problems? The bigger the liquidity pool becomes, the harder it is to remove liquidity without disrupting certain businesses or the economy in general. At least for the moment, the Fed seems to have no credible exit strategy or plan to reverse the unintended consequences of the monetary and fiscal stimulus; the consequences of excess liquidity and disrupted free markets could occur over a long period of time. This is a critically important issue and one to watch closely.

At the same time, Fed Chairman Ben Bernanke uses every opportunity he can to say that the Fed is in control and will do whatever it takes to avoid inflation to flare up. What else do you expect him to say? Do you expect him to say: "We have a major problem down the road, and frankly, we're not sure how to get out of this mess!" It turns out that the best statistic to forecast inflation is inflationary expectations. This seemingly circular argument applies because inflation feeds on itself: Once consumers and businesses believe there will be inflation, wage demands and price hikes will intensify. As a result, confidence in the Fed's ability is paramount to contain inflation. European Central Bank President Trichet called all the warnings about future inflation "extraordinarily counterproductive." He is absolutely right: the warnings about inflation may trigger more inflation. However, we would all be better off if the policies pursued were less inflationary.

The Fed and other central banks could prevent inflation from breaking out, I'm not doubting that. However, I do not think it is realistic that the Fed will raise interest rates or engage in other activities to mop up liquidity to the extent necessary, because those activities would throw the economy back into a tailspin.

A Choice Among Evils

Centuries of economic history and boom/bust cycles show that it's impossible to avoid financial crises altogether. That said, it is possible for the United States and other countries to decide what kind of crises they will get. The choice is between the up-and-down, crisis-prone nature of a lightly regulated society, an innovation-intensive, Wild West approach to finance, or a more tightly regulated but also more stable environment.

As a nation we've vacillated between the two. Before the Depression, it was Wild West, as most poignantly illustrated by the 10 percent margin requirement for buying stocks (you put up 10 percent, the broker puts up the rest). The Depression and resulting bank failures swung us back toward regulation and safety. Then, especially after 2000 and the full advent of the information age, the financial society crept toward less regulation and more innovation. The crisis that followed threatened to end all of that, and as I write this and in the wake of the Bernard Madoff and other scandals, there are calls once again for more regulation and safety in the financial system.

What's best? The answer depends on what is lost from crises versus what is gained from innovation. I tend to think that innovation, and further, the free and frictionless markets it supports, are a good thing. Regulation once again would serve as referee, not head coach and chair of the rules committee. The loss from crises is rather a natural thing and should be tolerated.

Policy, Complacency, and Sustainable Wealth

As a wealth sustainer, you must track which way the policy winds are blowing, and be sensitive to the long-term economic consequences they suggest. In today's fast-moving, complex world, it is no longer sufficient to stand by and trust the powers that be; too much hangs in the balance of their decisions. It is tempting to simply hold tight and wait for the Fed and other agencies to set things right when they go wrong, but as we've seen recently, it's dangerous to rely on these influences. It is also tempting to stand by and assume that our high standard of living is in everyone's best interest and will be sustained at all costs.

The temptations of credit, consumption, and policy have created a dangerous and volatile economic world, more so because of the speed of change and adjustment. The last temptation, the temptation of complacency, occurs when individuals, businesses, and governments take their greatness, standard of living, and financial stability for granted. That temptation is the subject of the next chapter.

4

The Temptation
of Complacency

Complacency is the enemy of study.

—Mao ZeDong

The *American Heritage Dictionary of the English Language* defines "complacency" as a "feeling of contentment or self-satisfaction, especially when coupled with an unawareness of danger, trouble, or controversy."

The temptation of complacency is the last and most abstract of the temptations we will address in *Sustainable Wealth*. Interestingly, complacency is to a degree a result of the other temptations (debt, consumption, policy) and to a degree a *cause* of those other temptations. We rest on our laurels. We become accustomed to certain outcomes. We take our wealth for granted. We're sure we're doing the right things; after all, our homes, bank accounts, and brokerage statements are growing in size, are they not? Easy and abundant wealth has made many of us into "Masters of the Universe," to borrow a phrase so eloquently coined by Tom Wolfe in his epic novel *Bonfire of the Vanities*.

It's bad when we as individuals, earning an ordinary salary and possessing ordinary talents, become Masters of the Universe. It's even worse when corporate executives in the highest position and even government officials and policymakers assume such a machismo and *modus operandi.* The specter of unassailability not only causes grievous errors (like overleveraging and subprime lending); it also creates a mentality in which, rather than preventing defeat, we only look for ways to explain it away, while expecting others to continue to come to our rescue. Those "others" include the government for individuals and corporations, and the Chinese for our government. As Hall of Fame NBA coach Pat Riley once said, "When a great team loses through complacency, it will constantly search for new and more intricate explanations to explain away defeat." In many ways we've become a society more geared toward explaining defeat and hoping the solution comes from elsewhere than one that embraces change and acts accordingly to deal with it.

I see five major areas where complacency and even arrogance have eroded our economic strength and long-term future as individuals and as a nation. They are all related. The first is the ongoing presumption of standard of living primacy and the drive to maintain it at all costs. The second is an underestimation and even an ignorance of risk; that is, the "look the other way" approach that has gotten so many individuals and the nation as a whole into trouble. The third is the tendency to take old business and leadership models for granted and the corollary unwillingness to adapt to change—when that unwillingness is passive, it is dangerous; but when it is active, as in the form of going out of the way to preserve out-of-date businesses or out-of-date ways, it is even *more* dangerous. Next is an overreliance on previously built-up trust, which manifests itself in a nation as an overreliance on our currency as a "reserve" currency sought by everyone, everywhere. Finally, complacency drives us to ignore the worst-case scenarios of our policies; the recent "brush with socialism" inherent in increased government activism in the business space could lead to dire consequences if we become overly complacent about it.

This chapter explores all five manifestations of the temptation of complacency.

Big Hat, No Cattle

The phrase "big hat, no cattle" refers to someone " . . . who presents themselves as a person of great importance, but whose actual credentials are spurious or questionable." The phrase is used in different settings; when it comes to money it was made famous by

Thomas Stanley and William Danko in their excellent personal finance classic *The Millionaire Next Door* (first edition: Longstreet, 1996). They used the phrase to describe individuals rich in possessions but poor in true wealth, that is, those whose possessions came about largely as a result of borrowed money.

Possessions coming about as a result of borrowed money aren't true possessions. Buy a $40,000 Lexus and borrow $35,000 to do so, and for all practical purposes, the bank owns the Lexus. That's fairly obvious. But what about illusory wealth—that is, wealth that falls short of being true wealth, illusory because you own assets that aren't really worth as much as they appear to be—because their value is inflated in a boom? Sure, it felt good when your house out-earned you each year during the credit bubble. But was that true wealth? *Sustainable* wealth?

The Complacency of False Prosperity

It wasn't sustainable at all, as many people painfully found out. Worse, if you had borrowed money using such "wealth" as collateral, you would be in far bigger trouble. Once the illusory wealth evaporated, the debt secured by that wealth would still be there. Your "prosperity" would have gone from positive to absolutely negative. Millions had this happen; in fact, an early 2009 account showed that some 14 million homeowners owe more on their homes than they're worth. Now those unfortunate owners not only have seen their prosperity evaporate, but they also have no money to spend. Their wealth, and now their borrowing power, are exhausted. And that had serious and lasting impact on the economy.

How did we get ourselves into such a mess? One reason is that we forgot one of the most important axioms in finance concerning assets and liabilities: *Asset values are subjective while liabilities are real.* If you own an asset—*any* asset—it is worth no more than what others are willing to pay for it. And that *price* can be driven by many factors and vary all over the place. Asset prices are high during boom times, when everyone has money and no one considers the full risks in owning that asset. Asset prices drop when no one has money and everyone thinks ownership of your asset and others like it is an inherently risky proposition.

But what about the liabilities? The debts that you hold, the mortgages, credit card debt, and so forth? Those values are fixed and real. If you owe $35,000 on your car, that amount is fixed; it doesn't go up and down with the economy, the value of the car, or anything else. If the value of the car drops to zero, you still owe $35,000.

A lot of people forgot this axiom during the 2005–2007 credit boom, and it has come back to haunt them. We became complacent about what we bought. We assumed that real estate prices could only go up. We assumed that incomes would stay steady or even rise—all of which made the debts taken on to buy all of our stuff seem like a minor, irrelevant detail. Our financial institutions and policymakers unfortunately assumed the same thing.

Tragically, that turned out not to be the case.

The Standard-of-Living Complacency

According to the popular Wikipedia definition, standard of living is " . . . the quality and quantity of goods and services available to people, and the way these goods and services are distributed within a population." Many Americans have become complacent about their standard of living. They live on the assumption that it will always get better, and worst case, it can never get worse. It's a dangerous assumption.

True measures of standard of living, like per capita GDP, tend to break down because of the more abstract overlay of "quality of life," which incorporates stress; cleanliness (as in water and air); availability of leisure time and things to do in that time; increased life expectancy; open space; short commutes; and so on. It does not account for distribution of wealth, that is, that some have a much higher standard of living than others. It also does not include the value of unpaid work, such as housework or volunteer work, whose availability and contribution both serve to enhance the perceived living standard. And it doesn't account for the quality but only the quantity of goods and services produced. So it becomes more a matter of perception than physical and financial reality.

On January 4, 2008, a Gallup Poll reported that 56 percent of all Americans thought their standard of living was getting better, while only 26 percent thought it was getting worse. On February 27, 2009, those figures had reversed; 33 percent of Americans thought their standard of living was getting better while 44 percent thought it was getting worse.

So why had the perception of standard of living become so much worse? Indeed, cracks had formed in the income base; our standard of living from a pure income perspective dropped a few percentage points, but something even greater was going on. Sure, stress levels were higher, as everyone suddenly started having to worry about their jobs and basic necessities. But the real key to people's appraisal of their own living standard comes from their wealth, or their perception thereof.

During this short time period between the two Gallup polls, we experienced an almost unprecedented decline in personal wealth—especially the "easy" wealth gained from real estate price appreciation and, to a lesser extent, the appreciation in the price of stocks. Wealth gained through hard work or prudent investing leads to a gradual improvement in living standards. People who have earned money that way typically have a greater appreciation for that wealth and are less likely to make sloppy investment decisions, because they know that wealth is earned the hard way; they are less driven toward "wealth-effect" confidence and complacency.

Sure, these people lost a lot of money, too, but they probably managed it better, lost less, and had a more balanced perspective on the whole crisis. They knew that an investment loss might mean working longer, and could accept the fact and plan accordingly. The individuals who amassed their "wealth" from overvalued assets driven by an overheated economy are the ones who really got hurt. They now live in fear of a permanent decline in their living standards. In my experience those folks were more likely to think they are invincible; nothing could happen to them, they were Masters of the Universe, their wealth was permanent and unassailable; they became complacent to the risks inherent in that wealth, and when it evaporated it was a surprise.

Wealth versus Sustainable Wealth

There are two very important messages here for you as a wealth sustainer. First, there's a huge difference between wealth and *sustainable* wealth. Sustainable wealth comes without serious risk to its demise; it is not built on the base of assets and especially inflated asset values driven by excessive debt and policy excess. Builders of sustainable wealth are keenly sensitive to asset overvaluation and the factors that can cause it.

The second message is that complacency about your wealth and wealth-producing ability will lead to adverse consequences unless you're lucky, and you don't want to depend on luck for your long-term financial security. You must stay informed and active to ensure that your assets are priced properly and not unduly influenced by artificial forces. You must see the risks in your investments and the income from those investments; the companies and entities represented by those investments must be capable of adapting to change. And your own personal income-producing ability must also adapt to change—as any autoworker or newspaper pressman can tell you these days.

The Big Hat, No Cattle complacency leads to other complacencies—the disdain of risk, the resistance to change and leadership, the assumption that America is great forever and can ignore economic realities, the complacency that government always should and always will bail us out. I will address each of those in turn in the sections that follow.

Complacency's Counterparty—Risk

I hear it again and again. People say they didn't see it coming. They didn't foresee the remarkable downdraft in the markets and the economy in 2008 and 2009. They knew the real estate and stock markets had been strong and might have expected a "normal" correction—but not anything like this. Not a 30 percent drop in real estate prices and 50 percent drop in stock prices. Real estate, of course, "always" goes up, and stocks, well, they pull back 10 percent on corrections, 20 percent in bear markets, and with the Fed in charge, surely that was about all that could go wrong this time around.

For that matter, some of the largest and most respected financial institutions in the world got it wrong, too. They, too, assumed the price of real estate would never retreat. Lenders lent, eager for the short-term fees generated by the transactions, eager to borrow short and cheap and lend long at a profit, eager to sell the loans—again for more fees—to someone else.

I don't need to share the rest of that story. Suffice it to say that individuals, major corporations, and the policymakers that let it all go largely unchecked all got it wrong. The part they simply didn't understand—or chose to ignore—was the risk.

The complacency of risk led to some remarkable bets, all built on the assumption that:

- The worst would never happen
- It wouldn't happen to everyone at the same time
- If it did, someone else would pick up the tab.

That led to some remarkable results. For instance, *one division* of the financial bellwether and Dow 30 giant American International Group (AIG) wrote some $440 billion in credit default swap insurance on U.S. corporate debt—in addition to the normal risk exposure such an insurer would take—despite having only $200 billion in net company worth. One small division put the entire company at risk two times over.

In some ways, it was inevitable. The Great Depression happened too long ago for anyone in the working world to remember. Wall Street was loaded with thousands of young, newly minted MBAs barely old enough to remember even the 1987 stock market crash. And everyone assumed the "Greenspan put," that the Fed would come to the rescue if anything really bad happened, although "really bad" was assumed to be something like another terrorist attack or oil shortage or some other terrible exogenous headline, not the fact that they themselves had taken on too much risk and created financial instruments nobody could understand.

The ignorance of risk clearly has its own perils—it's not hard to see that if you invest in something that fails, you lose your money. If too many people put too much money at risk, and entangle each other in a web of risk management transactions, the risk goes beyond the original risk taker; it becomes *systemic*. Systemic risk means that the failure of one entity can bring down several others; and maybe even an entire market or economy. It's what Warren Buffett was talking about when he referred to credit derivatives as "financial weapons of mass destruction" way back in 2002.

But arguably the biggest peril created by risk ignorance, one that played a huge part in the most recent boom and bust and most others before it, is the overvaluation of assets. It's not a hard concept to grasp—an asset *without* risk of loss is worth more than an equivalent asset *with* risk of loss, all other things being equal. People become complacent about risk and thus bid up the price of assets under the assumption that there simply wasn't any risk. It happened with tulip bulbs in the early 1600s, with stocks in the 1920s and with real estate in 2005–2007. It's a circle of irony: Complacency ultimately drove asset prices higher; the higher asset prices made us still more complacent. Such was the hubristic air that inflated these bubbles.

Any asset or credit bubble is accompanied by an expansion of risk *tolerance*, that is, contrary to intuitive logic, people perceive *less* risk as the bubble expands. When the bubble pops, there's an implosion of risk intolerance, risk aversion returns to the forefront rather abruptly, usually as a result of anything from an international event to a high-profile business failure. At that moment, the appreciation and even the dread of risk returns to its full girth, everyone suddenly pulls back into safe-haven investments, and asset values plummet. The observance of plummeting asset values causes individuals, corporations, lenders, and everyone else to fret more, lend less, and buy less, and so the cycle is perpetuated.

In short, the misappraisal of risk is one of the most important catalysts of any boom and bust cycle, and, most importantly, it is complacency that allows the proper assessment of risk to go off course in the first place. And the continued misappraisal of risk— one way or the other—after the bubble bursts causes continued maladjustments in the economy, which makes it all worse.

The Perils of Risk Modeling

The misappraisal of risk is most certainly behavioral. It starts with the feel-good mentality brought on by success, combined with policy and credit tailwinds and an absence of bad news. But it doesn't stop there. By nature, financial institutions, and especially investment banks, exist to make financial bets on the business world. They lend money to what they expect to be successful enterprises in the interest of generating profit. They buy and sell securities in markets in a bet on what will be higher or lower down the road. Every single product or service they produce has—or should have— a risk assessment; as a practical matter, financial services companies are in the risk management business.

As such, they have strict guidelines and sophisticated methods and models to manage risk. Financial institutions have relied more and more on statistical models and measures to appraise the risk, or safety, of a security or portfolio of securities. That safety is—at least in theory—balanced against the return of the security or portfolio and is used to determine how much risk capital a bank needs to set aside for a rainy day. In the old days, financial services companies had a chief legal counsel or some other officer who would serve as a chief risk manager and final arbiter of risk and deal making. These individuals could check whether a deal could jeopardize the franchise—but in many cases, they were replaced by the models.

The conventional value-at-risk (VAR) model is a normal statistical distribution, giving the highest probability to the most likely scenarios and steadily declining probabilities to increasingly less likely scenarios. Out at the extremes lie the "tails"—the very least likely scenarios. The scenarios are mapped according to what has actually occurred in the past.

The approach works well for the normal and close-to-normal sets of events, for which there is plenty of history. The problem occurs at the tails, where there isn't much history and where the complexities of the financial system add more systemic risk than might be measurable in the model. For example, the tail might predict a certain number of 300-point down days in the Dow Jones Industrial Average, but it has trouble predicting that ten such days in a row would lead to the ruin of many businesses and financial institutions, causing a far greater event than would normally be predicted.

To give an example, according to a report in *The Economist*, mathematician Benoît Mandelbrot calculated that a "normal" distribution would have suggested 58 days of 3 to 4 percent moves in the Dow between 1916 and 2003, but in fact it did so 1,001 times. A move of 4 to 5 percent should have happened 6 times, but it actually happened 366 times; a 7 percent move should have happened only once in 300,000 years, not 48 times during the period.

The standard mathematical practices of the day underestimated this so-called long-tail risk. Most likely, if risk managers at the purchasing financial institutions had fully appraised these long-term risks and fully appraised the inherent risks of the credit securities they were buying, the temptation to engage in these transactions would have been reduced. Instead, as one pundit put it, financial engineers designed and built a rocket and launched it high into space with great fanfare when things were good, but when the market turned, the rocket fell back to Earth and landed on the engineers who designed it and the risk managers who were supposed to understand how it worked.

Where Were the Risk Managers?

In fact, where were those risk managers, anyway? As we sorted through the ashes of the financial meltdown, we came away wondering who was really in charge of the risks that the major financial institutions were taking. Who made the decision to allow AIG to write all those credit default swaps, or Merrill Lynch to buy all those asset-backed subprime collateralized debt obligations (CDOs)? In the "old days," risk was closely controlled by a chief risk officer, usually a chief financial officer—someone far from the corporate limelight with ultimate authority to sign off on risky transactions. That system seems to have given way to a less rigid appraisal and control of risk, a "fox in the chicken coop" mentality in which those in the corporate hierarchy who were best positioned to reap the rewards from the added income also had the responsibility for controlling the risk. Complacency and the lure of wealth tipped their scales, and we all know where that rocket ultimately landed.

Fair Is Fair

I've said it before in previous chapters, and it bears repeating: I do not necessarily advocate low interest rates, low prices, and high credit standards. What I advocate is *fair* interest rates, *fair* prices, *fair* credit standards, *fair* everything in a free market economy. Why? Because with fair standards, the economy is allowed to function naturally. A transaction defined by fair prices, interest rates, and standards must earn enough return to support itself without intervention; thus, it is a proper transaction. Artificially low prices, rates, and standards lead to improper, unsustainable decisions.

What makes a price, rate, or standard "fair"? A price is fair if a buyer and a seller agree on a price based on their free and rational assessment of value, which is in turn based on a proper and realistic assessment of risk.

Moral Hazard

The term *moral hazard* comes from the insurance industry and can be defined as the possibility that a party insulated from risk may behave differently from the way it would behave if it were fully exposed to the risk. Moral hazard happens when that party—an individual or institution—is not subject to the full consequences of its actions; as a result it might act less carefully than it otherwise would. Some other party—an insurance company, or, in our case, a third party or the government—assumes some of the responsibility for those actions.

The packaging of debt securities did much to send risk downstream and to help lenders avoid the risks of their activities. Moreover, recent government actions, including liquidity injections, bailouts, and the TARP (Troubled Asset Relief Program) have given many a false sense of security that they will not have to bear the full consequences of their actions. That could be very dangerous as we move forward. As economist Paul Krugman put it, we've been led in the direction of "lemon socialism"—a two-tiered capitalist system where private enterprise reaps the benefits of a decision while the taxpayers pick up the risks.

The complacency brought about by moral hazard creates distortions in the economic system, engendering risks that might not otherwise be taken, and causing assets to be mispriced. Thus the danger is not only to the government and taxpayers who must bail people out of excessively risky positions, but to all of us who may suffer shocks to asset prices when these chickens come home to roost. Recognizing the evidence of moral hazard in the economy, particularly a *growth* in moral hazard (perhaps detected through cocktail party conversations or excessively cocky CEO comments in annual reports or quarterly earnings conference calls) is a hallmark of developing sustainable wealth.

Of course, sustainable wealth implies that it's just as important for you to avoid *individual* moral hazard; that is, you should not become complacent in the idea that someone is going to bail *you* out if your finances take a wrong turn.

The Complacency of Business Legacy

As we've discussed in previous chapters, the bust following the boom is economic nature's way of clearing the dead wood from the economic forest floor—that is, purging the economy of the effects of bad business decisions and bad businesses themselves.

Businesses come and go on their own, even without the assistance of a business cycle. Improvements in technology and productivity combine with changes in consumer tastes and needs to drive a persistent evolution and change in the marketplace; those marketplace changes then drive changes in the businesses themselves. Or at least that's the way it's supposed to work. Economist Joseph Schumpeter called this process "creative destruction" in his 1942 book *Capitalism, Socialism and Democracy*.

In Schumpeter's words, creative destruction is a " . . . process of industrial mutation that incessantly revolutionizes the economic structure from within, incessantly destroying the old one, incessantly creating a new one," and goes on to say that the "process of creative destruction is *the* [emphasis added] essential fact about capitalism."

The message, of course, is that in a capitalist system, businesses must reinvent themselves constantly. Moreover, the pace of that reinvention has accelerated dramatically over the years. The technology cycle for railroads, for instance, took 100 years to run its course, from invention to their economic peak in the 1940s. For radio, it took perhaps 40 years, starting in the 1920s; today, many technology cycles run 20 years or less. This, in fact, is Microsoft's predominant counterargument to antitrust actions against it; that while they are the masters of the PC software world today, that mastery is constantly under threat from new technologies, such as cloud computing.

The speed of change and the recent economic bust combined to deal a huge blow to corporate America—the corporate world, in fact—as we exited the first decade of the 20th century. The troubles at General Motors and Chrysler, the disappearance of several major retailers, the rapid decline of the newspaper industry, and several other prominent business failures were great examples of the inability to adapt to change. And it isn't just a U.S. phenomenon—banks and industrial conglomerates in Japan, for instance, failed to react to changed business conditions; many went out of business or hung on by government support for years. The willingness of the Japanese government to let them hang on as-is was one of its biggest policy failings. Even in "upstart" China, inefficient businesses with inefficient technologies are starting to be cleaned out in large numbers.

Thus, the cost of not responding to change—for individual, for business, for governments—can be very high. Jobs are lost, capital is wasted, products are made and sold at prices that don't generate adequate returns; the cycle repeats itself. But those costs are a necessary part of creative destruction and will lead to an improved, more efficient, more up-to-date economy eventually. The cost of not allowing that to happen may be greater; there is no better example than the delays in producing truly energy-efficient American-made automobiles.

When the government steps in, it gets even worse. As we saw in Japan and most notably in the United States during the recent credit bust, the government has a tendency to backstop these legacy industries in the interest of preserving jobs. That's an honorable objective, but if a business or a business model is flawed, it is flawed, and making it last longer still doesn't really work. If anything, it makes managers and shareholders even less likely to look for sustainable long-term solutions.

There are other unintended consequences. The rewards for effective business leadership are essentially destroyed, as rewards no longer match valid economic contributions. It also leads to misallocations of capital; for example, if the U.S. government effectively borrows to bail out inefficient industries, it crowds out proper funding of private sector investments or even appropriate public sector (e.g., municipality) investments. It becomes very difficult for anyone but the government to raise money. Indeed, Warren Buffett in his annual 2009 letter to shareholders, points out that the cost of borrowing for his AAA-rated enterprise is higher than for broken businesses that have received government support through implicit or explicit government guarantees. The government, with all its well-intended efforts, is destroying healthy companies, substituting rather than encouraging private sector participation.

Trust Must Be Earned Every Day

Voluntary exchange is the essential feature of any market economy. Voluntary exchange implies trust. Exchange takes place because both parties to a transaction trust the other to deliver the contracted good on one side and money on the other. Moreover, a market economy builds trust because it typically depends on repeated transactions. A failure in one transaction destroys trust; you would not do business with that person or firm again. The market economy rewards trustworthy behavior.

The best way to internalize this concept is to think about what capitalism would be like *without* trust. Without trust, even short-term transactional economic activity would come to a standstill, for someone would either have to supply a good or service and trust they would be paid, or they would have to pay up front and assume the good or service would be supplied. More importantly, in the long term, nobody would invest, nobody would lend; there would be no promise of ever getting a proper return on invested capital. The level of repeated, unhindered exchange would drop; the economy in such an environment would eventually falter or even cease to exist. World history has given numerous examples of countries and economies hampered by varying degrees of mistrust.

Trust is gained through fairness. Fairness in rules, fairness of enforcement, fairness of making sure rewards accrue to those who earn them. It is also gained through stability; that is, the knowledge that the rules will be essentially the same many years down the road. Trust is gained through solid, consistent leadership and through transparency—that is, the ability for all players in the market to know what is occurring in that market, at least to the extent necessary to make important financial decisions. Transparency of financial statements and financial reporting is but one example.

Once again, to explain how trust is gained, it helps to explain how it is lost. Trust is damaged by unfilled promises, unexpected outcomes, hidden activities, and indecisive leadership. Each of these factors effectively increases the risk of engaging in any form, especially in long-term economic activity. More to the point, when certain individuals in power—or governments as a whole—start to fiddle with the economic system by granting bailouts, modifying loan terms, devaluing currency, slapping heavy import or export tariffs, and so on, those actions clearly get in the way of trust. And the loss of trust can be swift and slippery; once it gets started, it's hard to stop, and most efforts to restore it are prone to failure. One only needs to look at the economic histories of Latin American countries for examples.

It's easy to become complacent with the idea that you have the trust of others. Building trust is a long-term, gradual exercise, but many forget how quickly it can be lost. As Warren Buffett said, "It takes 20 years to build a reputation and 5 minutes to ruin it. If you think about that you'll do things differently."

The Complacency of Reserve Currency

Quite simply, no other country on this planet would get away with the deficit spending and finance seen in the United States. Now, that's not entirely a bad thing, because the United States still enjoys reserve currency status—that is, it's still largely the world's most sought-after currency among all choices for safety, at least in the short term. That didn't come by accident; it's a result of long-term economic strength and reasonably good policies through the decade and the past in general. Contrast the United States' situation with that in the United Kingdom, where similar temptations and credit problems to those we've discussed in the first four chapters led to a dramatic 40 percent drop in the currency against the dollar in late 2008 and 2009 and a virtual loss of its world status as a safe haven.

Now that's not to say that the U.S. dollar hasn't depreciated in recent years. Indeed, the price of gold quadrupled from around $250 in 1999 to $1,000 an ounce in early 2009, and the dollar has lost about half of its value against major world currencies since 2000, although the dollar did rebound a bit in the risk-averse world financial environment of late 2008.

The 2008 rebound, and the endurance of the dollar overall, is explained by the fact that the United States is still the dominant economy and is still perceived to be the most stable, in political and economic terms, among world economies. Over a very long period of time, we've earned the world's trust. The dollar is still a "reserve" currency for public and private investors around the world, not quite as good as gold, but it's still a safe haven. Relative to Kenyan schillings or Argentine pesos, the U.S. dollar looks pretty attractive. Adding to the dollar's atypical strength is the fact that other countries, notably China, have found a strong dollar in their own economic interests to support exports, and so the dollar gets more support.

Reserve currency status brings with it the advantages of a constant stream of inflows—cheap money from abroad—which lowers the cost of doing business for both individuals and the government. The problem, of course, is that the reserve currency status has allowed the United States to get away with economic policies—including the perpetuation of consumption and easy credit—that wouldn't otherwise be tolerated. It isn't clear how long this situation will last; if something happens to cause the dollar to "break" lower, it could start a run against the currency with disastrous consequences, including massive inflation resulting from higher import prices. The temptation to rely on others to uphold our currency could be dangerous in the long run.

Reserve currency status made us complacent and perpetuated the other three temptations outlined in this book, which in turn represent a threat to our reserve currency status. It's clear that a different set of policies to support the dollar and encourage savings and investment, while painful in the short term to economic prosperity, would do a lot to reduce the threat to reserve currency status. Again, it's dangerous for us as individuals or as a society to take our greatness for granted.

As an individual investor, you must watch policy and the world value of the dollar for signs of trouble. If the dollar were to lose its reserve status and go into the possible freefall that would result, your dollar-denominated assets would be in serious trouble. In Part II, Chapter 7, we'll talk more about how to reduce this risk.

Live Free or Die

The phrase is the state motto of New Hampshire, coined by one of its favorite-son generals in the first decade of the 19th century. It speaks to independence and inherent trust in government, without intervention, without central control or planning. More than most other world nations, the United States has "walked the walk" of capitalist freedom and self-determinism, although policy at its highest levels has acted as an "invisible hand," leaning against the wind to move toward politically acceptable economic outcomes. In the aftermath of the credit crisis, though, that hand has started to become more visible. The fear is, of course, that once that process starts, once trust is replaced by government intervention, it can spin out of control; the world has ample experience with the iron hands of socialism and communism.

In dealing with the credit crisis, major sectors of the economy—the financial industry, the auto industry—effectively became wards of the state. They became dependent on the U.S. government for financial sustenance and even for leadership through the crisis. The state went further into the private economy by granting credit to specific industries and businesses, something that had almost never happened before in U.S. history—and certainly not on such a large scale. It was, in short, a brush with a planned economy.

By engaging in credit allocation to specific sectors of the economy, the United States is stepping into territory traditionally left to governments with a socialist or communist brand. Communism has shown us that planned economies don't work. "Live Free or

Die" implies that a severe recession ought to be a lesser evil than a planned economy. And to continue the parallel, when communism swept Eastern Europe, the standard of living for everyone dropped. In today's world, we already see that the "re-failure" rate of those who defaulted and then renegotiated their teaser rate loans, is above 50 percent. Yet all taxpayers have to pay the price for the bailouts.

To be sure, we are a far cry from communism. But we must keep our eyes open and not be blinded by the perceived "help" of money printed by the Fed. Debt is the origin, not the solution, to the problems we face. The Declaration of Independence's "life, liberty, and the pursuit of happiness" may be difficult to achieve when drowned in debt; building sustainable wealth without the shackles of debt may be the more appropriate path. It's not by mistake that the Founding Fathers decided that their currency would be backed by a precious metal that could not be inflated to give in to the temptation of the day.

We've come a long way from that day. Our economic lives have been permanently touched by the not-so-invisible hand of policy, so much so that if the potential inflation bomb ever goes off, we're in big trouble as individuals and as a nation. There is nothing in that scenario that we can be complacent about; preparing for that possibility is a critical part of achieving sustainable wealth.

I'll close by quoting a Scottish history professor named Alexander Tyler, who studied democracies existing until his time. He lived in the late 1700s, yet what he had to say was a strikingly prescient summary of the hazards of government economic intervention in democracy:

> A democracy is always temporary in nature: it simply cannot exist as a permanent form of government. A democracy will continue to exist up until the voters discover that they can vote themselves generous gifts from the public treasury. From that moment on, the majority will always vote for the candidates who promise the most benefits from the public treasury, with the result that every democracy will finally collapse due to loose fiscal policy, [which is] always followed by a dictatorship.

I cannot endorse the Scotsman's statement without qualification, but I do believe he rightfully highlights that we cannot take democracy for granted. We have to cherish and fight for our values and way of life; otherwise, complacency may lead to the downfall of democracy and society. It is clear that temptations have made today's world more volatile and unpredictable, and that as a result, you must more actively manage your assets to stay ahead of the game. At this point, it's time to close the discussion of temptations and how they *affect* sustainable wealth, and to switch the discussion to more active approaches to *achieving* and *managing* that sustainable wealth.

PART
II

ACHIEVING SUSTAINABLE WEALTH

In the introduction to this book, we compared the successful management of your personal wealth to flying an airplane. You, as pilot, are in charge of your financial destiny. Pilots cannot simply push a pause button to think about the next course of action; the plane continues to fly, and doing nothing is dangerous. Pilots must plan ahead and have a flight plan, and they must amend it en route as circumstances require. For example, if the en route weather is worse than anticipated, the pilot must make a decision before entering the bad weather.

Carrying the analogy further, Part I discussed the weather conditions you might encounter once you grabbed the controls and left the runway. Those weather conditions are analogous to the external economic environment of our times. Those conditions are responsible for much of the economic turbulence we've seen lately, and are to be watched carefully as you file your flight plan and embark on your financial journey. The four temptations—credit, consumption, policy, and complacency—describe meteorological forces that by themselves or in concert can cause heavy weather and choppy economic air.

Now, do pilots check the weather only after takeoff? No; they start with a goal, a place they want to go; then they check the weather conditions and other factors to determine the best way to get there. How to get there is the subject of Part II of the book. The task becomes to find the best and least risky way to make the flight.

Part II is about moving forward to create a financial flight plan with a clear and suitable financial destination and with weather conditions—the economic environment—in mind. It's about finding the best route to the destination with maximum efficiency and minimal risk or discomfort from turbulence. The plan allows change; that is, should you decide to change your destination midflight, you can do so with the same confidence you embarked on originally.

Chapter 5 provides some guiding perspective on the perils of conventional wisdom and what it means to pilot your own financial airplane. It covers how to properly assess risks and how to become a pilot's pilot, the Hudson River hero Chesley Sullenberger of the trade. Chapter 6 covers the tuning of expenses to income, how to avoid debt, and how to build wealth through savings.

Chapters 7 through 9 explain how to sustain and grow wealth once earned. I'll start with crisis investing in Chapter 7, for if you're a pilot and learn how to fly in choppy air, imagine for a moment how much easier it is to fly in smooth air. Chapter 8 is about investing strategically to profit in a volatile world, while Chapter 9 covers some of the tactics of sustainable investing. Finally, Chapter 10 puts the sustainable wealth framework together to motivate you to get started.

Keep this in mind as you read on: What lies ahead in the remaining chapters defines the difference between *illusory* and *sustainable wealth.*

CHAPTER

5

Challenging Conventional Wisdom

The conventional view serves to protect us from the painful job of thinking.

—John Kenneth Galbraith

The *depth* of the recent recession has been well-documented as greater than any since the Great Depression. What may be even more significant this time is the *breadth*—that is, the number of people caught in the perfect storm of excessive debt, declining asset prices, and job insecurity. As many as 20 million may now be "under water" with their primary real estate investments, and many more have lost countless thousands in net worth in the collapsing bubble.

The apt question is "Why?" Are recessions by design becoming more democratic, more likely to have greater effects on the larger masses, as though mass media and mass Internet connectivity spreads the "virus" further? No, not in my book. Instead, more people with more wealth were lured by the temptation of credit: They followed the conventional wisdom that real estate prices (among others) would rise forever and that borrowing huge amounts of money to buy homes or using them as piggybanks to fund other purchases was "risk free" and perfectly okay.

If you take away one message from *Sustainable Wealth*, it is this: Always challenge conventional wisdom. You're at the controls.

That means that if you hire an adviser or any investment professional, they may help you, but it's your responsibility to work with them and to determine whether what they say and do has value to you. It is your responsibility to understand the risks of any investment and to understand the folly when someone tells you "there's no risk." It is your responsibility to separate true wisdom from conventional wisdom and to avoid staying the course in the presence of storm clouds. You must adapt or face the consequences.

This chapter will help you to replace conventional wisdom with wisdom of your own.

Recognize Your Responsibility

When you're at the controls of an airplane, it is all about how you plan your flight and respond to the conditions once in the air. You, and you only, must make the decisions crucial to keeping the flight level and on course, and while you may receive instructions from a controller, the ultimate responsibility to follow or deviate from them rests with the pilot in command. If the controller tells you to do something that you won't, you simply say, "Unable." If the controller insists, you declare an emergency and deviate as necessary in the interest of safety.

However, that's not to say there's no help available in making those decisions. You have instruments. You have air traffic control, weather reports, navigational aids and other forms of information and decision-making aids, both on board and on the ground, to help you achieve a successful and safe flight. Executing a flight without these aids can be done, but it's a lot more dangerous than it would otherwise be.

And so it is with your finances. I strongly believe you should be in charge. I strongly believe that you and you only can make and implement the key decisions, based on your latest interpretation of the latest information from your instruments and from the ground.

That doesn't mean, of course, that you do it without help. You use the inputs and information gained from your instruments and others on the ground. That said, you must not take such inputs either as gospel or for granted. Instruments are measuring devices only—you must realize that they aren't perfect, and that they don't tell the whole story; you, as the pilot, need to put that story together. And, likewise, the help from the ground represents an interpretation of other instruments, radar and so on, and while it is surely of help, it won't fly your plane.

Where are we going with this? Simply, you need to be in charge. You need to be aware of what's going on in the outside world, and you should stay on top of what other experts say and do. But that doesn't mean you should act solely on the advice or prognostications of others. Once you recognize that you are ultimately responsible for your financial decisions, you will take greater authority in managing your investment adviser or broker. Have you noticed that in many aviation accidents, pilot error is the main or at least a contributing factor? That's by design: Because the pilot is ultimately responsible for all decisions, when something goes wrong, the pilot's actions have contributed to the outcome. If it were any different, aviation would be far less safe, as air traffic controllers and others would be more concerned with their own liability than providing a support structure for pilots. Of course, air traffic controllers, aircraft mechanics, and meteorologists have responsibilities, just as your financial adviser or broker does, but the help you get from them is directly related to the input you provide into managing the relationship.

What Happened to Independent Thinking, Anyway?

There's an old saying in the corporate world: If two people think the same way, you don't need one of them. That expression also has a lot of truth in the world of personal finance and investing.

Since the mid-1990s, there have been fewer differences in opinion about the markets. Many of those who were negative on the markets lost their jobs in the second half of the 1990s during the dot.com bubble. And few who warned of the perils of "financial weapons of mass destruction," including Mr. Buffett himself, who uttered the prescient words, were taken seriously.

As the money management business has matured, managers tend to have the same MBA type of education, applying the same investment tools and risk models, not to mention thought processes. The same trend also applies to the hedge fund industry, where the largest players tend to focus on the same ideas—commodities, energy, mining, and real estate plays in the recent boom. When everyone thinks the same way, markets are moved excessively in that direction and efficient markets break down, likely causing some assets to become overvalued. Additionally, there is the so-called "institutional imperative"—the "nobody got fired for buying IBM" mentality once pervasive in the computer business—which drives these investment professionals to think and invest like the crowd. Many advisers invest according to the same models in the pursuit of perceived diversification. Unfortunately, as 2008 showed, in a panic all assets tend to be correlated and converge in one direction—downward. While there may be more people investing in the markets, there may be fewer true decision makers and fewer independent opinions about the state of the markets or individual companies.

It isn't just about professional advisers, by the way. The way certain investment vehicles themselves are constructed lead people toward mediocrity—and worse. Indeed, before the 1970s, most investors used to pick—and had to pick—securities based on their personal analysis; now many investors buy mutual funds and exchange-traded funds (ETFs). Investing in a "market portfolio," an index, has its merits, but index investors quickly run into a chicken-or-egg problem. In a market-cap weighted index, the strongest companies comprise an increasingly large share of the index; the popular S&P 500 Index is a classic example. But as we saw in the 2001–2002 bust with technology companies and again in the 2008–2009 financial services bust, the weighting of these companies becomes excessive; and the unwary investor has really made a bet on the sectors at the end of their boom, sectors that have already made their run. Thus, especially in a bubble, the index may actually represent a poor investment allocation, being overweighted in what's *already* done well.

I don't object to index investing, but I would like anyone using indices to be aware of their shortcomings. You cannot expect to make big leaps by piggybacking on other people. If you have a view of what the world will look like tomorrow, by all means, put your money where your mouth is. If you have no idea, follow the herd but don't complain if your investments do poorly. Many argue against actively managed funds because, on average and after fees, they do not outperform the indices. True, but that's by definition, as the average cannot possibly beat the average. I hope that after reading *Sustainable Wealth*, you feel energized to be active in the areas in which you are comfortable and consider index-based investing for areas in which you would like to have exposure but haven't found a better alternative to an index-based fund.

If there was one good thing coming out of the 2008–2009 market turmoil, it was that investors disagree once again; there were widely differing opinions on what the markets would do, as well as what individual sectors and securities would do. Further, there were differing opinions on how things would shape up as we emerged from the bust. First, investors and institutions alike were becoming more risk averse, leading to a more balanced appraisal of the markets. Second, it signaled that investors were starting to think again, providing a key ingredient to efficient markets and the avoidance of future bubbles.

Bubbles happen when everyone thinks the same thing. Moreover, when everyone thinks the same thing within a given asset class, as happened recently with real estate, it's a sure sign of a bubble. In the years preceding the credit crisis, stocks, bonds, real estate, commodities, and international investments all rose: Money was created out of thin air and flowed into all asset classes. In a more balanced world, money tends to flow from one asset class to another. All asset prices rising in lockstep may be the most ominous bubble indicator. In a bull market, everyone feels smart—when that happens, it's time to consider becoming more conservative in your asset allocation.

Should You Use an Adviser?

You've probably already been asking, while you read *Sustainable Wealth*: "Should I, as an independent thinker and master of my own financial destiny, employ a financial adviser?

Just because you're in control of your finances and the decisions made about them doesn't mean that you have to do all the legwork. Many people find it outside their interests or skill sets to pore over financial data, investment analyses, and so forth; it just isn't what they want to do. They don't want to learn the ins and outs of financial statements, risk models, interest rates, and so forth—that's okay. I'm not so interested in the ins and outs of dentistry, likewise, I'd rather have someone else read the x-rays and do the picking and prodding. But I will still make the final decisions about whether to fix a problem with a filling or a crown.

Many of us simply don't have the time. I'm in the financial business, so reading financial reports, gathering financial data, and learning about the economy is all part of my job. But my dentist probably doesn't have the time to do this to the degree I do, even if he or she were interested. By the way, having said that, here is another bubble indicator: your dentist should be more interested in your teeth than the stock market.

Financial advisers come in many forms and flavors, and commenting on each is beyond the scope of what I'm trying to accomplish here. The important point is to grasp the idea that no matter what, or how much, of your financial life you decide to "outsource" to someone else, you are still at the controls. Working with a financial adviser is really not all that different from working with an interior designer at home, or, in the corporate world, outsourcing manufacturing to Asia: What you get out of the relationship is related to the effort you put into it. Do not expect to meet your investment objectives with a "check-the-box" approach. Look through the marketing message and try to understand the methodology the adviser applies. If it all sounds like rocket science, that's great—if you are a rocket scientist. If you are not, you may want to work with someone who speaks your language. Investment advisers fulfill an important function, but they can only perform it if they receive the proper guidance from you.

The recent experience with Ponzi schemer Bernard Madoff has sent shockwaves that go far beyond the investment business: Whom can you trust if a person that seemed highly reputable was able to commit massive fraud? Economic activity grinds to a halt without trust; you must be able to trust your doctor, your gardener, your financial adviser. If you don't trust anyone, you may be best off hiding your nest egg in bricks of gold under your pillow; although if you do so, you may still be haunted that someone may rob you. Thinking of it, that investment strategy would have outperformed many alternatives in recent years. That raises another point: Any adviser you work with is likely to promote investment choices he or she is licensed to sell to you. Few advisers receive fees based on the gold you hide under your pillow; some have licenses to sell you insurance products, most don't. A real estate broker will, quite likely, try to convince you to buy real estate. What about cash? Most investment professionals do not make a lot of money promoting cash in lieu of riskier investments. *The entire investment community is built around the concept of selling risky investments.*

Even if the adviser charges based on assets, many clients are less willing to pay the standard rate fees if the adviser holds cash for an extended period. I speak from experience, as I closed my separate accounts business in early 2008 after I held almost nothing but cash for my clients—mostly international cash, often in the form of foreign government bonds. I had held the cash for some time, refusing to give in to client requests to buy structured products or other forms of investment that I deemed inappropriate given what I considered a market in bubble territory. In retrospect, I should have doubled the fees as I discouraged clients to invest in the stock market. I was in the fortunate enough position to be able to do so, as I had positioned our firm in 2004 to go into the mutual fund management business, offering investors the opportunity to invest in funds with which I was comfortable, given what I saw developing in the markets.

An investment adviser can and should be a great partner; if you work with your adviser, and you understand and agree to the investment process applied, you can leverage on his or her skills. At all times, apply the common-sense approach; if it sounds too good to be true, it probably is. And remember that in a bear market, the person who loses the least wins; be realistic with your expectations. Many investors forgive their advisers for losing money in a bear market, possibly even underperforming; but many investors won't forgive their adviser for lagging behind in a bull market. Evaluate what sort of investor you are, and whether your expectations are realistic, and discuss your expectations with your adviser.

For all of these cases, a financial adviser can certainly help. But make sure you can trust that adviser to interpret your needs and to interpret the financial facts the way you would, or at least in a way that adds some light to your own interpretation (remember, again, you don't need two people thinking the same thing). Make sure they can gather the facts so that you can make your own assessments easily, quickly, and accurately, much as a pilot interprets instruments, weather data, and ground control to make rapid adjustments to a flight.

That said, it's extremely important that an adviser be able to help you understand not just the short-term market twitter but also the long-term facts and trends that will influence your financial destiny. What you clearly don't want is an adviser who simply dispenses the conventional wisdom, particularly without taking your individual goals, needs, and worldview into account.

Finally, and bottom line, the adviser should make you sleep better at night and not be a source of 3 A.M. worry. Here's a rule of thumb for your investment portfolio: If you can't sleep at night because of your investments, they are too risky for you, no matter what you told your adviser or what you convinced yourself of at the time you made the investment decision.

The Proactivity of Sustainable Wealth

One of the obvious problems with conventional wisdom is that it's typically a lagging wisdom, not a leading or foretelling or prescient wisdom. Conventional wisdom gets us to do things like "invest in stocks" because the markets have delivered an 11 percent return since 1929. Or to invest in real estate, because "they ain't making any more of it" and it never goes down. Or to invest in energy stocks, because oil is at an all-time high of $147 per barrel.

It's not hard to see that if you always chase yesterday's trend, you'll almost inevitably lose. As Buffett said, the worst reason to buy a stock is because it's going up. But it gets worse than that: It's easy to overreact not just to an individual stock but to a greater apparent trend—and be wrong altogether. And yet, over the years, many people do it, often on their own, at times guided by advisers who do the same thing—and fail to learn from it. At the risk of mixing metaphors, latecomers to any party get trampled when the herd reverses direction and crushes them.

So it is in this context that I introduce the concept of proactive wealth management. Sure, it sounds intuitively obvious and simple to do, but I truly believe that for wealth to be truly sustainable, it must be managed completely in a forward-looking way, looking out the windshield toward what's ahead, near and far. Looking in the rearview mirror has its purpose when overtaking, but ultimately, what's ahead of you is what matters. Understanding history, however, is different from believing history must repeat itself. Many believe that because we have tick-by-tick data on just about any security, we can build forecasting models. In reality, any statistician should be most careful of extrapolating based on the few economic cycles we have had over the past 100 years. Economists will counter this argument by saying that we have to work with the facts we have. I tell them that shouldn't mean we should ever throw common sense out of the window. As Yogi Berra might have put it, forecasting is very difficult, especially when it pertains to the future.

A Layered Approach

The challenge becomes one of staying ahead of the conventional wisdom being dispensed by everyone else. Sure, it's tricky; none of us can predict the future to any degree of accuracy, else we'd all buy lottery tickets and have little reason to read this book.

As one approaches the task of managing sustainable wealth, it's important to break the task up into two essential dimensions, or layers. Sustainable wealth investors must have a sense for the first layer, the future of the global economy and the markets within the economy, and the second layer, the future of their own personal situation, including their income, expenses, and investments. When one goes to bed at night thinking about sustainable wealth, one is thinking at both levels, though I stress that pondering sustainable wealth at bedtime should be because one seeks the challenge, not because of fear!

Operating within the global and personal economic layers, proactive wealth management proceeds with a plan containing objectives, constraints, and a worldview. You can develop all three of these components on your own (and with family) or with the help of outside experts; it's your choice, so long as you stay in charge.

Develop Objectives

To paraphrase another old Yogi Berra maxim: If you do not know where you want to fly, it makes it harder to get there. Successful personal finance and sustainable wealth start with a clear-eyed view of your personal and family objectives. Typically, they start out as a set of non-dollar denominated objectives. As an example, which I'll return to throughout the rest of the book, my wife Hanna and I are committed to sending our four children to college at the institution of their choice *without incurring debt.*

Now there are some key aspects of this commitment worth noting. First, it is somewhat specific—four kids, college of their choice. Implicitly, it is also *time*-specific, for we know when, or about when, college will happen and the funds will have to be in place to make it happen. Finally, there's a condition—without incurring debt. So before any dollar amounts are put on paper, you're clear, and in agreement, on what you want.

A good financial adviser can help you establish these objectives, or they can be done on your own. As many businesses do, this is an important enough exercise that it merits an "offsite"—some kind of time away from the daily routine to think clearly and independently about what you (singular or plural) really want. Also borrowed from the corporate world is the idea that you should probably have somewhere between three and seven of such objectives—fewer probably doesn't cover the breadth of your family needs, more is too much detail.

Make up your mind as to whether these objectives are "wishes" or hard constraints; the more seriously you take your objectives, the more likely you will adjust your lifestyle to achieve them. Likewise, objectives that focus simply on the accumulation of a sum of money don't work so well. For most people, if they can't see clearly what the money is for, they don't have as much motivation to accumulate it. Finally, objectives, once set, should be quantifiable in dollar terms, for that is the only way they can be determined as realistic and measured properly for achievement against them. So an objective like "achieve $1 million in net worth," while quantifiable, isn't motivating, and it will naturally conflict with another family objective, like "pay for our boy's tuition out of pocket." As stated, it also doesn't have a timeframe. Alternately, you can see how such loose panaceas like "get rich" or "be happy" don't work.

Examples of Good Objectives

- *Have no home mortgage by the time we retire*—There's a specific goal here but without a specific dollar amount (it depends on where you're living at retirement, among other things). And the timeframe also varies because you don't know when you plan to retire—but implicit is that retirement happens when the objective is met. So while not as precise as other objectives, this one works. Note that, as many baby boomers do not have the money to retire, they are likely to postpone retirement. While we consider this a failure nowadays, once society as a whole retires later, the perception of working into your 70s is likely to change. I bet that in 20 years, if you ask a 65-year-old whether he or she is retiring, it will be considered an insult. Society adapts. As far as you are concerned, however, your goals matter more than how others view them.
- *Have $1 million in our retirement accounts when we retire*—It sounds like "achieve $1 million in net worth," but it has a more specific timeframe and purpose.
- *Save enough to pay cash for a new Honda Accord by June 2011*—This is a smaller and shorter-term goal than others. It's good to have some shorter-term goals that can be checked off, giving a sense of accomplishment and allowing space for new goals that might come along.

Know Constraints

Constraints, as the term implies, work counter to the objectives; obviously if there were no constraints, all objectives would be achievable. Constraints recognize the boundaries of your personal financial situation and the boundaries of your risk tolerance.

Take the sample objective described above: send our four children to the college of their choice *without incurring debt*. The final clause, "without incurring debt," works as the first constraint, for it says that the objective is only fully achieved if it doesn't jeopardize or compromise the rest of your finances (and, likely, some other goals such as retirement) by incurring a load of debt. Beyond that, another constraint for this objective, and for your finances as a whole, might relate to risk, especially for funds to be accumulated *and sustained* for this objective. Since this objective is all-important, indeed your family's chosen "number-one" objective, you might specify that funds set aside to achieve the college objective cannot afford to be jeopardized, and thus are invested with the utmost prudence. That doesn't mean you have to invest all the funds in Treasury bills, but it does mean that to meet your objective, you must be willing and able to cover any shortfall because of investment losses by diverting money from other objectives or by generating more income, for example by working harder.

A constraint may be that you don't want to run out of money in your retirement. That sounds simple enough, except that you don't know just how old you will become or how long you will be healthy enough to earn an income. Something as simple as an annuity or cashing in on your own life insurance may not be adequate either as many of these insurances do not factor in cost of living adjustments; especially in a world where inflation may pick up, this is a very challenging task. This shouldn't stop one from trying to set targets, but with such "grand" targets, it is important to keep an open mind and be willing to adjust your lifestyle: When it comes to running out of money, in most cases, it's the expenses, not the income, that are the problem.

Develop a Worldview

The first four chapters of this book serve as a good example for the kind of worldview you can develop if you read the media and do a little homework on your own. You can get a pretty clear idea of how the various economic and political forces will affect your finances. You can appraise how we're doing as a society when it comes to sustainable wealth—are we consuming more than we produce? Is the economy moving in a favorable and sustainable direction? Are we in a healthy boom cycle, or are we forming a bubble? Can what's happening now last forever, or are we headed blindly down a path of financial self-destruction? And what are the risks? Are there specific event risks that we need to keep in mind? Or is the greater risk one of long-term malaise and loss of economic vitality to foreign nations? What about war? Commodity shortages? Political unrest? What about less dire, but still financially harmful, circumstances like inflation or higher interest rates?

Clearly you can't "know" about all of these things; nobody has the perfect crystal ball. But it's important nonetheless to evaluate your financial well-being in the face of what *is* going on, and what *could* go on, in the world. You can make this assessment independently or with the help of a professional; either way is okay, but again, remember that you're still in charge. And don't forget to stay in touch with the media to find out how that worldview is changing. The more diverse views you read, the better; the Internet is an excellent resource here. If there is only one newspaper you subscribe to, let it be the *Financial Times*: the paper is based in London, but covers the United States and the rest of the world from a global perspective. The *FT* covers not just business, but also world news and politics. Having said that, many local, often free, newspapers, have good articles: In recent years there has been a trend to have staff journalists cover local stories, but also buy articles from major syndicators, such as Associated Press, Reuters, *The New York Times*, or smaller but high-quality players such as *The Christian Science Monitor*.

It is important you also read views you disagree with, if only to sharpen your own arguments. *It is a form of complacency to listen only to those you agree with*. This may mean surfing the Internet to news sites in the Middle or Far East.

Closer to home, public radio—especially Marketplace and National Public Radio—has excellent coverage of domestic and world affairs. A few years ago, I started noticing that cab drivers increasingly listen to public radio, whereas 20 years ago, they would primarily listen to music. To an extent, it's a reflection that many cab drivers are educated people who have emigrated from countries experiencing unrest; public radio has extensive news coverage of their home countries. While such coverage may have little impact on your portfolio tomorrow, it does provide insight into the shape the world may take.

Just as when you talk to an adviser, be aware of where the journalist or analyst is coming from when you read or listen to them. An investment professional is likely to have strict rules on what he or she can say or write, based on regulations; a journalist, conversely, sometimes veers into the realm of giving investment advice without necessarily being qualified. I am not suggesting that the investment professional will necessarily have something smarter to say than the journalist—many journalists are great researchers—but it helps to put what you read, hear, or see into context.

The online world has changed the way we gather news and information. Because there is so much information available, make sure you go beyond the core sites you typically visit; make an effort to read other views. Many Americans get their political and business education on late-night comedy shows. Conversely, policymakers increasingly talk in sound bites to control the headlines in the media. We can do better than that. The world of news has penetrated mobile devices as well. On the iPhone, for example, Bloomberg offers a free application that not only gives you a market overview, but also will give you news headlines and stories based on parameters you select.

Then there are investment newsletters. I read many of them, typically not for their buy or sell recommendation, but because the writers are themselves well read and speak to a lot of people. If I take just one or two good ideas from a newsletter writer a year, sometimes from people they quote, the newsletter tends to be worth the fee (if it charges one). If nothing else, please follow my publications. I write a personal finance blog at www.sustainablewealth.org; I also provide in-depth analyses on currencies, global imbalances,

News You Can Use

Now, recognize that I'm not just sustaining my own wealth; I am in the profession, so therefore I am also sustaining the wealth of others. Staying on top of the news is one of my biggest and best investments in this endeavor. Here are some selections from what I follow. I don't expect that you have time to check out all of these resources all the time, but I recommend keeping your eyes and ears open to the following:

Print and online publications: *Asia Times* (online); *Barron's*; Bloomberg; BreakingViews.com; *BusinessWeek*; *The Christian Science Monitor*; *MarketWatch*; *The Economist*; *Financial Times*; *Forbes*; Free Market News Network; *The Globe and Mail*; *Investment News*; *The New York Times*; *San Francisco Chronicle*; TheStreet.com; *USA Today*; *The Wall Street Journal*

Radio: American Public Media's *Marketplace*; BBC; Bloomberg; FinancialSense.com; KCBS/KNX (news talk radio with business reports); The Korelin Economics Report; National Public Radio; RTTNews.com

TV: Bloomberg; CNBC; FoxBusiness; PBS's *Nightly Business Report*

Online news aggregators: 321gold.com; CaseyResearch.com; finance.yahoo.com; FinancialSense.com; Kitco.com; Safehaven.com; USAGold.com; 24hGold.com; Marketthoughts.com; merkfund.com/money; ResourceInvestor.com; LeMetropoleCafe.com; RealClearMarkets.com; RealClearPolitics.com; The Gold Report (theaureport.com)

Newsletters: Richard Russell's *Dow Theory Letters*; Bill Bonner's *The Daily Reckoning*, Bill Fleckenstein's *Daily Rap*; Lance Lewis's *Daily Market Summary*; John Mauldin's *Thoughts from the Frontline*; Terry Savage's *The Savage Truth*

Books: *Manias, Panics, and Crashes: A History of Financial Crises* (Kindleberger, Aliber, and Solow: Wiley, 2005); *When Genius Failed: The Rise and Fall of Long-Term Capital Management* (Lowenstein: Random House, 2001); *Fooled by Randomness: The Hidden Role of Chance in Life and in the Markets* (Taleb; 2nd ed. Random House, 2008); *America's Great Depression* (Rothbard; 5th ed. Ludwig von Mises Institute, 2000)

While there's freedom of speech, I would like to mention that regulation does not allow me to mention authors who work for brokerage firms that also sell our firm's mutual funds (the reason is that it would be considered a benefit that goes beyond the distribution agreement, and as such could be construed as a bribe to favor our products over others). It's a pity, as there are further good commentaries and books out there.

When there is news on a specific region, I visit news Web sites based in places such as Pakistan, China, Germany, France, or the Middle East.

Keep this in mind: A comprehensive worldview is one of the key differences between wealth and sustainable wealth.

and the socioeconomic impact of the U.S. administration's policies with *MerkInsights,* a newsletter available at www.merkfund.com/newsletter. *SustainableWealth.org* and *MerkInsights* are both available free of charge.

Low-Probability, High-Risk Events

Chapter 4, in its exploration of societal and personal complacency, brought us into the subject of risk and, in particular, the under-appraisal of risk and how it led to bad decisions. Bringing that discussion forward, it is imperative to challenge conventional wisdom when it comes to the subject of risk.

It's human nature to ignore that the risk equation has two sides. This is most profoundly illustrated by considering the line most people heard from real estate and mortgage professionals in 2004–2006, that real estate could "only go up." Such conventional wisdom at that time completely and unabashedly disregarded the downside risk, but that's not the only time we've seen it. Most remember the near absence of "sell" or negative recommendations for stocks in 1999. Ratings agencies giving a negative rating to a financial services company or a mortgage-backed security could hardly be found in 2005. Few were bearish on the price of oil in 2008. The list goes on.

The point is, particularly during boom times and especially bubble times, people forget about the other side of the equation. They get caught up in the herd mentality; they respond to peer pressure; they figure if everyone else thinks real estate can only rise, everyone else must be right.

Managing sustainable wealth, of course, requires a constant vigil on the downside risk of any global or market situation and any individual investment. That vigil may be helped along by credible comments from others, but you, as sustainable wealth manager, must learn to separate true wisdom from conventional wisdom.

Additionally, sustainable wealth investors must be careful not to rely too much on traditional risk models. As we learned in Chapter 4, traditional risk models often come up short; they're based on a statistical interpretation of what *did* happen before, not what *could* happen. None of these risk models would have predicted a price for GE shares in the single digits, nor a retreat in oil prices from $147 to $32. But these happened. Understandably, such events are more probable for an individual security than for a market as a whole, but very few models called for a 50 percent drop in the markets overall. That didn't even happen in the wake of the 2001 terrorist attacks, which were overlaid on a recession that was already under way.

That's not to say that managing sustainable wealth means living in an underground silo with all of your assets stuffed into the proverbial mattress. Instead, it simply means realizing that these events are possible, and in fact may even become more likely when the conventional wisdom maintains that "it could never happen." Managing sustainable wealth means taking these risks into account and investing no more than you think you can afford to lose in a "low-probability, high-risk" scenario.

The best known low-probability, high-risk scenario may be the "nuclear risk" scenario; I would like to encourage everyone to visit the Web site www.nuclearrisk.org, where Stanford Professor Emeritus Martin Hellman discusses this risk in great detail. Interestingly, especially when it comes to nuclear disarmament, it is mathematicians that promote awareness. Professor Hellman invented public key cryptography—a cornerstone of secure Internet transmissions. Einstein is another mathematician who devoted a lot of effort to warning the world about nuclear weapons. A Russian chess master is also part of the movement. While my own mathematical skills are far more modest, mathematics and statistical analysis have been an important part of my college and graduate-level education. What's the relevance to sustainable wealth? Once you understand that low-probability, high-risk events can happen, you take them seriously and into account in your investment decisions. Call them flat tails or black swan events if you prefer, but ignore them at your own financial peril.

This thought process must extend beyond investments—what if you lose your job or a major source of income? What if you have a sudden and unexpected expense, like a chronic illness, that simultaneously costs money and reduces your income capacity? Examining such scenarios is an important part of challenging conventional wisdom and managing sustainable wealth; we'll return to this idea in a moment.

Adaptive Investing, Rather Than Staying the Course

Buy and hold. That was the conventional wisdom about common stocks—at least until recently. Buy and hold, and your stocks will grow with the U.S. economy. The combination of gross domestic product (GDP) growth, dividends, and a little bit of inflation would almost guarantee an 11 percent or so return if you held on for the long term. Indeed, many studies concluded that such returns were almost automatic if you looked back to 1929.

Staying the course makes sense if both the world and your priorities and constraints don't change. The French journalist Jean-Baptiste Alphonse Karr said: "Plus ça change, plus c'est la même chose"—the more things change, the more they stay the same. But the world did change, even if the cartoons from the 1930s lamenting the course of the economy look all too familiar. A key attribute of the markets that did change was risk assessment; as risk was priced back into the markets starting in late 2007, volatility surged. If the risks in the markets change, your portfolio allocation should also be revised. That's because most invest according to their personal risk/return profile. Well, if the risks in the markets change, but your personal tolerance for risk hasn't, then it's only logical that you need to make adjustments to your portfolio. If you don't, the market will make those adjustments for you. And, oh boy, the market did so with a vengeance, sharply reducing the value of your risky assets. You would have been far better off moving risky assets to less risky ones once you realized that the world had become a riskier place. When an investment environment is perceived to be risk free, that should be taken as a warning sign to start early in taking chips off the table.

Your personal situation can also change. Let's assume you did lose a lot of paper wealth as major stock market indices were cut in half. Rest assured, you are not the only one: The wealthier people were, the more they lost. The billionaires lost billions. Still, most billionaires won't have to worry about retirement savings, as they continue to have a substantial cushion. However, if you lost a lot of money, re-evaluate whether you can still lose the risky assets you have left. Many argue that you should ride out any storm. But can you still sleep at night knowing that you lost a big chunk of your money and could lose more? If you are young and will make up any shortfall with more work, by all means, feel free to stay the course. But if you previously had capital you could put at risk, but are now down to the bone with your savings and cannot afford to lose more, it is prudent to scale back your risk profile. It is always more prudent to build wealth the slow way, using compounding; just because money

Nothing Has Changed

Source: *The Chicago Tribune*, 1934.

moves fast doesn't mean you should try to repeat the mistakes and chase the next trend—otherwise, sustainable wealth may remain an illusion forever.

Even if the world or your personal situation does not change, the speed of business and the pace of business *change* have accelerated.

It's almost impossible to find a true "buy and hold" with an individual stock, as even such stalwarts as Procter & Gamble and Coca-Cola are dealing with change, and anyone who thinks Microsoft is here forever in its current form needs to take another look. Sure, P&G is still the detergent king, but having shed steady brands like Folgers, Spic and Span and Jif in favor of Olay and other more trendy cosmetic concoctions, one can hardly say it's the same company it was 20 or 30 years ago. True, it may be a *better* company; that's for you to decide. But it isn't the same company, and today's retail and consumer environment is hardly the same as it was in 1975.

The point is that you can't become complacent and stay the course on much of anything these days; instead, you need to adapt. I choose Procter & Gamble because it is a more surprising illustration than most; the point is, if P&G can change so much, what does that mean for other businesses and the economy in general? You can't just "stay the course" with anything—the winds, the weather, the turbulence, the other aircraft will sooner or later require a change in altitude, attitude, airspeed, or direction. Notably, these changes can be for the better, not just to defend against the worst.

Many investors also forget that you need to consider changing course if your portfolio, or an asset in your portfolio, rises. Even the smart professionals managing a good many hedge funds forgot this in early 2008—they were sitting on significant gains in their mining stocks, mining equipment makers, fertilizer, energy and ethanol stocks. Did they think about changing course? Did they think about greater risk inherent in an inflated stock or an inflated industry, and the greater proportion of their asset base they had locked up in these inflated investments? Did they think about shifting some of that to cash for the "just in case" outcome of increased market volatility and related withdrawals? No; in fact, their compensation structure motivated them to stay the course and continue to reap their "2 and 20" fees (2 percent of asset value plus 20 percent of portfolio gains, for those unfamiliar). There was no incentive to sell, especially in a market where everything was rising and there were few undervalued alternatives to choose from. An investment philosophy based on buying an overpriced security in the hope of finding someone else willing to pay even more for it is bound to backfire.

The point is, again, that it is dangerous to blindly stay the course. Now I must emphasize that just because I advocate not simply "staying the course" all the time, that doesn't mean I don't advocate patience; indeed, short-term trading is not the answer. Just as when you fly an airplane, quick decisions with poor rationale will typically bring more trouble than staying the course. Instead, it means that one must keep track of conditions and watch the instruments while avoiding peer pressure, blind complacency, and conventional wisdom. One must be continuously willing to adjust finances, to adapt the goals and techniques involved in managing those finances, and to "downsize" when necessary.

I applied that philosophy in a hedge fund I ran for many years—I felt (and continue to feel) so strongly about the need to adapt that I called the fund the Adaptive Growth Fund. I closed the fund as part of my firm's transition to the mutual funds business. I apply the same philosophy to my investment advisory firm as I do to my personal investments. Always a believer in prudent diversification, I invested in technology stocks in the mid-1990s, but diversified to other industries to manage volatility. As the tech boom ensued, I noticed that diversifying to other industries no longer provided the desired benefit, as early signs of the bubble caused securities throughout different sectors to move more and more in tandem.

As a result, I expanded by diversifying internationally. Toward the peak of the bubble, even such diversification no longer provided the desired effect. I adapted by applying more of a macro approach to investing, now moving more toward cash management—including international cash—and precious metals. Over time, my investment approach became more conservative, as I did not like how the dynamics of the world were unfolding. While my advisory business was profitable, I noticed a warning flag: As my strategies became more conservative, clients started to inquire about discounts in the management fee I charged. At the same time, various scandals on Wall Street caused regulations to increase. From a business point of view, this meant that margins were declining. My marketing was based on word-of-mouth marketing. There were a number of directions I could have moved the business. The most obvious would have been to invest in riskier assets, something many of my clients would have been fine with; indeed, some were pushing me in that direction. Instead, I decided to give up clients with whose desires my outlook on the markets was not compatible. In early 2008, I closed the last separate client accounts I managed; I was almost exclusively holding cash in these accounts (again, including non-U.S. cash or equivalent such as short-term government securities), as I did not like the markets a bit. But I did not phase out my hedge funds (I had managed three small hedge funds) and separate accounts without an alternative. The alternative was to build a mutual fund company that reflected my investment philosophy. While a mutual fund business is a high fixed-cost business, it is far more scalable than the separate accounts business I had been engaged in before. Regulations prevent me from discussing our mutual funds in this book, but in Chapter 10, I will discuss elements of running the business that are applicable to sustainable wealth building.

All too often, we start defending our investment choices without rational reason. The best example may be your home: When you look for a house, you look for the best deal in town and argue that the price should be lower. The moment you own the property, you find every reason in the world that your neighborhood is the best one and that the value of your house should go up. Keep cool as you evaluate your home; think as if you were the homebuyer, instead of the homeowner, in evaluating whether your home is a good investment.

When you choose an investment, always remember why you bought it. If those conditions prevail, then the current market price is secondary. Say, for example, you bought a stock because the company is cash-flow positive and pays a healthy dividend; your decision to continue to hold the security should then be based on those factors. If the firm starts paying the dividend out of capital rather than earnings, you should question your investment. Conversely, if you bought a stock because you think the firm has great and innovative products, revisit this question periodically; don't just get complacent because the firm receives cash flow from legacy products. Or you really like the management of the firm; this may be more difficult to evaluate, as it can be rather subjective, but do consider whether the current management is the right one for the new challenges ahead. Even if you base your investment decision on technical factors, stay true to your philosophy.

The Sustainable Wealth Lifestyle

Sustainable wealth itself means avoiding the temptation to accept conventional wisdom. Conventional wisdom feels good, it sounds good, everyone's doing it, why shouldn't we? We can't go wrong buying IBM, right? What makes it worse is that, for long stretches of time, this approach can actually work, for markets move in the direction of the herd, at least for a while. Accepting conventional wisdom built a lot of paper wealth for a lot of people during recent asset bubbles, and everyone felt good, spent more, and became masters of their universes. As we found out, the sense of security, and even of mastery, can be horrifically off target.

Sustainable wealth is a lifestyle. It isn't just about spending a few hours each week or month reading the financial press, reviewing investments, developing a budget, or balancing a checkbook. The lifestyle is carried out at two levels. At the high level, it means staying on top of the economic world and proceeding with life with a clear worldview. At the detail level, it means making prudent financial decisions to control expenses and liabilities and influence income and asset values in such a way as to consume less than you produce; to save and invest toward goals; and thus to sleep at night. At both levels, you avoid the trap of following conventional wisdom and, in so doing, assume full control of your airplane. Do it right, and you'll sleep better at night and leave a legacy for your family—the twin promises of sustainable wealth from the beginning.

The remaining chapters examine the key building blocks of the sustainable wealth lifestyle.

CHAPTER 6

Saving and Spending in a Volatile World

Because of deep love, one is courageous. Because of frugality, one is generous.

—Lao Tzu

Chapter 5 covered the notion that the creation and preservation of sustainable wealth starts by challenging conventional wisdom. Those who follow the prevailing winds blindly will inevitably find surprises when the wind changes. They are most vulnerable to boom/bust cycles. Further, without a plan that incorporates a worldview and specific objectives, sustainable wealth is difficult to achieve; to quote a harsh adage, those who fail to plan plan to fail.

These general principles, if followed, will certainly get you started down the right path toward sustainable wealth. But the real differences between sustainable wealth management and other forms of personal financial practice start to emerge—and become more specific—when we talk about managing income and expenses successfully on a day-to-day basis, and how to build those principles into a sustainable wealth *lifestyle*.

The sustainable wealth lifestyle is a backdrop, a prevailing philosophy and thought process that governs daily thinking and daily activity with an eye toward a comfortable present and future (i.e., sleeping well at night and leaving a legacy for your loved ones so

125

they can sleep well at night). The lifestyle governs your thought and activity toward producing more than you consume. It aims toward being prepared, should the relatively uncontrollable features of your financial life go out of control, namely income and asset prices. The lifestyle takes aim at what you can control—expenses and liabilities—to achieve the most favorable outcomes later on with the least risk and exposure to a volatile world.

So how does one control those expenses and liabilities? How does one earn the most, then keep the most of what is earned? How does one avoid the temptations of consumption and credit to maintain flexibility and an edge necessary to avoid trouble and to prosper? Why does it all start with proper management of saving and spending?

These are the important questions answered in this chapter, which is ultimately designed to help you switch from a mentality of playing catch-up to one of staying ahead while still being able to collect the rewards of your hard work.

The Sustainable Wealth Grid

Business consultants around the world have long reaped considerable rewards by assessing and assigning all sorts of business matters and prospects into four-quadrant grids. I won't argue with that premise. In fact, I've seen excellent analysis done with the so-called *SWOT* grid (Strengths, Weaknesses, Opportunities, Threats) pioneered by the Boston Consulting Group years ago. Following in their path, I will introduce a four-quadrant grid of my own, which I will call the *sustainable wealth grid* (Exhibit 6.1).

Some of you may recognize this framework as part of personal finance author Robert Kiyosaki's cashflow quadrant diagram. I am

Income	Assets
Expenses	Liabilities

Exhibit 6.1 Sustainable wealth grid.

not going to get into the dynamics within this grid, that income less expenses equals either assets or liabilities depending on the size of income and expenses. I consider those dynamics fairly obvious.

What is more relevant to the notion of sustainable wealth is the essential nature and behavior of each quadrant on the grid—and your ability to manage and control that quadrant. What do I mean? Let's lay out a key maxim of sustainable wealth management in simple terms:

- Income and asset values will fluctuate beyond your control.
- You, meanwhile, have full control over expenses and liabilities.

Income, of course, depends on how much and how effectively you work, but many uncontrollable factors can happen to cause it to decline or go away altogether. You can influence, but not control, those factors by choosing jobs wisely, controlling the quality of your work, and so forth. Likewise, and more obviously, you can manage your assets, but not control their price; that price is determined by markets. We saw the dire results of those who took their asset values (really prices) for granted and proceeded in the world as if they did have total control.

I maintain that as sustainable wealth managers, you do have complete, or nearly complete control, of expenses and liabilities. That's an important statement; let's examine it further:

You might argue, "How do you control high housing costs and rising gas prices? I need to live somewhere, and I need to drive to work." Agreed, you don't control the prices—but you do control the amount you spend and how you spend it. In the long term, your choice of standard of living and lifestyle (e.g., what kind of house, what kind of car, how far you live from work) becomes the lever to manage your expenses; in the short term, those "smaller" expenses are all controllable. Not 100 percent controllable, I'll agree, but controllable to the extent that, in the sustainable wealth context, you're the pilot, you're making the decisions, you're in charge.

The control of liabilities is even clearer. Liabilities are incurred when expenses exceed income; you're in control of expenses and the timing of those expenses. Liabilities represent decisions about:

- How much you spend
- When you spend it
- How you pay for something

I maintain that outside of some kind of "nuclear" event like a cancer treatment, you are in control of your liabilities based on the spending, timing, and payment decisions you make.

So, very importantly, the fatal flaw—and conventional wisdom— I often see in how people manage their finances is this: They focus too much on income and assets (which they don't control), while not paying enough attention to expenses and liabilities (which they do control). Further, people tend to fail to plan sufficiently for the *contingencies*—the unexpected outcomes—in the income and asset quadrants, and in the expense quadrant as well.

I'll echo this key sustainable wealth principle again:

- Conventional wisdom: Focus on income and assets
- Sustainable wealth wisdom: Control your expenses and liabilities

I have had clients who earn twice as much as others, yet who save far less. But I have also seen many build financial security with a modest income through better expense management and the avoidance of debt. Good expense management, while using debt only when you can afford to and when the rewards are likely to be higher than the cost, can go a long way toward achieving sustainable wealth.

With this wisdom in mind, we should re-examine the sustainable wealth grid (Exhibit 6.2).

Exhibit 6.2 brings to mind the ancient prayer "God grant me the strength to change the things I can, the serenity to accept the things I cannot change, and the wisdom to know the difference."

Income	Assets
Influence	*Influence*
Expenses	Liabilities
Control	*Control*

Exhibit 6.2   Sustainable wealth grid, influence versus control.

Much of what I advocate about sustainable wealth management clings to that principle. I strongly advocate using your strengths to change the things you can change—expenses and liabilities; the rest will fall into place, especially with your influence. Moreover, if they don't fall in place as you would like, you'll be less vulnerable.

Become a Scenario Planner

One of the critical dangers of following conventional wisdom is the failure to adequately take alternatives into consideration. People tend to believe so wholeheartedly in the prevailing view of the world that they fail to examine what happens if this view doesn't work, or worse, doesn't work by a wide margin. Once again, the worldview that real estate prices could only go up got a lot of smart people into trouble.

Sustainable wealth management requires adequate and consistent consideration of alternative scenarios, exploring not only likely, but also less likely ones. Such scenario planning occurs at a *macro* level ("What if inflation were to rise to 6 percent annually?" "What if taxes were to increase to cover government spending?") and at a *micro* level ("What if my son's college tuition doubles in the next five years?" "What if the equity portion in my daughter's college fund loses 20 percent in value?"). A wealth sustainer walks through these scenarios. There may not be time and bandwidth to produce a detailed plan for each scenario, but the wealth sustainer should at least have them in mind while proceeding through financial plans.

A scenario-based approach makes sense, in part, because it will provide you with a comprehensive view of your investments and the world. One of my professors in college used to say, "On average, it's 12 o'clock." This paradox expresses the notion that mean forecasts of the future are inherently flawed. If you buy a lottery ticket, you will either make lots of money or zero, but unfortunately, not some sort of average in between. The "high-risk/low-probability" discussion from the previous chapter is really only a specific example of what should be part of your every analysis. I have long and strongly felt that your finances, investments, and the world as a whole should be seen in scenarios: Back at university, I wrote my master's thesis in computer science on a probabilistic decision support system. In plain English, that's scenario planning for geeks. But you don't have to be a geek or a statistician to develop reasonable scenarios and think through their consequences.

To put some flavor to this concept: If you think we may be faced with a serious inflation problem, don't wait until it is all too obvious, but take it into account in your investment allocation today. Or if you think a currency crisis is possible, don't wait until it has happened, but position yourself, even if the odds are low.

Scenario plans should also be inner-directed to a degree—that is, not just to cover exogenous events like changes in the economy, prices, or asset values. They should consider the possibility that your family's needs, or even wants, might change over time. They should also be fairly time-specific, so that you can properly assess risks during the period. For example, the risk horizon for a college savings plan suggests less risk immediately before your kid starts college, because lots can happen in, say, a year or less. That risk rises if the horizon is perhaps three to five years, because a lot can happen in three to five years. If you're just starting out with college savings, you might have a 15- to 18-year horizon, so while there's risk, there's plenty of time for adjustment and recovery. In fact, your scenario plans may be done as a set of scenarios, short-term (maybe two years or less), mid-term (two to seven years) and long-term (seven years and beyond).

Interestingly, many scenarios you come up with can be counterintuitive, and often these counterintuitive outcomes can be very revealing. Take the issue of being self-employed versus employed. Many think that being self-employed is the riskier alternative. I beg to differ: As an employee, you can lose your job at any time. When you are self-employed, you are in charge of your destiny; your clients can fire you, but most of the time, they don't all leave at once, which gives you clear warning signs that you have to adjust. Because I am in charge of my destiny, I believe I have greater visibility on the scenarios that confront me.

No matter how you go about scenario planning, the important part is that you do it and avoid the temptation to accept the conventional wisdom. In my newsletter at sustainablewealth.org, I frequently discuss different scenarios for how the economy and the markets may unfold given the latest developments; make sure you visit the site to subscribe to the blog and newsletter.

Sustainable Wealth: A Store of Value

You, as sustainable wealth captain, have control over the two ships of expenses and liabilities, while the values of the other two quadrants, income and assets, are more subject to the winds and waters of the external environment.

Why are expenses and liabilities so important? The first and most obvious answer is that you can control them. Yes, that's true, and indeed, as the prayer goes, it is good to have the ability to change the things you can, while accepting the things that you cannot change. But just as importantly if not more so, an individual or family with low expenses and no debt enjoys comforts not otherwise enjoyed, both of which go a long way toward fulfilling the twin promises of sustainable wealth: being able to sleep at night and leaving a legacy for your family. The two comforts are:

1. *Stored wealth.* Grain farmers measure success in the form of stored grain in a silo, ready and waiting to take to market when the conditions are right and when they need or want the cash. Similarly, the ability to "store" financial potential for the moment most needed or wanted is an important attribute of sustainable wealth.

   Note that during times when an increasing number of currencies are at risk of losing their function as a store of value, storing wealth becomes a very challenging proposition. I have long argued that there may no longer be such a thing as a safe asset, and investors may want to take a diversified approach even to something as mundane as cash—central banks are increasingly doing it by diversifying their reserves. The grain example illustrates a way to address this challenge: You can control the amount of grain, but not the current market price. Don't lose sleep over the current market price if you are satisfied with what you hold. The same applies if you buy gold: Count the ounces, not the current market price—the volatility in these markets may otherwise drive you crazy. Similarly, Warren Buffett buys entire companies so that he does not need to lose sleep over share price fluctuations, but can focus on the cash flow the firms generate. Indeed, in his letters to shareholders, he discusses how he has grown earnings for Berkshire Hathaway more than the S&P 500; he typically does not discuss how the share price has done versus the index. Most of us are not in the position to buy entire companies, but we can still apply the same philosophy by focusing on tangible, stored value, such as owning a (small) percentage of a public company; if the firm dilutes your holdings on a regular basis by issuing additional shares, you may not be storing wealth, but rather being taken for a costly ride.

If you keep your expenses low, you'll be able to save money, which makes you more able to buy the things that you want or need *without incurring debt.* The ability to buy something when you need it *or* when you want it, in the sustainable wealth lifestyle, becomes just as important as the actual act of buying something itself. That is, knowing that you can buy a second home or a new car or an airplane if and when you want to do so.

2. *Absence of debt.* Most obviously, debt is what you owe someone else, and for most of us the idea of owing something to someone is a bit unsettling. Conversely, freedom means not owing anyone anything, financially speaking or otherwise. From experience (mine and that of others) there are few things more liberating than the notion of debt freedom—that is, not owing a thing to anyone, now or later. Further, that absence of debt gives you financial potential, just like the savings and stored wealth noted above, to buy something when you *do* need it. Additionally, debt freedom give you flexibility, as well as the ability to absorb the *unexpected* when it happens. All while sleeping well at night. Remember, it's a volatile world out there.

These two comforts are central to the notion and experience of sustainable wealth. If we turn our attention to the things we can change, expenses and liabilities, and attend to them correctly, we should be rewarded with the comforts of debt freedom and stored wealth.

The sustainable wealth grid lays the foundation for sustainable wealth management, starting with control of expenses and liabilities, and moving on to what can be done to influence income and asset values. From here, the main point becomes not why but *how* to manage expenses and liabilities. That discussion starts with another conceptual model, which I'll call the individual wealth cycle.

The Individual Wealth Cycle Model

The earlier chapters on the temptations shed light on the *business* cycle and particularly the boom/bust cycles that can emerge from

As Richard Russell Sees It

At age 85, Richard Russell publishes a daily market commentary, and with over 10,000 paying subscribers, he could afford a lavish lifestyle.

At a recent tribute dinner celebrating 50 years of writing the *Dow Theory Letters* (www.dowtheoryletters.com), Russell attracted 450 guests, including some of the brightest minds in the newsletter and money management business. As part of the celebration, one of his daughters provided quotes from Richard about his rigorous management of personal expenses. Bottom line—he lives what he preaches:

- What kind of person would need to use a heater in San Diego (he lives in La Jolla, California)? If you insist on turning on the heater, set a timer for 15 minutes.
- Water is the best drink there is.
- When you go to a restaurant, you are there to eat, not waste money on drinks.
- Soda pop? You know how much that costs them to make? Probably 3 cents.
- Restaurants? About twice a year is enough.
- When you're at a movie theater, you're there to watch a movie, not buy popcorn or other junk. That's how they make all their money: selling junk.
- (On his daughter's wish to have a horse): You can have a horse when the price of gold doubles . . . gold is the only real money. (She eventually got a horse before the price of gold doubled.)
- Buy things used. Let others spend all that money to buy things new, and then you save money from their mistakes.
- *Don't buy anything until you can buy it with cash.*

Russell grew up during the Great Depression. He bought his silverware at Goodwill, and never bought a new car. He never bought a house until he could pay cash, and this was in the days when he didn't have much money.

The point: Sustainable wealth is more than an approach to investing; it's a lifestyle.

it, helped along by the temptations of credit, consumption, policy, and complacency. Individuals and families are economic entities, too, and I believe all such entities have a boom/bust cycle of their own. The ability to understand, visualize, and manage that cycle is key to the creation of sustainable wealth, in particular, the stored

Is Frugal Cool?

It's always interesting to follow larger economic and social trends to see what people are thinking and are interested in. In early 2008 "green" was in, as more citizens became aware of the long-term perils of global warming and its consequences. As energy costs skyrocketed, this green imperative strengthened, as Americans started to see the connection between going green and saving money. In fact, the green movement reached a tipping point when, for the first time ever, going green was perceived as being less expensive, not more expensive—a legacy from the days of buying more expensive organic and recycled products.

Interestingly, in just a few short months, the brief commodity and oil-induced inflation, particularly in food prices, turned us all from energy misers to misers in general. Suddenly it became cool to shop at warehouse clubs again, and even to shop at Wal-Mart and eat at McDonalds. Indeed, as most other retailers were folding their tents, these two companies beat the market averages handily. In a March 2009 survey, only warehouse clubs showed year-over-year sales and traffic gains out of 28 retail categories. The personal savings rate hit a 16-year high.

Frugal seems to be "in." Americans, struggling with the twin perils of uncertain income and declining asset values, have finally gotten the message to control what they can—the expenses and liabilities quadrants in their grids.

It remains to be seen whether this trend continues when policymakers provide incentives to have consumers keep up or even increase their levels of debt. In my view, we will only see lasting change when policies are introduced to encourage consumers to save and invest rather than spend. Spending should be the natural result of wealth, not the pre-condition of economic growth. That's also what the Chinese are telling Americans; however, if it were up to American advisers, the Chinese would give each one of their citizens a credit card. Even if they did, American policymakers may be disappointed: The Chinese love American brands, but most of them are made in China!

wealth and debt-free existence discussed above. Understanding the ups and downs of the cycle and positioning your expenses accordingly is the next step in the sustainable wealth–building process.

The fact of the matter is that individuals, like economies, endure up and down cycles, too. Up cycles, the personal booms, occur when incomes are strong, that is, helped along by wage increases and bonuses if the individual is employed, or by sturdier profits, dividends, or other forms of income if not employed or in supplement to employment. Wherever an individual derives income, there are almost always ups and downs to that income stream.

In addition, the asset values for most individuals will also rise and fall, usually but not always coincident to business cycles. Stocks rise and fall, real estate prices rise (and as we now know, fall), even the value of fixed income investments can rise and fall, though not to the degree of other asset classes.

Income and asset highs and lows usually coincide with one another, for the factors that drive income expansion usually also drive asset expansion. So the ups and downs of personal wealth can be fairly sharp; indeed, in 2008 alone, the bear market destroyed almost 20 percent of U.S. household wealth—some $11 trillion, and that's not to mention the effects on income, nor the carryover into 2009.

Not only can we identify a clear cycle in personal income and assets, but notably, the cycle and its ups and downs are getting more volatile. First, on the income side, job duration is shrinking, and a greater number of individuals are self-employed or working as contractors to larger firms; thus, income streams are less certain and less regular. (Indeed, I mentioned earlier that self-employment may reduce uncertainty, but that only applies if you are reasonably established in what you do.) Additionally, dividend cuts, rental vacancies, and other factors have made investment income more volatile. Asset values themselves, too, have become obviously more volatile.

An individual's or family's financial well-being, therefore, can be defined by matching income and asset values to expenses. Granted, this approach does not fully capture *future* income and liabilities, but it serves an important purpose, as our daily income and expenses are happening *now* (future modeling is important, too, but you need to feed your family now; you need to save now). When income and assets are strong while expenses are steady or even declining, the individual or family is becoming wealthier; it is saving, at least in some form. When income and assets are on the decline and expenses are steady, the family starts to feel the pinch, and if income and assets decline faster than expenses decline, eventually the difference will produce "losses," which on the personal balance sheet translate to liabilities.

You'll probably recognize that businesses go through such cycles all the time, and the natural reaction to a downturn in income, and less often, to asset values, is to decrease expenses—to cut costs. Layoffs and other business process improvements occur, which often put the business in a better position to capitalize on the next upturn.

On the personal side, I think it's important to manage to these cycles, much as a smart business does. Beyond that, I believe sustainable wealth can be created by reducing and *keeping* (emphasis important) costs at a low level, at the level of the "worst-case scenario" for income. Living below means—especially when things are good—makes it possible to achieve goals, and just as importantly, to avoid creating painful debt when things go bad. Not all of us will go as far as Richard Russell does above, but we should always be aware that many expenses are a choice, not a necessity.

I've put the individual wealth cycle into three pictures, shown in Exhibits 6.3 to 6.5. These three models are necessarily oversimplified—assets and income don't rise in such neat curves, and expenses don't flatline as I've shown. But I recommend internalizing these as conceptual models; the closer you can get your financial situation to Exhibit 6.3, the closer you are to achieving sustainable wealth.

The Sustainable Break-Even Cycle

First comes the *break-even* wealth cycle, where wealth is neither created, sustained, nor destroyed. In Exhibit 6.3, the curved line shows income and asset values conceptually; the flat line shows expenses:

In Exhibit 6.3, the income/asset line rises and falls with the cycle, while expenses are managed "in the middle." So when things are good, as in the B portion of the chart, income and asset values exceed expenses, and the individual or family can spend more or pay down debt. The latter—pay down debt—is most likely, because some debt was created in the first part of the cycle (A). If the individual or family can achieve payoff, they accumulate some savings during B, leaving them less vulnerable to the next downturn (C). But human nature suggests that when things get good in the B timeframe, many will spend more instead—on a new car, going out to dinner, home décor—you name it. Over the long run, the

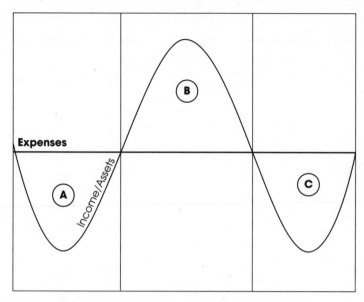

Exhibit 6.3   Individual wealth model, break-even case.

individual or family will survive financially, but will be hard-pressed to create any lasting wealth or family legacy. Whether the family sleeps at night depends on how predictable the cycles are and where they are on the cycle. Such a cycle is probably typical for most Americans, although most likely too many find themselves in the *chronic debtor* cycle, shown next.

The Chronic Debt Cycle

The chronic debtor tends to tune his or her expenses and standard of living to the highest level of income and assets. The chronic debtors get a nice job, cash a few paychecks, and before long, they're living in a large home, eating out four nights a week, and getting to the restaurant in one of two or three new cars. They feel great—for the short duration of time where their income and assets match their expenses. In the other periods, A and C in the chart in Exhibit 6.4, they run up sizeable debts with little hope of actually paying them off.

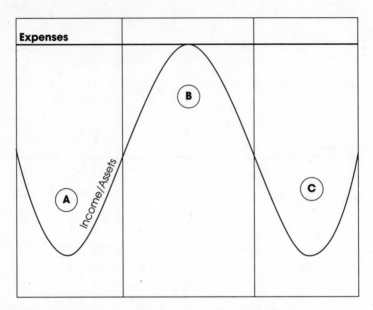

Exhibit 6.4   Individual wealth model, chronic debtor.

The implications of Exhibit 6.4 are obvious; this individual or family is going nowhere financially unless expenses are brought down to a reasonable level, allowing at least some savings or debt payoff. Additionally, individuals and families must make a conscious effort not to allow expenses to ratchet up to match the highest income levels, particularly expenses that are relatively fixed in nature. (Once again, the chart is an oversimplification; not all costs are fixed.)

The Sustainable Wealth Cycle

Finally—and it probably won't come as much of a surprise—we get to a wealth cycle model capable of creating sustainable wealth. (See Exhibit 6.5.)

In the *sustainable wealth* scenario, expenses are held down to the level sustained by the *lowest* point on the income and wealth cycle. So expenses match income and assets in the down cycles; nothing is saved, but no debt is incurred. When things get better, in the up cycle, what happens? The true wealth sustainer books some of the surplus into savings toward long-term goals, like

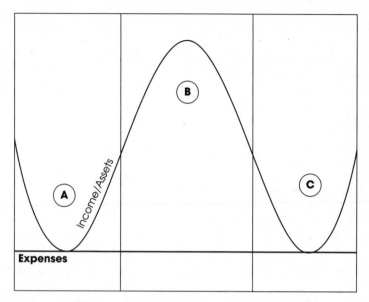

Exhibit 6.5   Individual wealth model, sustainable wealth.

the college education goals described in Chapter 5. The wealth sustainer may also set some aside as cash, waiting for the next downturn, to acquire important assets at a lower cost. Finally, the wealth sustainer chooses this as the time to make a few purchases, to reward him/herself and the family for sticking to the principles of sustainable wealth.

Now I'll once again stress that these diagrams are conceptual; they aren't this precise and pretty in real life. Indeed, one interpretation of the exhibit might be that you will never increase your standard of living as expressed by the flat expense curve; that's not my intent. Surely, you can enjoy the fruits of your labor; the slope and position of the expense line and income/asset curve can change. The point is to grasp the importance of the *relative* position of these lines.

The ups and downs don't move in clean, predictable waves as shown; neither are expenses totally flat at all times or in all scenarios. As a wealth sustainer, it's your job to keep the big picture in view and to "see through" the variations and ambiguities of real financial life as they overlay these diagrams. The main point still stands: if you manage expenses to break even at your minimum income and asset levels, you shouldn't accumulate any debt, and you'll have more room to enjoy any up cycle or any upside surprise that happens. If you aren't successful at keeping expenses at this "low tide" level, you'll incur debt, and will be more or less successful at paying that debt off, depending on the variations in your cycles and where your "expense line" really lies.

The rest of this chapter is largely aimed at explaining how to manage the expense line for success.

The Importance of Pay As You Go

The wealth cycle models show a "big picture" premise for sustainable wealth. First, and most obvious: Keep expenses below your worst-case income level. Likewise, and this is a bit more complex, you should make sure that your assets, when at their bust lows, don't put you in panic mode insofar as covering your objectives. In addition—and this is important—your assets at "low tide" should still be able to cover all but the most nuclear emergency expenses.

But big-picture premises don't always turn into achievable small-picture promises. What do I mean? It's not easy to whip out a meaningful wealth cycle diagram every time you have to make a purchase decision. It would be neither practical nor realistic.

So on a day-to-day, week-to-week, month-to-month basis, I recommend adopting "pay as you go" as an operating mantra. That is, if you have to borrow to buy something, you need to think twice, and you probably shouldn't do it. There are, of course, some exceptions, and we'll discuss them in this section. The main point is this: If you pay as you go, you preserve flexibility, you can adapt to any future need or contingency, and you can avoid debt.

Rewarding Yourself

If it sounds like I advocate hoarding cash and living like a church mouse, the proverbial miser, eating nothing but canned beans, wearing nothing but thrift-store clothes, and furnishing rooms with particleboard and concrete block furniture, that isn't my intent. Believe me, I do not advocate this.

If you're reading this book, you most likely work hard for your money. There is a time and place for rewards; rewards are what keep you going and keep your family cooperating with the notion of sustainable wealth. Achieving goals is important, as are the accumulation of potential wealth and the avoidance of debt. But to not have *any* rewards *any* time defeats the purpose of working hard to achieve something; those rewards may also consist of rewarding others you care about, as we will discuss in Chapter 10.

So—and this is important—you need to create and preserve a reward system. Rewards stimulate sustainable wealth behavior on both sides of the equation—the production of income and the control of expenses. The point about rewards is this: They still happen, but they happen when either (a) a specific goal is achieved or (b) more generally, when you can afford them.

Good Debt, Bad Debt

So what if you *can't* pay as you go? That's a very important question, and it confronts all of us from time to time. Buying a home for most of us requires a mortgage; it would be a very difficult "pay as you go" accomplishment for most of us. Then there's the unforeseen medical emergency or car repair, if not accounted for through savings or some other resource, which becomes debt. It's a sudden blip in the expense line in the wealth diagram. These are all good questions, too. Of course, if you can stay out of debt altogether, that preserves the most options, and it saves in interest costs, too. Zero debt is the surest way to achieve sustainable wealth objectives of sleeping at night and leaving a family legacy. But I realize that "debt-free" just isn't reasonable, possible, or even smart in some circumstances. Debt is appropriate in the pursuit of sustainable wealth when the return on investment is higher than the cost of debt.

Quite simply, except for emergencies, this is the only time you should consider taking on debt. I am not talking about investing on margin to seek higher returns in the stock market because of a tip received.

In certain circumstances, it makes sense to incur a little short-term debt to get a super deal on something. If you need a lawn-mower and see one in a store as an "open box" return in November, selling for $160 instead of the intended list of $380, using some short-term debt makes sense. Buying out of season usually makes sense in general. Having said that, don't just buy because of the advertisement: Do you really need the item now? Or soon? Do you need the extra features of the more expensive item on sale now? And do you really need to go into debt to afford it, or can you sacrifice another purchase decision instead? Only go shopping for items you need; plan ahead to buy out of season or on craigslist. Do not be tempted to buy all those other great offers while you are in a store—most of the "deals" are for items you don't need.

Now, we come to a big question: what about using credit cards? Credit cards are not only a handy way to pay for things, they also give a clear record of expenditures and have certain protections that make them safer than using cash everywhere. Use credit cards so long as two conditions are met: (1) they are paid off every month without fail, so this month's income meets this month's expenses ("pay as you go"); and (2) credit card users stick to some sort of budgeted guideline or allowance (covered below). Treat a credit card like a charge card (requiring full monthly payment), but take advantage of any "benefits" that come with the card. These benefits, as you may imagine, are not freebies, but the lunch you pay with your credit card includes a markup that allows an airline to offer your miles that

Drive-by Borrowing

I have to confess that I have taken out a loan to buy a car. It was in 2006 when my family needed to upgrade to a van to have enough seats for our four children and to carpool. I had done extensive research on the Internet; picked the model; called several dealers; negotiated on a price over the phone on a specific car; then went to the dealer to sign a check and leave with the car. As you may know, car sales people have as their primary goal to get you into the shop; when I arrived and was ready to sign on the dotted line, the price had changed. Typically, I would have walked away from the transaction, but the manager came and offered a 0 percent loan deal over five years, just slightly above my offer. I calculated that his offer had an overall cost significantly less than what I had offered, considering that I could invest the additional cash in Treasury bills. Having surveyed other dealers, I also knew the offer was competitive. For my personal cash management, I opted for a 3-year, 0 percent loan, as it still offered an attractive advantage, but would allow me to eliminate the loan faster. In my view, the industry has done itself a major disservice by providing loans longer than four years.

you may or may not be able to use; you might as well take advantage if you can. However, if you don't use your credit card, you still have to pay the premium to finance everyone else's bonus programs.

Using a mortgage to buy a home can, but doesn't always, meet the positive return-on-investment criterion, especially lately. When real estate was rising, the prevailing wisdom was that it always made sense to get a mortgage; the increase in real estate prices and the leverage involved almost always produced returns greater than debt costs. It can still work that way, but doesn't always; you must be careful. I'll come back to that later when examining the rent vs. buy decision.

If you have a business idea that requires financing, taking out a loan may be appropriate. If you were to buy an investment property, the property itself can serve as collateral for a loan; for most small business loans, you will need to personally guarantee the loan. The banks love that personal guarantee, because it puts your personal credit line and financial well-being on the line. It is important that any such projects don't jeopardize your overall sustainable wealth plans, even if they turn sour.

Here are a few places I would *avoid* using debt if possible:

- *Purchase of any short-term consumables (e.g., groceries).* The general rule of thumb for both business and personal finances: Never finance any purchase for longer than that purchase will last. Corporate financiers speak of using short-term debt for short-term asset costs or expenses, and long-term debt for long-term purchases. If you mix the two, using long-term debt to finance something short-term or immediately consumable, the item is gone, but the debt is still there for you to cover. This is a complete no-no. Incidentally, the credit crisis might have never happened if corporations had not financed long-term obligations with short-term commercial paper. Unfortunately, many of the emergency credit facilities provided by the Federal Reserve encourage such irresponsible behavior, rather than forcing companies to break bad habits.
- *Buying a car.* Listen to the ads or most of your neighbors, and you'll swear it's okay to borrow to buy a car. Everybody does it, right? I actually think it's a bad idea. First, the car depreciates, especially if you buy a new one. So you pay twice—once for the depreciation, again for the interest. Unless you're really in a business where having a certain kind of car produces a return,

owning a car, or at least a newer or better one, doesn't really produce a return. I believe all cars should be paid for with cash, and if you can't afford what you want, you should get an older, cheaper, less stylish car, and save the difference in cost until you can afford what you want. Leasing a car is a tad more complex. If you like the certainty of your monthly expenses and the ability to return the car, it is something to consider; be aware, however, that there is a lot of fine print to consider in lease agreements—if you don't understand a contract, do not sign it.

- *College education.* Just like buying a car, borrowing money to go to college, with today's college costs, has become more the rule than the exception—some two-thirds of all four-year college graduates have some debt, and the average debt amount exceeded $19,000 in a 2004 survey. I'll grant that college is an investment that produces a return, and that return may exceed the cost of borrowing. But saddling a student just starting out with debt should be avoided, for with the student loan cost in the student's expense line, it takes a lot longer for the *student* to build sustainable wealth through retirement savings and so on. The greatest gift—the greatest legacy—a parent can give a kid in college is to put him or her on the path to sustainable wealth right out of school. We will discuss college savings without going into debt in Chapter 9. When it is not possible to follow the plan, a reasonable amount of debt may be appropriate. However, always be realistic about your ability to pay back such loans and whether there are alternatives, such as grants or part-time work that help supplement the cost of tuition.

Getting a Handle on Expenses

In *Sustainable Wealth,* it isn't my intent to bog you down with detailed analysis of your past, present, and future. What's most important as you read along here is to grasp the underlying concepts, premises, and philosophy of sustainable wealth.

That said, the expression "the devil is in the details" enjoys no finer hour than with the analysis of your household expenses. Before any effective household financial plan can be put together, you and your family need to get a fluent understanding of your family expenses. Not to the nearest penny—that's too much detail—but to a degree sufficient to make plans and to make decisions.

The first step involves a process called *financial forensics,* a concept discussed extensively by budgeting authors Peter and Jennifer Sander (*The Pocket Idiot's Guide to Living on a Budget,* 2nd edition, Alpha Books, 2007). Financial forensics is essentially an end-to-end analysis of past spending behavior. In that analysis, best done over a year's time, you're looking to categorize expenses in the following ways:

- *Regular vs. irregular.* Your mortgage or rent is regular, occurring in the same amount every month. However, your car insurance may be paid twice a year, your property taxes twice a year, your homeowner's insurance once a year (unless part of your mortgage payment is paid as an impound). Irregular expenses, in particular, have a tendency to turn into debt, because we don't have the discipline to save in advance of their occurrence.
- *Expected vs. unexpected.* A mortgage payment, an insurance payment, gifts, or even your favorite morning coffee beverage may be regular or irregular, but they are expected. Unexpected expenses include car or home repairs, doctor bills, and so on; once again, these have a tendency to turn into debt if not understood or planned for.
- *Discretionary vs. nondiscretionary.* Your morning coffee, a night out at a restaurant, or a bottle of wine are discretionary, while your mortgage, groceries, and utility payments are not. However, some portion of nondiscretionary expenses might be controllable, that is, how large an apartment or house you rent or own; how much electricity or gas you use; or how much you spend at the grocery store.

As a wealth sustainer, you'll want to round up all your expenses and categorize them as such. This doesn't have to be done to the nearest penny—to round it to $30 a month for the morning coffee buzz is okay, so long as you're comfortable with that estimate. Such approximations make things easier to understand and manage, as we'll describe further in a minute. You'll find that the financial forensics exercise can actually be fun if done right and without any finger-pointing. You'll discover that the clear view of the past gives you a clearer view of the future.

At the risk of repeating, the point is to understand your financial situation well enough to project it forward into the future; to understand where your expense line really is in the above wealth cycle diagrams. To be sure, like any forward-looking exercise, the past is hardly the only source of information for the future; in fact, if you confine the future by only what's happened in the past, you'll make some big mistakes. Expenses change as we change, our families change, our needs change, and as prices change. A good expense plan carried forward covers these things, and you must additionally incorporate known and planned major expenses like college education into your thinking and into your expense planning.

How to Spend Less Than You Earn

It should be quite clear by now that one of the keys to unlocking the door to sustainable wealth is to *consistently* spend less than you earn. Not just sometimes, but consistently. Spending less than you earn provides the seed capital to invest and compound the income you earn; it makes you less vulnerable to "budget shocks" that can get you behind and put you into debt. Finally, the practice gives you the financial fortitude to reward yourself and buy the things you want to buy without unintended financial consequences later.

Moving forward, the next task is to develop a plan to spend less than you earn, and a lifestyle to support that plan. There are many ways to get there, many of which involve the construction of a budget for current and future income and expenses. This is what small businesses, large corporations, and governments do. But they spend a lot of time and energy (and often have a full-time staff) to do it, and the process, not the result, often becomes the important thing.

Budgets are, at the end of the day, a tool. They help you understand behavior, and they help you plan behavior. They help you figure out where your expense line is, and how it relates to your income. They help you plan for irregular income and expenses, and they can also help plan for longer-term purchases or goals. They can help you understand the size of the surpluses during the good times, so you can plan your purchases, your rewards, and your longer-term savings. But budgets aren't the only way to get there—if you have a good notion of your expenses, and if they're in the right place with respect to income, and everyone commits to staying the course, you can get away without a budget. I do not want to take you through a detailed examination of budgeting; for that I refer you other books, such as the Sanders' book; or you can come up with your own process. The important point is that it works for you, not how you do it.

However you decide to approach expense, income, and savings planning, the following points are important to follow.

Don't Be "Penny Wise and Pound Foolish" or Vice Versa

As I've watched others assume greater control over their finances, I've noticed a tendency to take an unbalanced approach to understanding and controlling expenses. I've seen many people go into great detail to capture the small expenses, the day-to-day pocket money expenses like lunch, coffee, a newspaper, while at the same time they are not able to capture the larger expenses properly, like a kid's college tuition, the full cost of owning and running a car, the true cost of home ownership—or worse, they ignore these expenses altogether. These oversights lead to disruptive financial behavior in a family situation, as family members are called onto the carpet for buying two lattes in a day instead of one—while the financial horse escapes the barn because they drive 50 percent more miles in a year in a car twice as expensive as what they need or plan for. Such behavior may give a sense of purpose and control in the beginning, but tends to bring trouble later on.

Likewise, and almost just as common, I see people focus on the big-ticket items, only to lose it on the small stuff. They get the house payment, housing expenses, car payment, college savings, and so forth right, but they proceed with life with little knowledge nor control of the small stuff, and are continually surprised every month by credit card bills and checking account overdrafts.

Not surprisingly, both of these imbalances—oversights, really—are in conflict with the ability to achieve and preserve sustainable wealth. If you absorb sustainable wealth as a lifestyle, it becomes more meaningful and effective.

Make the Important Standard-of-Living Decisions

It should be clear that sustainable wealth is about planning and also about discipline and financial self-control. As we'll see in the next few chapters, it is also about managing the resulting wealth generated by discipline and self-control. But there is an important controllable factor that goes a long way toward defining your ultimate financial destiny: *standard of living*. More specifically, the *choices* you make with respect to standard of living are at the forefront of your overall financial well-being.

These choices can include large purchases, like a home or vehicle; they also relate to a more abstract set of lifestyle choices that might dictate whether you buy the best brand name of clothing or dishes or are willing to settle for more utilitarian choices. Do you need to spend $100 on your cable TV subscriptions, in addition to Netflix and Blockbuster memberships? Mobile phones have almost become a necessity, but do you need these expensive plans? There are those who can live off a $100 prepaid plan for a year. Think about the small print on your mobile phone contract—many of them set you back $2,000 over the term of a two-year contract.

Toward the Not-So-Big House?

The most important standard of living choice you'll make is about your home—the size of home, the location, its style. In recent decades, Americans have had a love affair with large homes; this love affair has only recently shown signs of receding with the recent real estate and financial bust. More room, more size, farther out in the suburbs; extra-large kitchens and bathrooms, three-car garages, a pool in the backyard. American expectations for the scale and scope of that castle had grown for years, and new homes constructed had accommodated those wishes, doubling in size from the 1960s to more than 2600 square feet in the early part of 2008. Needless to say, the cost of these new homes grew substantially. The largest of these homes earned the sarcastic moniker of "McMansions" because of their size and mass-produced character. These homes were hardly constructed as unique statements of prestige on enormous land estates as in yesteryear, but as entire subdivisions full of them.

Of course, what many people forgot is that there's more to the cost of such a home than the cost of the home itself. For example, in France, you can buy a chateau at what appears to be a ridiculously low price. The real cost is in the maintenance, not the purchase price. Higher utility costs, insurance, costs for furniture and upkeep, and long commutes (as these homes were inevitably placed far out in the suburbs in McMansion communities such as Castle Rock, Colorado; Grapevine, Texas; and Lake Zurich, Illinois), not to mention the high-interest costs of a jumbo loan: These all served to put great numbers of people in negative financial territory.

Also note that a larger house doesn't automatically translate to more upside when you sell the home. Consistent with the sustainable wealth theme, a larger home means greater risk. If you can afford it, by all means, indulge. But also consider the fact that as the baby boomers are retiring with too little savings, they will be downsizing. The next generation has fewer kids and may—out of necessity—be more prudent with their expenses. That doesn't bode well for the value retention of McMansions.

The financial crisis started out as a subprime crisis; many pundits argued the crisis would be contained. Instead, it spread. High-end real estate held its value better than other areas as of this writing. But that's only because the demographic of those owning higher-end homes is likely to be hit later by the credit crisis. In the jumbo loan market, you typically have to pay 30 percent down these days; in times when the savings of many have been cut in half, that's no small feat. Stock options are generally worthless, taking away an important driver of the higher-end housing market.

Further, we have yet to see some of the worst in the housing market: Three-year adjustable-rate mortgages that were taken out at the peak of the housing market in 2007 will reset in 2010. Those folks will be unable to refinance, as the value of their homes quite likely will be less than the value of the mortgage. The government support programs have been geared at the low end of the housing market; even there, my view is that market forces may be stronger than the hand of the government. But if you are considering a McMansion, make sure you can afford it with today's volatility.

The wealth sustainer should approach the housing decision carefully, for it is likely the biggest financial decision you will ever make.

The Own-or-Rent Decision

For the greater part of the last 60 years, Americans have been sold on the idea that home ownership is practically a sovereign right granted to everyone as if by the U.S. Constitution. Most recently, the Bush administration touted nearly 70 percent home ownership rates as both a goal and an accomplishment of the administration. Unfortunately, a few too many bought into that idea, enticed along by government-backed loan programs; they bought far more home than they needed and were most vulnerable to the coming crash.

More importantly, unless you hold your mortgage free and clear, the bank, not you, owns the home. You are in servitude to the bank; as long as you can manage to pay the mortgage, this is a great deal for the bank—you put your personal credit and your reputation on the line and will work hard to make those payments. But is it such a great deal for you? It might, but run the numbers as to what it would cost you to rent versus what it would cost to buy. Be sure to add all the cost and factor in that, as homeowners, you have to pay real estate taxes, unexpected expenses, and are more likely to make upgrades and spend money on maintenance.

In Germany, a country with an extremely low rate of home ownership, buyers take out a calculator to gauge how much they will bid for the home. One of the many reasons that Germany has such a low rate of home ownership is that tenants have lots of rights and can only be kicked out of their homes if they don't pay or if the landlord wants to use the unit for his or her personal use. For many in the United States, the uncertainty that one may be kicked out at the end of the term of a rental contract is a motivation to buy a home. You should take into account how much it's worth to avoid this hassle.

As a wealth sustainer, and especially in these times, you have choices not only about what to buy, but whether to buy or rent. I have lived in the San Francisco Bay area for about nine years, and I have rented rather than bought through this period. You may say: Wait, had Axel bought when he first moved here, he would be ahead, as prices may have fallen, but not that much. Maybe so, but

Dead or Alive

We haven't spent much time discussing taxes, but let me add a word about real estate taxes. These vary from state to state, but if you pay 1 percent of your property's value (or purchase price) in taxes per year, that number adds up. It's like paying estate tax once a generation, except they take it from you alive, year after year.

I am in the sustainable wealth–building business, not in the gambling business. It is no secret that houses in the Bay area are expensive. Buying a house is foremost a risk assessment decision: How comfortable am I affording the risk? I did not want to tie up financial resources, as I was investing in my business. Now the situation is different, as I can afford to make a purchase decision even if the real estate market were to go against me. To restrain myself, I locked myself into a rental contract until the summer of 2010, as I believe the real estate market is unlikely to bottom out significantly before then, if at all. This timeframe may still be too early for the neighborhoods I am evaluating, but my family will make the decision to buy closer to that date.

However, that doesn't mean I wanted nothing to do with real estate—just that it didn't make sense to live in your own property. I own an investment property in a real estate market that is stable and cash-flow positive. As economic times have become less certain, I reduced the mortgage to make cash flow more positive. I also owned a condominium in southern California that I sold as prices were reaching the stratosphere. I did not catch the top of the market. I was early in selling; but, again, gambling was not the purpose. I decided that I would have much better use for the money in my business than in an inflated real estate market.

As far as a bottom in the real estate market is concerned, I do not think we will have a sustainable bottom unless and until home buyers have incomes to sustain their mortgages—without government subsidy. Unfortunately, policymakers bend over backwards to keep the markets highly unstable. While that could end up as political suicide, a homeowner who cannot afford his or her home is best served by downsizing. Someone will have to take a loss in the process—the homeowner, the bank, or you (the taxpayer). Only then can that now-former homeowner build up equity again, invest, and possibly afford a larger home down the road. If, however, such a person receives a subsidy, not only has history shown that he or she may yet again fall behind on the mortgage (the re-failure rate is more than 50 percent of those who had their mortgage terms amended), but that person is unlikely to be able to fix the roof when necessary or cater to other scheduled or extraordinary expenses. By extending the term of a loan, the person only enslaves himself or herself further.

Sustainable Wealth in a Volatile World

Sustainable wealth is more than budgeting and spending less than you earn. It is also about making prudent decisions in the context of where you see the economy and your personal financial needs evolving. In the remainder of the book, we move on to what to do with wealth once produced through prudent spending and saving habits. I also discuss prudent risk taking, and how to adjust both your investments and personal financial decisions with the knowledge you have gained in Part I and so far in Part II of *Sustainable Wealth*.

CHAPTER

Crisis Investing

If you're not confused, you're probably not paying attention.
—Tom Peters

Earn it, keep it. That was a central theme of Chapter 6. Achieve short-term financial security by tuning expenses so that you aren't dependent on every last drop of income, every last drop of a *second* income, or even worse, going into debt to survive. Beyond that, tune your income and expenses to build savings and you may be able to indulge in a reward or two along the way. If you get this far, you've accomplished a lot. If your finances are running smoothly and more or less according to the sustainable wealth principles outlined so far, you and your family are on the path to achieve lasting sustainable wealth.

But there's more to the puzzle. The next step, and the goal of the next three chapters, is to finish out the *earn it, keep it* picture by adding the third step in achieving sustainable wealth: *grow it.* These chapters take a closer look at building and protecting the value of those assets created through prudent income and expense management.

The *grow it* part of building sustainable wealth is done primarily through investing. However, rather than taking the typical first step of discussing general investing, Chapter 7 takes special aim at *crisis investing*—that is, managing personal wealth and investments during periods of considerable uncertainty and volatility. You may have seen the slogan "Don't lose it"—the Richard Russell quotes in Chapter 6 also list "hold on to your capital" as the number-one priority. That's of course easier said than done, especially taking the erosion of purchasing power into accounts typically associated with "safe" strategies.

You may notice that I'm not only covering crisis investing first, but that it is also the longest chapter. That's because holding on to your savings in times of crisis is a key ingredient to sustainable wealth. Again, consider the pilot analogy. An experienced pilot is one who has experienced choppy air; who has diverted during flight; who is willing to make a no-go decision (i.e., stay on the ground) and let an "opportunity too good to be true" pass, because the risks are not worth it. Choppy air and unpredictable conditions force you to respond to change, make prompt judgments and adjustments, and put safety at the forefront. It is pretty much the same story with crisis investing versus investing as a whole.

We will examine how to think about the external perils and how to best play defense so that you can sleep at night. From there, Chapter 8 turns the corner from defense to offense, giving insights on how to profit from different global environmental scenarios; and finally, Chapter 9 shares best practices for investment choice and portfolio construction.

Chapter 7 characterizes crisis investing: what makes it a crisis, what special risks are posed during a crisis, and how you as a wealth sustainer should respond.

Signs of Crisis

The first step toward successful crisis investing is to identify the crisis. Sure, it seems obvious, but it's always surprising how many smart people get "blindsided" by the unwinding of an economic boom and the consequences of that unwinding. And we are not just talking about an economic crisis; personal financial crises are also not always easy to identify, although they may appear all too obvious with the benefit of hindsight.

Why are people surprised by crises? It usually starts with an overdose of conventional wisdom. Such conventional wisdom can take the form of overreliance on the correction model (e.g., a 10 percent dip in stock prices and then we're on our way again). The "Greenspan put" idea is another dangerous conventional wisdom—where the Fed always can, and will, come to our rescue just in time and with enough power and influence to pull our chestnuts out of the fire. Especially when our personal finances and investments are going well, there's a natural tendency to feel invulnerable, to feel that problems will take care of themselves or be taken care of by the system and we'll be on our way shortly.

Such a feeling of invulnerability was characteristic of the brief market drop that occurred in February 2007. That sharp 5 percent dip, in just a few days, made a lot of headlines and brought real estate lending and derivative concerns to the public eye for the first time. But did the markets—the stock markets and real estate markets—roll over just then? No; most took it as a brief correction—a blip. They felt that delinquent subprime mortgages were but a small minority and well-contained problem, and went on their giddy way, driving the Dow to new highs that October. Real estate prices had already flattened, but, in part due to the opacity of the mortgage-backed securities market and the accounting for these securities, there was little to signal the precipitous drops to follow.

Still, the sustainable wealth manager had good reason to be concerned at that moment. The events that followed would quickly bear that out, although it took six months or more for many of those signs to become obvious; even at the height of the crisis, however, many pundits said it would be contained if only the government would do this or that. Using the piloting analogy, we hit a strong and turbulent bump that February 2007, which should have made us more alert for changing weather ahead. That changing weather did come eventually, after a period of smooth air. Economic growth started to slow, delinquency and foreclosure rates started to rise, consumer debt reached an all-time high, and real estate prices started to fall. The Fed had reduced the target funds rate 50 basis points by September of that year, and the rest is history. Notably, it took until the September–October 2008 period, a year later, for the crisis to "mature," although the Bear Stearns collapse in March 2008 provided a sharp squall; by then, any wealth sustainer would have already looked for a place to land and take cover—preferably in a shelter that could weather the storm. In the fairy tale of "The Three Little Pigs," only one of the pigs was able to withstand the huffing and puffing of the wolf; the third pig not only built a better shelter, but was smarter and always a step ahead of the wolf. Trouble is that the wolf is the market, and in a crisis, it is no fairy tale.

No two crises are the same. The details of what fails when, and what triggers the failure, are often quite different. In some cases, the stock market leads the way down, as in 1929, creating collateral damage along the way in the form of failed margin debt, deleveraging, and hence, failed banks. The 1997 turmoil was made apparent by the Long-Term Capital Management hedge fund collapse, and the 1998 Asian crisis could best be observed through currency speculation and devaluations. The dot.com collapse came after a period of extreme stock overvaluation; the 2008–2009 crisis was similar except that residential real estate, not dot.com stocks, were the protagonist. Like the 1929 crash, the 2008–2009 collapse was driven by overextension of credit and subsequent deleveraging. You are unlikely to find a big red flag waved on CNBC at the top of the market (nor at the bottom); some will alert you, but listening to the right voices will always be easier with the benefit of hindsight. Often, there is no simple trigger to show you that the market is turning. What makes it even more difficult, in the current environment, is that policies seem to change every other minute; in this case, looking for clarity of policies and judging their effectiveness may be providing clues about the developments of the markets. For example, unless incomes can afford mortgages without immense government subsidy, any recovery in the 2008–2009 environment may be unsustainable.

Very few will be able to identify the top. If you are lucky, you may be able to do this on a specific security or the market in general once, twice, or—if you are really good or lucky—three or more times in your lifetime. You want to start shifting into crisis mode when you see warning signs, before the crisis has fully erupted. By the time the crisis is completely apparent, it may be too late to leave the party, and few plausible investments remain. The goal is not to be a market timer, but to preserve what you have. In a bear market, those who lose the least win. Don't get depressed over losses, but always think ahead on how to be prepared for what may lie ahead.

Economic crises have common traits; I'll review some of the obvious signs, some of which will show earlier than others:

- *Asset prices rise in unison.* Booms are characterized by widespread asset price increases, whereas under normal circumstances money tends to flow from one asset class to another. A bubble is forming when all, or nearly all, asset classes rise simultaneously. When stocks, bonds, commodities, real estate, international markets, and so on all go up simultaneously, as they did during the credit bubble, be on alert. Booms and bubbles feel good, and there's an argument to be made that some of the best gains can be made during the blowout phase of the bubble. When you start taking shelter depends a lot on your risk appetite, but don't expect to be able to call the top. When things seem too good to be true, they probably are; start taking chips off the table. Don't expect to be able to run for cover if you are pushing your luck—others may be running for the same exit at the same time. Bear Stearns and Lehman Brothers learned this lesson the hard way. Apply common sense, not sophistication; listen to yourself and apply what you have learned in this book. Ignore the pundits.

- *End of a parabolic uptrend.* The recent decade's boom in asset prices, and real estate in particular, showed a parabolic upward trend before the bust—as had 2008 oil, dot.com stocks, 1929 stocks, and tulip bulbs some centuries before. Prices simply aren't supported by fundamentals, whether it be corporate earnings, home buyer incomes, or simple supply and demand economics. Uptrends are hard to sustain for long periods, but parabolic uptrends signify a mania in which those late to the party or those who prematurely "short" the market clamor to get on board. Demand begets more demand, and price and value are further separated. That pattern will typically end and unwind very rapidly; when it does, look out below.

- *Stock market behavior.* In a bull market, stocks tend to rise gradually, with the occasional sharp correction. In a bear market, gradual declines tend to be interrupted by vicious rallies; there are no faster buyers than short-sellers covering their positions in a short-squeeze. The stock market is there to cause maximum frustration and pain to those who follow it closely. The stock market can forecast economic events to come, but be aware of economist Paul Samuelson's quip: "The stock market has forecast nine of the last five recessions." If you read too much into the market, do so at your own peril. While you may not want to panic in a correction in a bull market or jump into the market based on a rally in a bear market, staying the course can be hazardous to your wealth when fundamentals in the markets change. Please see Chapter 5 for more details on the perils of staying the course.

- *IPOs that don't make sense.* Raising money or going public should serve a purpose that benefits shareholders. Going public merely because you can get the money, not because you need it, is often a sign that we may be nearing the top in a market. In the latest crisis, the fact that private equity firms were engaging in IPOs was a clear warning sign that the stock market was overvalued. Similarly, if a firm merely goes public so that owners can sell out, that's usually a bad sign, no matter how wildly successful the IPO may be. Don't mistake investor greed with opportunity.

- *"Darling" investments peak and fall.* Every boom has its darling can't-miss investments; most recently, oil, metals, energy stocks, mining and construction equipment, fertilizer, and basic materials. The play was that China would maintain or even accelerate its rapid industrial and infrastructure growth, adding to an already stretched commodity supply picture in a booming economy. Investors, and particularly hedge funds, played this aggressive trade and were forced to sell when leverage and redemptions caught up with them. The reversal of tech stocks in 2000 and "nifty-fifty" stocks in the early 1970s signaled similar crises. These aren't necessarily bad long-term investments, as China will indeed use more resources in the years to come and the United States won't revert to the Stone Age but will require more computer technology in the future. But there can be too much of a good thing when everyone piles into the same idea; moderation is key to sustainability. In fact, I do believe that the world's reflationary efforts will prove inflationary and cause commodities to recover; but if a good story turns wild, it's time to take chips off the table, and especially to avoid using leverage.

- *Fear, uncertainty, doubt.* In the boom, everyone is optimistic, and there is convergence of belief among most financial commentators and observers. When the boom turns to bust, fear replaces greed and optimism, and convergence turns to divergence. Talking heads argue. Everyone watches every move of the Fed and Treasury closely and there are frequent hearings and testimony before Congress. Policy is ambiguous and continuously changing; witness the changes in the TARP program after its unveiling in late 2008 or the conflicting message of bailing out some homeowners (encouraging debt) while threatening to reduce tax deductibility for others (discouraging debt). Markets can't move, and many assets can't change hands or even be priced because of uncertainty. Fear alone is not bad—it can show that there may be a market bottom; however, uncertainty in policies is poison. Often, bad policies are better than no policies. With bad policies, you can still determine who the winners and losers are. But when trillions are thrown at a problem with conflicting signals, the best we can hope for is anemic, then unstable inflationary growth.

- *Deleveraging.* During the expansion everybody borrows cheaply to buy assets. Companies borrow to buy back shares. When the crisis "tipping point" hits, suddenly individuals and businesses reverse course to strengthen balance sheets. Some can't, and those weak debtors and, ultimately, financial institutions are left holding the bag. When news headlines suddenly shift to covering bankruptcies and companies struggling to sell or refinance debt, the crisis has started. The deleveraging process creates a still-greater crisis when assets used to secure debts decline in value, as with stocks in the 1930s and real estate more recently. As a result, crises caused by overleveraging and debt can be the most severe, hardest to fix, and longest lasting. Note that the markets are generally stronger than government policies, but government interference increases volatility; when government policies appear stronger, the recovery is likely to be unstable.
- *Central bank props up system—without effect.* When the central bank throws money into the system without a concrete plan and without effect, that's trouble. The trillions recently injected into the economy did little to jump-start the economy; never confuse the clinging to good news with a sustainable recovery.
- *Deliberate devaluation.* Any country that deliberately devalues its currency, either by decree, as Mexico did in 1994 and Thailand in 1998, or through monetary policy, as the Fed may be doing today, is admitting economic trouble. The idea is to export more and, eventually, attract more foreign investment, although the latter goal is compromised if devaluations are too severe or unpredictable. The United Kingdom has already pursued policies similar to the United States, flooding with liquidity and bailing out banks, and as their currency doesn't enjoy "reserve" status on the world stage, these actions brought a swift decline in the British pound.

When the Government Says It's a Good Investment

By now, you know that I believe the government should stay out of micromanaging the economy. It's bad for resource allocation and bad not just for the government's, but also your own bottom line. Remember when Congress wanted to invest Social Security funds in the stock market? Greenspan did a good deed when he stopped that nonsense in its tracks. Even the fact that it was seriously considered was a warning sign that stocks were becoming overvalued. Unfortunately, the government is now taking stakes in firms anyway through its bailouts—a bad omen for long-term growth. Or take the Bank of England's sale of its gold reserves, pretty much at the bottom of the market; now the British government is leading the calls for the International Monetary Fund (IMF) to sell its gold—another sign that we were closer to the bottom than the top? The government does set trends, and when trillions are thrown around, it will affect markets. Take the government-sponsored ethanol mania—the move fizzled, because ethanol is neither efficient, green, nor cost-effective. Government policies that allow the markets to allocate resources tend to have lasting impact; direct subsidies tend to be counterproductive in the long term.

- *Protectionism.* The first policy concern in most crises is the protection of jobs and asset prices. Soon the conversation shifts to protecting entire industries. When trade protection hits the agenda, and especially when trade wars erupt between countries, it signifies trouble. Once started, protectionism is hard to stop, and historically leads to more of the very economic decline policymakers were trying to avert in the first place. All countries lose with protectionism, but those with a current account deficit are particularly vulnerable, as they depend on inflows from abroad to prop up their currency. Something as little as restricting financial institutions that received government help to hire foreigners is already highly problematic. As Goldman Sachs' CEO pointed out, they have 200 foreign employees affected by the rule in the United States, but if other countries retaliate, 2,000 Americans that pay U.S. taxes are affected in Goldman's overseas offices.

- *Bailouts.* Along the same lines as protectionism, when policy-makers are confronted with calls to subsidize or bail out large corporations or entire industries, the crisis is in full force— especially if they agree to do it. Bailouts serve as an admission of the possibility of systemic failure, or, more cynically, fear of political consequences if an industry is allowed to fail. They are an admission of unwillingness to let the system work out its own problems. But they create substantial uncertainty about the future, which can cause normal economic exchange to slow or become extremely cautious for a long time to come. For example, banks became even more reluctant to give up their toxic assets, for fear they might lose a better deal through an eventual bailout. Such a standoff can prolong the crisis considerably.

Many of the traits discussed above are particularly applicable to the 2008–2009 crisis. Every crisis will have its own symptoms; I hope the above gives you a flavor of what to look for. The art is, of course, to see these characteristics and act on them before the crisis feeds on itself and takes your personal finances down with it.

Hope Is Not a Strategy

Sustaining wealth means keeping a close eye on conditions, watching the instruments, and finding and staying in smooth air, all necessary to avoid a crisis. This approach applies not only to your investments but also to your day-to-day finances—income, spending, and debt. I'm always amazed at how some people choose to ignore crises altogether, spending anyway because they can't stop, or they still have income, or they think they must "help the economy." Further, when things get bad in the markets, they stop opening their brokerage and 401(k) statements, preferring instead to stand by and wait for the storm to blow over. If you piloted an airplane with this attitude, you wouldn't stay in the air for long.

Those who ignore the warning signs or try to ignore the crisis altogether do so at their own peril. Economic crises jeopardize income streams and reduce asset bases, while expenses typically stay the same or may even increase. Notably, college and health care costs did not come down one bit during the most recent downturn. We do not have widely spread "deflation" as many want us to believe—has your cost of living gone down? Has deflation brought more purchasing power to your savings? Do you feel like your savings can take you further? Lower commodity prices are a stimulus, not part of a deflationary spiral as policymakers discuss.

With the Fed printing money to finance government spending, the seeds for Great Inflation may have been placed. In 2003, referring to the global imbalances, the former head of the European Central Bank said, "We hope and pray that the adjustment process will be slow and gradual." When central bankers refer to hope and prayers, I take notice and act. I changed the business model in my firm to prepare for what I saw as the risks ahead. Strategy is about long-term planning, not tactical maneuvering. Note that the credit crisis is a symptom of the global imbalances, but by no means have we addressed and developed mechanisms to manage them. Of course, I didn't take my savings in 2003 and place them under a mattress; but one must be prudent and adapt the sorts of risks one is taking.

If you don't keep an eye on your finances, crises can easily cause you to take on more debt. If expenses stay the same (or increase) while incomes drop, either debt or a drop in savings is the necessary outcome. By the same token, even if debt doesn't increase in absolute terms, it rises *as a percentage* of your asset base if your asset prices drop. Just like a corporation, the more debt you have as a percentage of your asset base, the more leveraged you are, the less flexible you are, and the less prepared you are to handle a crisis. This problem can happen covertly without you doing anything.

Yet many people reach for the financial "autopilot" just as things get tense. They now want to allow the airplane to take care of itself, so they do not touch the controls. They want to maintain a steady course, they want to stay focused on the long term, they want to avoid the stress of tracking events and making frequent adjustments. That is exactly the wrong thing to do.

To sustain wealth during a crisis, you need to keep your eyes glued to the horizon and the instruments more closely than ever, and take safety into account even more than usual. Following are six sustainable wealth principles to be followed at all times and especially in times of crisis:

Don't Put the Crisis on Ignore

Ignoring a crisis will not make it go away; it will simply bring more unpleasant surprises later. Even more than usual, it is important to stay tuned to the news and media reports to understand what is changing, why, and how it will affect your investments. As hard as it is, it's important to keep looking at your investment and broker-age statements—in contrast to many people I've observed, who only look at their financials when things are good. It doesn't stop with investments—a crisis merits a closer look at all parts of your sustain-able wealth grid: assets, income, expenses, and liabilities. Don't just look: Evaluate rationally and act as necessary.

Earn Your Job Every Day

Many people worry about their assets and especially their stocks during a downturn, but are less worried about their expenses and their job. They fail to take decisive, proactive steps to make their jobs—or their businesses, if self-employed—less vulnerable. They worry about how their "401(k) has turned into a 201(k)," not about what they could be doing to make themselves indispensable to their boss or clients.

A crisis is a perfect time to take inventory of the value you really bring to a job. If you're in a job that inherently doesn't add much value, it may be time for a change. Crises, especially if allowed to run their course, naturally shake out inefficient, low-margin, low–value-add players. If, by self-assessment or the judgment of others, you aren't in a good "value-add" position in the food chain, it's time to make some adjustments.

I am not trying to depress you, but I believe that you should always be on the lookout to add value to your firm. If your firm does periodic reviews of your work, embrace them, as they are the best opportunity to learn about your standing. Some firms do peer reviews, top-down and bottom-up reviews (i.e., everyone you work with reviews every-one, no matter whether they report to you or you report to them). Traditionally, only consulting firms (which love doing surveys and evaluations thereof) go to such extremes. But if there is no formal process for this, take the initiative. Investing in yourself is the best pos-sible investment.

Income isn't just about jobs, either. You must also pay attention to cash flow received from investments. Only cash received, such as from dividends, is cash in your pocket; everything else is just a paper gain that may evaporate.

Focus on the Future, Not the Past

It's easy to get too caught up in past spending and investing decisions. It goes something like this: "I lost 40 percent on company XYZ; if I hang on long enough, it will come back." Such an approach can get you in trouble, for the decision to buy XYZ is past and irreversible. All that matters at this point is what will happen to XYZ in the future, and that must be compared to *the future of* any alternative investment. Always think about why you purchased an investment in the first place—if that condition is no longer met, move on.

Reduce Exposure

Now I arrive at one of the most important principles of sustainable wealth: Spend only what you can afford to spend, invest only what you can afford to lose.

These phrases sound fairly simple, but are in reality more involved than they sound for two reasons:

1. Determining what you can really afford isn't simple.
2. That amount changes as the crisis deepens, your situation changes, and your need for safety increases. As a wealth sustainer, you must keep an eye on both the afford-to-spend and afford-to-lose figures, and adjust those figures for the situation.

Prepare for Extremes

The recent downturn was unusual in its depth and speed, once it gained momentum in the fall of 2008. As pointed out in Chapter 5, many behaviors and combinations of behaviors fell outside the market's normal statistical boundaries one would have expected from history; it busted the models. Markets tend to overrun reality both to the upside and downside; but in this case, we had some real black swan events—for instance, the collapse of Lehman and AIG on the same weekend—causing extreme panic in the markets. This downturn generated more black swans than most.

The expression "black swan" comes from an old belief that all swans were white, which was dismissed forever when black swans were discovered in Australia. As a wealth sustainer, you must always keep the black swan possibility in mind. Keep this in mind, too: If you're investing only what you can afford to lose, black swans won't destroy your wealth.

Act as Necessary

Some people put the crisis on "ignore" altogether; others watch what's unfolding, but, like the proverbial deer in headlights, they find themselves unable to act. Whether it happens out of hope, complacency, or fear of making a mistake, doing nothing can be very dangerous. Many investors have lost their heads trying to avoid taking a $500 investment loss.

Don't Become a Boiled Frog

A very nonscientific survey of my friends and colleagues during the 2008–2009 bust indicated that many, if not most, are holding on to their stock portfolios. While the values of their portfolios were down 35–50 percent from their peak, even after the March 2009 recession rally, they must have thought that things were more likely to get better than to get worse in the future. Why else would they be holding on to their stocks?

When I asked my friends for their rationale for holding on to their stocks, their responses could be grouped into three approaches as follows:

1. *The eternal optimist*: "Things will surely get better tomorrow! My stock is up 40 percent from the lows!" Yeah, right, but a stock that fell 50 percent, from 100 to 50, then recovered 40 percent, is still only at 70, or 30 percent off the precrisis level.
2. *The worrywart*: "I cannot bear the thought of missing the eventual upswing, especially since I have already lost so much."
3. *Those in denial*: "If I just put my head down, focus on my work, ignore the news, and do not even look at my investment performance, one day I will wake up and things will have fixed themselves."

Group 1 was obviously holding out for a recovery, although the definition of "tomorrow" needed work, with the recession likely to last another year or more. Group 2 wasn't so sure that the recession would be over soon, but was instead waiting for the market to act upward in advance of a Main Street bottom. The only problem, of course, is not knowing how low Main Street really will go, and when. Those in Group 2 are also worried about recovering past losses instead of focusing on future gains. About Group 3: I have yet to find a good economic foundation; it probably has more to do with the psychology of survival than investment logic. Perhaps they just have a much more long-term approach to investing than the rest of us can afford to have.

All this reminds me of the boiling frog story. If you put a frog into a pot of boiling water, it will jump out. But, if you put it into a pot of cold water and heat it slowly, it will never jump out. The poor frog surely feels the water getting warmer, and warmer, and warmer. Perhaps he is thinking that the water *must* get cooler tomorrow? But, before he finally gets the smarts to jump out, it's too late.

Don't let this happen to your investments.

About Insurance

What about the use of insurance to protect you from crises? The wealthier a nation, they more its people are typically scared of losing what they have, and the more they can afford to spend to protect themselves. The Swiss are said to spend almost a quarter of their disposable income on insurance.

You should consider insuring a risk you cannot afford to bear on your own. These days, you also need to consider whether your insurance firm is able to shoulder the risk. Theoretically, insurance regulations help ensure that your insurance is safe; but there may be limitations on amounts, and the regulation isn't national but state by state.

Please note that insurance is a complex topic; I will only touch on a couple of aspects to show their relationship to sustainable wealth. This is not meant as a complete insurance guide. I encourage you to seek expert advice on any particular type of insurance you are considering.

Insure Yourself, When You Can

Insurance is like a prepaid service; you lend the insurance company money to pay you when certain clauses in your policy are triggered.

As a result, you should never feel bad about submitting an insurance claim!

Because insurance firms are paid in advance, a well-run insurance company can be highly profitable. And that's the rub: Your policy pays for the profits of the insurance company and sales commissions for agents. The commission for insurance agents is high: For annuities, for example, commissions can easily reach 10 percent or more of the amount you invest. That means the insurance company receives only 90 percent of the money to work with to cover its promises to you, as the commission is often paid up front. The insurer also needs to cover its overhead. In fairness to annuity brokers, they may only be paid once for a 10-year annuity (and they may share the commission with others on the food chain); in contrast, your friendly investment adviser may charge you 1 percent each year. But with health insurance, high commissions are paid year after year.

If you can bear a risk you consider insuring—like the first $500 of an auto accident, the first $2,000 of health care costs, or the first $5,000 of a major home loss—you may be better off investing the money you would spend on a premium. This is called *absorbing* the risk, or self-insurance if you will. The same logic applies to

Insurance Through Uncle Sam

You may also be better equipped than an insurance company to compensate for inflation. If you buy a $100,000 life insurance today, what about its purchasing power when the policy is paid out? Some policies adjust for inflation, but typically with a cap.

For many, the best insurance bargain in town may be Social Security. Social Security can be looked at as a form of annuity, except that benefits have a cost of living adjustment without cap; one can argue whether the published cost of living adjustment fully captures increased cost, but the formula currently used by the government yields payouts that are currently not met by the private sector.

It may also make sense for you to postpone receiving Social Security benefits. That's if you have pursued a sustainable wealth lifestyle and your Social Security income is a nice addition, but not a necessity for you. Delaying receipt may also pass the higher delayed benefit on to your spouse.

extended warranties: Risks add up when you buy an appliance, a toy for your children (or yourself), the latest electronic gadget, a large-screen TV, a computer for your home. Some of these purchases may break, but it's unlikely all will at once. On a very small scale, just like an insurance company, you have a portfolio of gadgets; periodically, something will require repair or replacement, but if you have assessed the risks you want to take prudently, you can afford to take those risks. You may even say that if this video game console breaks, the best choice is the dumpster—you don't need an insurance policy for that one at all. And you can set aside some savings to cover the larger deductibles on health and casualty loss policies.

Liability Insurance

In a simple world, if you break something, you pay to fix it. In today's litigious society, however, the actual damage caused is less relevant; what is relevant is the amount for which you can be sued. Referencing yet another pilot analogy, flight instructors in recent years have been sued when allegedly responsible for damage to property or students (physical or emotional). Flight instructors get sued more frequently nowadays because they tend to have insurance, whereas in the old days, they did not. Without insurance, it is not worth suing someone unless they have assets.

Similarly, you have to make a choice as to whether or not you need liability insurance. If you have assets, you'll have to make a risk-driven decision about protecting those assets. The details are left for consultation with insurance professionals, but I would like to point out a quirk about liability insurance: If you are in a legal dispute, your insurance company typically will defend you up to the policy amount; it will use this amount either to defend you or to settle any claims. In practice, it turns out that settlements are frequently exactly the amount of your policy, because the person suing you knows he or she can get that amount. However, that doesn't prevent a litigant from pursuing your wealth further; more of your assets can be at risk.

Conversely, if you have no liability insurance, all your assets may be fair game in a lawsuit. As a result, liability insurance may serve as an important and often sufficient buffer. It's these quirky characteristics of liability insurance that make it a little different from other forms of insurance. Liability insurance can be obtained at reasonable cost as a rider or "umbrella" to a homeowner's or renter's insurance. As with any policy, read the small print and only sign what you understand.

Health Insurance

Health insurance needs to be mentioned in the context of crisis investing, as the cost of health care can ruin even affluent people if they are not properly insured. I put health insurance into the bucket of risks I like to have insured, as hospital bills or the cost of managing a lifelong medical condition can be astronomical.

You have to make a choice about how much insurance you need; if you stay true to the theme of only insuring what you cannot afford to pay, you may want to consider a high deductible.

Because I want insurance to pay for things I cannot afford to pay, I want insurance companies to live up to that promise. I am very troubled with policies that have a cap on what they will pay. I am also concerned with insurance companies that can reduce or eliminate coverage out of no fault of your own; you are prepaying for services, they are making a commitment. In practice, that's not necessarily the case.

However, as this is not a book on health care reform, I will not step into this minefield any further at this time. The point is to make sure you have the right amount of insurance to sleep at night, not to buy and pay for more insurance than you need. In addition, you should evaluate and track your insurance investments just as you would any other investment.

There's No Such Thing as a Safe Asset

I have long argued that there is no such thing as a safe asset, and that investors should take a diversified approach to something even as mundane as cash. Even "safe" long-term Treasury bonds aren't so safe if inflation wipes out any gains, and they are further jeopardized if purchasing power erodes as the dollar plunges.

Moving away from bonds, it isn't hard to see how even less steady returns for stocks, stock markets and their indexes, commodities, and now even real estate require a constant vigil—compounded growth can find many ways off the tracks and into the weeds with such investments.

But what about cash? What's the risk there? Your grandfather told stories of hiding cash in his mattress to get around the obvious threat of bank insolvency during the Great Depression. But today? What really can happen?

The answer, of course, comes from considering the greater economic environment and the volatile world we live in. Central banks have always had the ability to influence the value of their currencies and should do so prudently. But in recent years, they've given in to the temptations discussed in the first part of this book, and to politics, and to the increasing imperative to "do something" and reflate the economy any time the markets catch a cold. That tendency can first hurt your investments, then hurt you again should you decide to turn your investments into cash. Worse, even a migration to foreign currencies doesn't help much unless done very carefully, for an increasing number of foreign central banks may be given to similar temptations. One may be able to mitigate these risks by diversifying toward a basket of hard currencies, or even to a country like China, which has an interest in less reliance on the U.S. dollar and the creation of a hard currency. You knew it was important to find leaders with stocks and the best locations with real estate and safety with bonds, but now it's important to be prudent even with cash, because these investments, too, have their risks.

Some consider gold the ultimate safe haven; it may be so, but the price of gold can also be highly volatile; further, even staunch gold bugs rarely have all of their money in gold. At the time of writing this book, I have taken steps to hedge the dollar risk of essentially all my assets. I am not alone in my concern; at a conference of foreign exchange professionals I spoke at in April 2009, I received confirmation that an increasing number of U.S. institutional investors are hedging their U.S. dollar risk. It's almost unheard of in a first-world country that institutions hedge their domestic currency exposure.

My views may change by the time you read this and should by no means be construed as investment advice; what may be appropriate for me may not be appropriate for others. What I am trying to get across is that you should put your money where your mouth is. Diversification has its value, but if you see the risk of negative scenarios unfolding, don't resort to hope—act, and take it into account in your portfolio allocation.

With any kind of asset at any time, and particularly in a crisis, I see at least four sources of risk to consider, each of which can temporarily or permanently cripple an asset or an asset class. These factors increase the risk of any investment, but not always in a negative direction. The goal is to consider the factors and consider how asset classes and individually chosen investments will behave in normal times and during the "stress test" of a crisis. These aren't the only factors that can affect your investments, and naturally they will affect different asset classes differently.

The Price of Policy Change

As described in Part I of *Sustainable Wealth,* governmental policy, of the U.S. government and others, can have profound effects, especially on the long-term value of many of your investments. First and foremost, monetary policy can erode cash value, and, of course, any asset denominated in cash value. At the same time, that cash or monetary devaluation can increase the price of hard assets such as gold, other commodities, and even real estate, provided that real estate is properly priced to begin with.

Monetary policy decisions may also be disruptive to fixed income asset prices. The Fed's policy of buying bonds to increase liquidity gives a boost to bond prices, but the eventual financing of all the debt required for stimulus programs will bring a flood of bonds to the market, likely lowering their prices while raising interest rates. Likely in addition or instead, the flood of government bonds could crowd corporate debt out of the market as new funds to purchase debt dry up; corporate bond values could suffer as a result. Another possible result is that foreigners will stop buying U.S. government bonds, causing a severe dollar decline. Indeed, the dollar may also decline if Americans sell their bonds to take their money abroad; in early 2009, reports have been increasing of U.S. institutional investors seeking ways to hedge their U.S. dollar risk. Usually, you hedge your foreign currency risk, not that of your own currency. The government may also increase taxes to finance the deficit. None of these scenarios bodes particularly well for the purchasing power of your investments.

Notably, policy and monetary measures do not motivate people to save; in fact, a downdraft in interest rates is more of an incentive to spend than to save. Such a policy fails to move people toward financial prudence and also fails to provide adequate private-sector investment capital. Worse, if and when inflation really does take hold, the

Fed may be unable to raise interest rates sufficiently to stop it, for the economy is likely to be too fragile to raise rates, and the cost of debt will be excessive.

The term "policy" does not stop with deliberate monetary economic measures taken by governments. Tax policy can affect entire economies or sectors within an economy, as investment tax credits can affect industries and capital gains taxes can affect individual investors. Regulation and trade policy complete the picture; one must always keep feelers out for policy changes. Importantly, not all policy changes come with clear and loud headlines; the recent Fed policy to reflate the economy by flooding it with liquidity has come in small increments and has been referred to euphemistically as "bank stabilization," "Term Asset-Backed Securities Loan Facility (TALF)," and similar.

In summary, crisis-driven policy changes have become more frequent and more wide-ranging in their effects on different asset classes. As you can see, the effects of policy, and especially policy change, are numerous and complex—investors find it extremely difficult to make long-term investing decisions. In my assessment, as government policies are aimed at propping up a broken system rather that providing incentives for more sustainable economic growth, we may be faced with increasingly less stable economic cycles.

Business Cycles

The business cycle is both a child and a parent of policy, and it helps to be able to map the booms and busts as they happen and as they are moved along by the powers that be. Business cycles can undermine the value of even the safest assets (and may enhance the value of some, like gold). Policy can, and often does, make business cycle effects stronger.

Quite clearly, business cycles have a great effect on corporate profits and thus the price of corporate assets. Beyond that, cycles affect the industrial demand for commodities both up and down— as observed when the China demand factor suddenly went away, exacerbating the slowdown of demand from other geographies. Commodity prices tumbled as a result, and, in my view, the cycle was further sharpened by investors, particularly hedge-fund investors, chasing these trends.

Business cycles affect businesses and even public sector entities in more subtle ways than the simple decline in unit sales or revenues.

Most businesses have fixed costs; some have substantial fixed costs. The greater the fixed cost as part of the cost structure, the more vulnerable the business is (correspondingly, a high fixed-cost percentage can lead to greater operating leverage and profits in favorable time). Debt works similarly as a fixed obligation that must be paid with a fixed outlay for the interest. So investors invested in high fixed-cost, high-debt businesses must be acutely aware of business cycles; crisis investing requires being nimble on your feet or avoiding these businesses altogether. It should be noted that some businesses can be negatively affected by "up" cycles if labor costs, energy, or other resource costs escalate.

During the 1990s and the early 2000s, we went through a period of relatively moderated business cycles, due in part to the "soft landing" policies of the Federal Reserve. But as the Fed and other policymakers lose control and run out of resources to make the corrections they want to make, and as the pace of business change quickens, I think that the effects of business cycles on asset prices may become stronger, making asset prices more volatile.

Commodity Cycles

If you think gold is pretty safe in a crisis, I would agree with you. But not even gold is 100 percent safe. Indeed, some of the safest assets may be hurt by their own success, even in crisis times. Gold and other precious metals are good examples. Suppose a crisis and the resulting "flight to quality" drive up the price of gold, as it did in 1979–1980 and again in 2007–2008.

Traditionally, jewelry demand dwarfs investment demand; when economic times are tough, jewelry demand plunges. It is remarkable that the price of gold has gone up despite a collapse in demand from India, traditionally the largest market for jewelry. Investor demand has taken the place of the traditional market and kept the price of gold high, even in light of central bank selling of reserves. If the markets stabilize, some safe-haven buying may reverse as money flows to riskier assets. Some say the central bank selling may put downward pressure on gold; it may, but I see that as a positive development, as money moves into private hands, giving less significance to conspiracy theories about governments trying to manipulate the gold price. Although just as the West has reduced its gold reserves, China is actively building them. I would not be surprised if China offered to exchange a good portion of its massive holdings of U.S. Treasuries with the United States–owned gold reserves held at the International Monetary Fund (IMF).

Many don't realize, however, that the gold market is small compared to most other markets in the world; all gold mined throughout history could be stored below the Eiffel Tower. As a result, if and when there's a flight into gold, we can see extreme moves, such as in 1979–1980.

One reason that commodity cycles tend to be longer than business cycles is because of the dynamics of mining. It takes years to increase production, as most people don't like to have a mine in their backyard. Mining is also capital intensive: In the aftermath of the credit crisis, there simply is very little, if any, financing available, especially with the price declines we have seen. But make no mistake about it: volatility in commodities—even during "normal" times—can be enormous, even without using leverage, as do many who use derivatives to buy these commodities.

As a slightly more complicated example, rising oil prices have *caused* crises, which in turn have further driven up oil prices as energy refiners, large consumers, and, eventually, speculators "pile on" in that market. You might think that in an energy-driven crisis, owning oil would be a safe bet. But the dynamics in the oil markets are complex; supply and demand depend not just on production and consumers but on weather and geopolitics, to name a few factors.

Gold is far more sensitive to the monetary and fiscal stimuli; other commodities have more industrial use and are thus more dependent on the cyclicality of the industries where the commodities are used. Similarly, during a depression, silver turns into an industrial metal and may suffer even as gold thrives. Silver is particularly volatile and periodically experiences 10 percent intra-day price fluctuations.

Creative Destruction

Business, product, and technology cycles are getting shorter and faster; radio, word processors, and PCs have shorter cradle-to-grave cycles as new technologies replace them or as needs change. The process of natural business and technological evolution and destruction was appropriately labeled "creative destruction" by economist Joseph Schumpeter. The reason that this concept is raised here is that crises tend to speed the passing of older, less efficient businesses and technologies (unless policymakers intervene). The dot.com bust hastened the demise of legacy phone-switching technologies, independent bookstores, and the Oldsmobile, not to mention thousands of Internet applications that probably served little to no economic purpose. As a result, corporate investments, which aren't so safe in the first place, become even riskier in a crisis if the company is producing legacy products and services vulnerable to change.

Finding a Place to Hide: Depression Investing

Early 2009 was characterized by a particularly unsettling confusion and inefficiency in government policy, one that seemed oriented to fighting deflation or even a depression while largely ignoring long-term inflation threats. I believe that it is appropriate to fight against depression, but doing so by throwing money around hoping something will stick and bailing out inefficient businesses was the wrong way to go; it will only serve to prolong the downturn and increase inflation risks later.

But even if I have been more involved in the public policy debate than many, my influences are rather modest; what I can do is have you consider whether some choices may help you sustain wealth if the bad scenarios play out. The big question, of course, is: Where should investors hide? Saving money is a good and healthy thing, but with such threats lingering to the purchasing power of the U.S. dollar, simply piling money into savings or money market accounts or even U.S. Treasuries would be a difficult way to sustain wealth and particularly to meet investing goals. Naturally, gold is attractive in such scenarios, for any currency is merely a medium of exchange, not inherently a store of wealth, since the world moved away from the gold standard. In the depression-to-inflation scenario, I have encouraged investors to consider adding a diversified selection of currencies to investor portfolios. Doing so wisely requires careful consideration of the alternatives. I submit the following analysis of some of those alternatives done in the spring of 2009 as an example:

The Euro

Many love to hate the euro; they shun the euro because of weak economic growth, internal discord caused by fiscal problems in weak member countries, and concerns about the solvency of the banking system. But in my view, the Eurozone will be far more reluctant than the United States to try to devalue their currency; the European Central Bank (ECB) is likely to show more restraint. The ECB's policies have long induced Europeans to save, driven by the twin motives of higher returns (higher interest rates) and concern about retirement security—in clear contrast to their American counterparts. Growth may indeed be subdued, but the currency can remain strong, even in face of a serious recession or depression. That would seem to go against conventional wisdom, which holds that one needs growth to have a strong currency, but it's only countries with significant current account deficits that need growth to sustain their currency, as that growth attracts foreign capital. Fed Chairman Ben Bernanke, an expert on the Great Depression, notes that countries that went off the gold standard but did not devalue their currencies recovered more slowly but had stronger currencies. So, if the rest of the world reflates their economies successfully, the Eurozone may experience stagflation (recession, slow economic growth, inflation "imported" from abroad), but the currency may stay surprisingly strong and would be a good bet against depreciated U.S. currency.

I should add a little here about other countries "abandoning" the dollar as the world's reserve currency. While I will never say never, I will say that it is unlikely to happen overnight, because of the lack of alternatives. Even if we lament the lack of liquidity in the markets, the U.S. market is far more liquid than any other money market in the world. Second comes the Eurozone, which is one reason that I am more optimistic than many on the euro in the long term. But there is simply no third in line—if you need to deploy central bank reserves, the world becomes a very lonely place if you look to diversify your holdings. Central banks can and have done so using derivatives (swap agreements), but the development of domestic money markets is likely going to be at the forefront of many countries' agendas as they want to reduce their reliance on the United States. On the one hand, these steps will likely be gradual, although you wouldn't think so if you looked at the pace at which China is moving to allow trading in the yuan with other countries.

Be aware, however, that prices are set at the margin. The current account deficit is exactly the amount foreigners need to invest in the United States to keep the dollar from falling; every day, more than $2 billion must be invested in the United States to keep the currency from falling. During good economic times, that is not a problem, but a current account deficit makes a currency vulnerable when foreign investment drops or when massive fiscal deficits need to be financed. It is changes in the marginal allocations by foreigners that put pressure on the dollar.

The Swiss Franc

The Swiss franc had long benefited from its reputation as a safe haven, but for many months after the peak of the credit crisis, the Swiss National Bank (SNB) had been issuing Swiss franc–denominated Treasury bills at par—that is, at 0 percent interest, producing a negative yield after commission. Now, one can criticize gold because it produces no cash return as interest, but was the Swiss franc in this scenario as good as gold? Further, Swiss banks had been quite active in lending to Eastern Europe; that may backfire as those economies and local currencies decline, and those loans must be repaid in Swiss francs.

As of early 2010, the Swiss National Bank will have a new chairman, Philipp Hildebrand; he is an aggressive advocate of unconventional monetary policy, including aggressive intervention in the currency markets to keep the Swiss franc weak. To me, this is very worrisome: While Switzerland depends on exports, its main export is tourism, something unlikely to benefit unless we have a recovery in the rest of the world. Swiss multinationals are all very sophisticated when it comes to managing exchange rates, and have manufacturing facilities outside Switzerland; a weaker Swiss franc may not help economic growth as anticipated. Conversely, however, the banking sector—the most important sector to Switzerland's economy—is likely to suffer, as investors have traditionally put money into Switzerland because of its appeal as a potential safe haven. The Swiss banking system has already had a multitude of blows due to the weakening of bank secrecy.

The Swiss, by the way, have not only talked about currency intervention, but done so. Their interference in the currency markets in early 2009 may encourage others to follow suit.

The Japanese Yen

As the recession lingered in 2009, the Japanese yen became a "panic trade" currency—that is, a currency with apparently little risk. After years of malaise, the Japanese banking system emerged from the crisis as one of the world's healthiest. But at the same time, the Japanese economy was in a depression, with industrial production down some 40-plus percent from peak levels. The risk was that the Bank of Japan would intervene to depreciate its currency and stimulate exports; that hadn't happened, largely due to comparatively weak leadership. The yen is a good example of how one can have weak economic growth (or a depression) yet a strong currency. However, just as the risk of currency intervention is growing, money may be flowing more into countries that benefit from attempts around the world to reflate.

The Norwegian Krone

Norway is in good position to replace Switzerland as the place to take refuge in Europe. In part because of its status as an oil exporter, Norway has been a surplus country, an enviable position to be in should we face an extended depression. Norway could afford to get through the crisis and fix any problems in its economy or banking system. The Norwegian krone has never been particularly sexy; indeed, it is highly correlated with the euro and Swiss franc; and if the markets recover, there would always be the risk that friendly money may move toward other currencies again. The Norwegian krone may be the most appropriate depression trade, set up well to lose the least (there is no winner in a depression).

How to Invest in a Bust

During a boom, everything moves up in parallel; then, sometimes with, sometimes without a triggering event, the markets reverse. The pattern accelerates as everyone realizes the risks, then heads for the exits. It happened with tulip bulbs, Florida land, 1920s stocks, and 2006 real estate. The downside is amplified by leverage (as was the upside) and the deleveraging process, as investors are forced to sell or sell ahead of being forced to sell, because of debt. The downward spiral takes liquidity away, further aggravating the contraction.

Unlike the boom, in which all assets tend to move in the same direction, the bust usually triggers a "flight to quality," as investors simultaneously seek to reduce risk, so supposed safe havens such as gold and Treasury securities rise, at least in the short term. The bust is, at times, easier to recognize, but only once it is in full swing, after having already done a lot of damage to your portfolio.

Both boom and bust are characterized (and accentuated) by investor psychology. In boom times, investors feel invulnerable; they behave as though anything works; they get giddy at published projections of a 35,000 Dow or a $400 Amazon share price. In a bust, psychology completely reverses course, and investors shy away from almost everything except Treasuries and gold, and some very good long-term investment babies are thrown out with the bathwater or ignored altogether. Patient bargain-hunters can win big in such an environment; the wealth-sustaining investor should always keep some spare resources for these opportunities. More specifics on how to identify and evaluate these opportunities are presented in Chapter 9. The point is this: Prudent investors should continuously look for good investment opportunities—even in a difficult investment environment.

Here are six suggestions:

1. *Diversify your income stream.* Don't just think of your stock portfolio, think of your income streams. If you have incomes from different sources, you are better equipped to handle any downturn. Good corporate managers and investors alike focus on cash flow—so should you.

2. *Consider a steady asset allocation.* If you choose to always have a fixed percentage of your portfolio invested in stocks, then the process of maintaining that allocation will defend you against busts and make the most of booms—automatically. If your stock investments grow during a boom, trim the allocation. Likewise, in a bust, buying stocks to keep your allocation steady will "force" you to buy some stocks at a relatively cheap price, effectively dollar-cost-averaging your investments. Over the long run, such a disciplined asset allocation has been shown by some studies to beat the markets. One of the tricks, of course, is to decide on the percentage (some advisers suggest the stock allocation to be 100 minus your age, so it would be 50 percent if you're at age 50, 40 percent if you're at age 60, and so forth). The other trick is to review your portfolio on a regular basis, regularly enough (at least a few times a year) to make the adjustments. I have to confess that I personally deviate from this rule, as I tend to have strong convictions and put my money where my mouth is; for example, my personal stock allocation during the first three

quarters of 2008 was essentially zero (but I'm not 100 years old, in case you do the math). If you have good reason, it is okay to challenge conventional wisdom or a rule of thumb such as this one.

3. *Take less risk.* Just because there may be bargains out there doesn't mean you should throw caution to the winds. It's time to re-evaluate the risk of all investments in your portfolio; if the risks in the markets increase, but your attitude toward risk hasn't changed, you should consider paring down the risk profile of your portfolio. If you don't do it, the market will do it for you.

4. *Don't expect to find the bottom.* Bear markets end in exhaustion, that is, when there is no one left to sell. Just as markets can overreact to the upside, they can do the same to the downside. Just as you can't rely on finding the top, you also can't reliably find a bottom. Don't catch a falling knife—in a bear market, there are plenty of sellers that must sell even their good holdings to rebalance their portfolios or meet margin calls. Be patient.

5. *Put money on the table slowly.* If we are in a bear market and you are convinced a security is too attractive to pass on, consider cost averaging by buying only a portion of the shares you considered now. Just as it makes sense to sell partial amounts during a boom to reduce exposure but still keep some skin in the game, it also makes sense to make partial commitments on the buy side, to put some skin in the game while also preserving capital for what might be a better moment while also not taking on too much risk.

6. *Invest what you can afford to lose.* It's a cardinal truth of investing, and it's important to realize that the amount you can truly afford to lose may have declined. As a rule of thumb, if you have multiple income streams and expect many more years of income, you may be able to afford to lose more. If you need the money within one to two years, do not put that money at risk. If you saved enough money for a down payment on a house, but are waiting for just the right house to come to the market, do not gamble with that money. The same applies to college tuition; or a tax bill you know is coming; or any other known expense.

Toward Sustainable Wealth

Investing for—or during—a crisis is like learning to fly in bumpy air. If you can master that, you'll become a much better pilot and will be more comfortable in smooth air. To the contrary, if you gather all of your flying experience in perfectly smooth air, you'll be ill-prepared for the bumps and bad weather. In the next two chapters, we'll broaden the discussion to cover investing in all types of conditions and ways to implement investing to achieve the sustainable wealth lifestyle.

CHAPTER 8

Profiting in a Volatile World

Price is what you pay. Value is what you get.

—Warren Buffett

For investors, the first decade of the twenty-first century has been a difficult and challenging ride. The booms and busts in the economy have become more rapid and pronounced. Many are wondering what will be the next shoe to drop—will it be the bond market? Will inflation finally rear its ugly head again? Will the dollar plunge? Will the economic stimulus finally start to stick and pull us out of this mess, only to lead to a bigger crash later?

Such are the kinds of questions people are asking, which are far removed from the buy-and-hold, everything-will-come-out-okay mentality that was characteristic of the investment world just a few short years ago. It takes a crisis for many to realize that "you'd better be prepared in case things get worse." It's an unfortunate reality, because the best time to prepare for a crisis is when you are not confronted with one.

Indeed, just a few short years ago far fewer people would have been interested in reading *Sustainable Wealth*. Everything was working okay, stock prices were increasing, house prices were increasing (in most cases, faster than incomes); there was a strong sense of enduring personal financial security. What was there to change? Who really cared about those derivatives, about Fed policy, about expanding trade and budget deficits? That was all Wall Street

183

and Washington stuff; we had it made, our McMansions were our castles, and each day we threw away two or three second mortgage offers arriving in the mail.

Does this mean applying sustainable wealth principles now is too late? Not at all. Sustainable wealth is a lifestyle that helps you navigate through both booms and busts. I would not have written this book if I believed the credit crisis was a one-off event; instead, I feel that the current financial crisis is a symptom of an increasingly unstable financial world. The world is not less stable because of globalization, but because of policies pursued to prop up a broken system, rather than working with market forces. The public—not just in the United States, but around the globe—may not make that distinction; as a result, I am afraid that populist politicians will gain more influence, only exacerbating any instability.

Now, most of us are wondering how our 401(k)s have become 201(k)s, and millions of us are wondering how our mortgages can exceed the value of our homes, and we all want to know what to do about it. The global economic stage has once again become important, for we all in some way are part of it, and our futures are determined by it. We're hunkered down, defending what we have left, saving what we can (that's good), and wondering what's next.

In any market, within the boundaries of overall economic growth or decline, there are winners and losers. As the rate of change increases and forces external to the financial markets become more active, the winners will be the ones who weather the storms by investing prudently. The challenge is to correctly see the long-term trends and to skate to that part of the arena with your investments.

It should be clear by now that I see two major trends baked into the U.S. and global economies for the future. The first is the increased tendency for governments and central banks to use—overuse—monetary and fiscal stimulus to give relief to the effects of bust cycles. Those policies, rather than reducing volatility, extend the busts and make recoveries less stable. The struggle during these busts becomes one of reflating the economies where—in the most recent case—trillions are thrown at the economy.

The other major trend I see is the greater separation of corporations according to those who adapt their business models to the current age, technologies, and tastes—and those who don't. Physical geographic separation, sheer size, tradition, and legacy have kept General Motors and Sears Roebuck and most of the newspapers of the world going, but whether that can continue raises considerable doubt. Corporations will evolve in many different ways and quite rapidly; concepts such as "big is best" and "too big to fail" are likely to succumb to the new forces of the global economy. Think of GM as a big ship: It is simply not possible to steer it through the waters swiftly enough to avoid the currents, which means that a wrong turn taken ages ago is deadly.

Diversification

A lot has been said and written about diversification. In practice, the financial crisis has shown us that the correlation of most asset classes converges to one—that is, they move together in a panic. Diversification has its value, but only when it works. That may sound like a cyclical argument, but here is what I mean: Monitor your investment portfolio whether it delivers the sort of diversification you desire. If you love tech stocks, but hold securities in other industries to diversify, do the stocks move in tandem or not? *The single best bubble indicator may be the breakdown of diversification in a boom.* It may be tempting to let your portfolio run when all your securities go up in value, but always be critical about whether your investments are serving the purpose for which you bought them. If you bought a company because of the yield it pays, ask yourself: Have the dividends increased as the stock participates in the bull market? Analysts often refer to the share price of a firm relative to those of its peers; that's not good enough. You need to appreciate the value of a firm or security on its own merits. That implies you must be willing to let some perceived opportunities pass. Consider Warren Buffett's example: He has never invested in securities of high-tech firms, as he didn't understand the value proposition; he has been just fine not investing in the tech sector.

Some say diversification is easy—you just buy a basket of exchange-traded funds (ETFs) and you're done. I beg to differ. Take China as an example. I praise the Chinese government elsewhere in this book, and believe the Chinese yuan may appreciate in value. However, I don't own any Chinese stocks. I generally like to know what I buy and, to me, the Chinese market is still too opaque.

I tell people that if they want to invest in China, they should roll up their sleeves, move to China and start a business. Actually, I'm not joking. You simply cannot expect that your investments will thrive if you outsource the entire process. In the United States, we have scandals from time to time, but generally, executives are held accountable. I am not trying to single out China; I have my problems with the executive culture in Western countries, as well. For example: In Germany, a couple of years ago, the CEO of a DAX-listed public company (DAX is Germany's major market index) I held a stake in lied to the public. The lie became apparent the next day, as he had already changed his posture. I filed a complaint with the German regulator; and the response was: They will only investigate whether any insider trading took place.

While I will encourage everyone to consider building a global portfolio, you must be aware that the rules and culture are different abroad. As you can imagine, if I am reluctant to trust a DAX-listed German company, I have reservations about investing in emerging markets. In practice, it means that my international investments are typically based on macro factors: Anything a company management says has to be taken with a grain of salt. A decision to invest outside the United States based on macro factors is fine, but it does generally limit your investment universe to larger firms that are influenced by macro factors. You may say, "Great, I can now use the ETF anyway, as ETFs and international mutual funds tend to invest in the largest companies in their respective regions." That may be the case, but the largest international firms tend to be multinationals that often make a significant portion of their sales to the United States. There's nothing wrong with these firms—indeed, some are excellent companies—but aren't you buying these firms to gain international diversification? If a significant portion of the firm's sales is into the United States, you might already have that exposure in your domestic portfolio, with fewer risks.

After providing this caution about ETFs, I still feel that for most people a traditional diversified portfolio, such as an index portfolio, is the appropriate starting point. I will refer you to a standard textbook on asset allocation, which explains how you may want to have a greater weighting on stocks when you are young and slowly reduce your risk profile as you get older, to be able to rely more on income. While this approach works in general and is better than having no plan, much of this book is about how to question a traditional asset allocation to make it suit your needs, to build sustainable wealth. My approach is to shift the focus from how risky your investment must be to achieve your goal (thereby ignoring the downside risk by assuming prices always go up in the long term) to investing only what you can afford to lose.

You may take a traditional portfolio allocation as your starting point, then amend it to suit your needs. Consider the discussion that follows as an encouragement to challenge conventional wisdom to make your investment portfolio work for you.

Whether a boom, a bust, or something in between, it is never easy to figure out how to allocate and deploy your investment assets. There are many, many choices, and you may not have the time, the knowledge, or the bandwidth to analyze each to the degree that you probably should—and would, if you were a professional investor. One approach to allocating your portfolio is to create tiers within the portfolio—a low-risk tier comprising the bulk of it, which I'll call the *foundation* tier; a smaller middle or *rotational* tier that moves with the current market cycle and trend; and a still-smaller top tier, the *opportunistic* tier, to capitalize on short-term opportunities. The bottom low-risk tier is the largest, changes least frequently, and is

Index Funds: A Chicken-and-Egg Problem?

What about index funds? The average investor cannot beat the average (index), especially not after fees. Should one conclude that one should invest in the average (index) as a result? In the 1990s, I had a discussion with William Sharpe, the Nobel Laureate and former Stanford professor who made great contributions to modern portfolio theory and reinforced the idea that you might as well invest in the market portfolio. I told him that index investing had a chicken-and-egg problem: The index is supposed to represent the best companies, but by investing in the index, you are distorting the index, as you are indiscriminately rewarding the companies already in the index. His reply was that he agreed, but because index investing comprised such a small portion of overall investing, one could ignore this. Since that conversation, growth in index investing has exploded. As I argued in Part I of the book, I believe we have fewer decision makers today than we used to, as more people invest in mutual and index funds and those who manage money tend to have the same opinion. Index funds have their place, but always be critical of whether the composition of the index reflects your own view of the world tomorrow.

typically invested in the least risky assets—cash, long-term low-risk bonds, gold or conservative stocks, stock funds, or index funds, as you feel comfortable. The middle rotational tier capitalizes on near-term cycles and may be invested in sector ETFs or commodity funds. The top tier, your smallest tier, contains the "risk" capital you can most afford to lose, but could boost the returns of your overall portfolio. This portion could be invested in individual, beaten-down stocks or sectors in a bust, or rising-star stocks or commodities in a boom. All invested money is money you can afford to lose, but this top tier is riskier, more rewarding, and perhaps more "outside the box" than the rest.

Scenario-Based Investing

In Chapter 6, we talked about how you should become a scenario planner for your personal expenses. The same applies to your investments. Assess whether government policies will pull us out of this crisis and at what cost to inflation? What are the odds that things will turn out better than expected and we have a sustainable recovery? What about the opposite—anemic growth is followed by a severe recession or depression?

I have my views on how things will play out, but I constantly re-evaluate them. But you cannot only listen to those with whom you agree. Capital misallocations happen because too many are in agreement on the outcome.

Do not disregard extreme scenarios—hope is not a strategy. I am not going to repeat what I have said in previous chapters: Implement what you have learned and be prepared for the unexpected. If a weaker dollar that erodes your purchasing power is a scenario you deem likely, consider taking it into account in your portfolio allocation. If you think the recovery will take some time and may fail, do not put all your chips into a reflation trade.

The ideas presented in this chapter may be outdated by the time you read this book. These are not investment recommendations, but food for thought. At the same time, I try to stay general enough that the themes I mention may be applicable for some time.

Investing in the Future

Efficient equity markets ought to reflect the present value of future cash flows (earnings). If you disagree with where the market prices a security, by all means, put your money where your mouth is. Be aware, however, that stock prices never reflect the actual value of a firm, but always the expected future value. You may be right about a company's future earnings, but by the time the earnings are released, that's old hat and the market will yet again focus on the future.

Generally speaking, why should you be right and the market wrong? True wisdom comes to those who are humble. Here's my approach: If the market prices something differently than I would, I first try to understand why. Once I have a handle on the reasons, I try to assess whether that market psychology is likely to prevail or whether it is possible that the market will come in line with my views; and similarly, I try to assess the odds that the market is right and I am wrong.

You don't have to be a stock picker to apply this philosophy. If you believe that a few years from now, some industries will be more important to the economy than today, odds are that those industries are going to make up a greater portion of the S&P 500. Of course you should check that this future industry—let's use "industries supporting green technology" as an example—isn't already priced at very high levels. If everyone else thinks that green technology will be the hip thing in the years to come, well, maybe that fact is already priced in to the markets. I didn't say this was easy. But especially young and coming industries tend to have some setbacks along the way; that risk should be priced into the market as well. If you believe that there's a good chance that the industry will make it through likely rough patches, your forecast is likely more optimistic than that of the market and you should consider deploying your money. If, however, the market ignores the risk of rough patches—say, the market prices in that ethanol-based fuel will rock the world with little competition—then caution is warranted.

If you invest according to how you imagine the future will look and you are right, you have a good chance of outperforming the markets.

Stock Investing: Investing for Value

You hear so often that you should buy something that's good value. Is "cheap" good value? An old joke holds that a stock that's down 90 percent is one that was once down 80 percent, then fell by half.

The question you need to ask yourself is what a security is worth to you. You then compare it to the market price, and if the market price is lower than what the security is worth to you, consider buying it.

Sounds simple enough. You don't know how to value a security? Then don't buy it.

In my opinion, the best way to value a security is by assessing its cash flow potential—the cash a firm generates and returns to shareholders. Apply this calculation to a home—evaluating the rental income a house would generate—and you are less likely to overpay than you would be if you factor in emotions.

Ideally, you should apply the same approach to a firm. What is the earning potential of a firm over the coming years? Add to that the assets of the firm; then deduct liabilities. If this sounds very much like discounted cash flow (DCF) analysis, it's because it is. Discussing the details of DCF is beyond the scope of this book. You don't have to be a math wizard (to understand the formulas) or have a crystal ball (to make all the forecasting assumptions the formulas require) to make decisions based on value, but I do want to drive home the point that you should only buy something that you have evaluated to be of value. I say it again: the basis of value-based investing is about values—determining the value of a security.

When forecasting the future potential of a security, the DCF model applies a discount factor to any cash flows expected in the future. Just as interest rates are compounded, the discount factor is compounded (i.e., cash flows received in the distant future are discounted more heavily than cash flows received next year). The discount factor reflects uncertainty about the cash flow, and a premium is applied to what is assumed to be the risk-free rate of return. A risk premium should be demanded by an investor, as otherwise there is no point in taking on the risk, as the money could be invested risk free.

Whether you are a math wizard or not, I would like to share some lessons from the basic concept of discounting. A mature firm with stable cash flow tends to have a lower discount factor than a young firm with uncertain cash flows. This is not rocket science, but explains a lot about the dynamics of share prices. When high-tech firms release earnings, the share price often reacts rather strongly, even if earnings estimates are beaten or missed by a small amount. In contrast, large multinationals may be off target by a significant amount, but the share price reacts in a far more modest fashion. The key point to understand here is that this is perfectly rational and expected: The high-tech firm's future is considered to be much less certain; thus, a higher discount factor for future earnings is applied. What that means is that the earnings for the next couple of quarters weigh far more heavily in the value calculation than earnings that are further out, but discounted heavily. The future path the young business may take is far from certain, so any clues provided in this quarter's earnings release may have far-reaching implications about investors' assessment of the firm's value.

Conversely, with a mature firm investors trust that the firm's business model is predictable and stable; it may have a bad quarter, but investors rationally look beyond the hiccup of the quarter to see the whole value of the firm. It's rational for such firms to be given a break.

A big part of analyzing the value of a firm is to assess the value of information about and from the firm. When Intel tells you that things look good, what do they know? They may have stuffed their inventory channels, but get returns and cancellations within a few days of the earnings release. Conversely, when a company like Caterpillar tells you things are good or bad, take note, because much of their heavy equipment is made to order; they too may face cancellations, but they are much closer to the customer than Intel. CEOs are paid to be optimistic; your job is to be critical.

As you analyze companies, always be cautious about what the companies want you to look at. Picking on Intel once more, analysts seem to look at nothing but their gross margins; sure enough, Intel will deliver margins whenever possible, although it may mean that inventory channels need to be stuffed. At other firms, the focus is on sales; well, have you ever wondered why you get so many mail-in rebates? Part of the goal of these mail-in rebates is that many are never able to comply with all the restrictions; but, importantly, they allow firms to recognize the gross sales in their quarter; never mind that the balance sheet deteriorates as the rebates are accrued as liabilities! IBM, for many years, told analysts to focus on "constant currency" earnings: When the dollar was appreciating in the 1990s, foreign earnings translated into fewer U.S. dollars earned. Guess what, when the dollar reversed that trend, IBM gave up on that concept. Remember—top management is in the business of placing their firm in a positive light.

Characteristics of Value

As you may have gathered, my approach to stock investing is rather cautious, and I only do it when I see uncommon value opportunities in the market and when the time seems right. For example, in early 2006, the only stocks I held were select mining companies, as well as a foreign real estate investment trust (REIT); I sold the last mining company later that year. I liquidated as the prospects of a credit-driven recession loomed and as good value was all but impossible to find. That said, it's important to share some of my perspective on value, particularly that which goes beyond the traditional fundamentals-based models easily found in other books and materials.

I believe a company's value lies not only in fundamental financial characteristics, which are mainly backward looking, but in its intangible qualities, which drive future value. As such, I look for strength in its market position (not the stock market, but the Main Street market) and its overall leadership. And that strength must play out in today's and tomorrow's world, not just yesterday's.

With that, many indicators of corporate success, such as brand strength, cannot be ignored but also sail pretty close to the "conventional wisdom"—which may or may not be the right wisdom in the eyes of the astute investor. Brand strength is yesterday's strength—the ability to compete on a retail shelf and to occupy space in the distribution channel. Today, the Internet has leveled the playing field and put consumers in control, and it isn't good enough to have the strongest brand; you must have loyalty, too, which can come and go in a heartbeat, especially with the grassroots consumer-to-consumer buzz now available in the marketplace. Kevin Roberts, CEO of the British advertising firm Saatchi & Saatchi, calls this the "lovemark" effect.

So now brand strength must be supplemented with another factor: Are consumers *in love* with a brand? Chevrolet or Safeguard or Home Depot may be strong brands, but ask yourself—are consumers in love with them? If not, the next aggressive marketer—Toyota or Axe or Lowe's—can emerge out of nowhere and do damage, as we've seen in these examples. Apple may be the best example how consumers not simply like the product, but love the brand. I bought shares of Apple in 1997 when the CEO Steve Jobs returned to the firm; I kept the shares for many years. Apple is a firm that builds a relationship with consumers that goes far beyond the product or service that they are selling. And they've made excellent use of the Internet to deliver those products and services, bringing creative destruction forces to their full girth in wrecking the conventional CD distribution industry. You may want to consider companies with this sort of combination of market savvy and forward thinking as part of a diversified portfolio—and it doesn't have to be a business as glamorous as Apple. To learn more about the coexistence of brand strength and brand love, check out a clever site set up by advertiser Saatchi & Saatchi, www.lovemarks.com.

Please understand if I cannot formally endorse a specific stock in this book—I cannot possibly know whether the firm will be a good investment by the time you read this, not to mention whether the investment is suitable for you. Again, please consider all of this discussion as food for thought, rather than specific investment advice.

Incidentally, I do believe the CEO is very important for many companies. My ownership of IBM pretty much coincided with the reign of former CEO Louis Gerstner, who took the helm in 1993, turned the ship at "Big Blue" and then retired in 2002. I also believe in long-term ownership when the management is the right one. I owned shares in one electronics firm for more than 20 years—you likely wouldn't recognize the firm's name, and that was before lovemarks were as relevant as today.

Bottom line: The companies with the smartest business models—not just the ones with the lowest current stock prices—may be good values. Look for *sustainable comparative advantage*. And two more points to consider: First, while index funds provide a good investing base, you cannot align yourself to such excellence by investing in index; and second—and I can't say this enough—always invest for the future, not the past or the present.

Putting the Value in Value-Add: Cash Is King

There is a fundamental principle of sustainable wealth that works both for companies to invest in and for your own place in the financial world, and it is simply this: To prosper, to even survive in the long term, we all, corporation or individual, must add value to something. The more value we add, and the more unique that value, the more we will be rewarded.

The test, at a corporate level, is to assess just how much value is being added. How much real value did the financial services industry add to the economy during the boom? Sure, there's a role to be played in allocating scarce capital effectively, but was it worth some 40 percent of all profits earned by U.S. corporations in the middle part of the 2000–2010 decade? The financial reward was out of line with the value-add; the wealth wasn't commensurate with the worth, and one or the other had to correct. The tide washed out on the financial institutions and their workers, as big money no longer accrued to those who simply generated transactions and shuffled money around.

The main message for investors is that companies that deliver real, strong and growing value will win. Any investor must be convinced that the company in question is delivering value and delivering it well. The companies that meet this test tend to be those that stay close to customers, deliver products and services people want, respond to change, and make operations more flexible and efficient, consuming less capital in the process. Such companies are congruent to the notion of sustained wealth.

There is a simple way to measure value: cash. Today's generation has forgotten that firms are in the business of creating value for their owners—you, the shareholder. We have fooled ourselves into thinking that share buybacks are a main source of creating shareholder value. Share buybacks are a way of hiding the dilution brought by options awarded to shareholders. I don't blame corporations for pursuing such policies, as tax policies discourage the payment of dividends and encourage share repurchases. But as an investor, I can look for firms that pay dividends. If you are not actively involved in the running of a business, I do think it is not too much to ask that you get a portion of the earnings paid out to you. You may choose to give the firm the benefit of the doubt from time to time that they indeed have some great investment opportunities planned, but I find it rather arrogant that most firms believe they are better at managing your earnings than you are. As you are an owner of the firm, it is your money they are playing with.

Given that I am rather cautious of the value of U.S. dollar cash in the environment I foresee, investing in companies paying dividends in hard currencies is something you may want to consider. As I mentioned earlier, you may not necessarily achieve that by investing in most international mutual funds or ETFs, as they tend to invest in large multinationals that in turn extensively sell to the U.S. consumer. You want to look for companies that have sustainable business models and present true diversification to any domestic securities portfolio. As you may be aware, international stock markets are highly correlated to the U.S. markets. But you can mitigate some of that correlation by choosing, for example, an Australian utility company. Such firms tend to pay high dividends in a currency that may appreciate. Keep in mind, however, that many utility companies rely on credit, and credit is tight in this environment.

One reason that I emphasize the value of cash is that in my current assessment (which may change by the time the book is published), the business model of many firms that depend on cheap financing is broken. Take GE, which for over a decade relied almost exclusively on the availability of cheap credit; GE is mostly a hedge fund that happens to make aircraft engines. While GE shows signs of focusing on its industrial heritage, it will make a very different firm than the one with which investors have been familiar. Ten years ago at GE, the present value of expected future cash flows of any mortgage product was recorded the quarter the product was sold. What that means is that the current quarter may have shown great earnings, but the firm is left with no upside potential, only downside risk on these products. The managers have long gone with big bonuses; the new managers inherit the risk. The subprime crisis is not something that came out of nowhere, but a result of a breakdown at many, many levels.

Diversification with Real Estate and Land

Diversification extends beyond your stock portfolio, but to your entire sustainable wealth lifestyle. I repeat what I have said before: It is important to have multiple income streams. Following is my assessment of real estate, followed by a discussion of alternative investments.

If you feel comfortable managing real estate, consider buying an investment property. But only do so if you can earn a positive return on your investment and can afford extraordinary expenses. Take the opportunity cost of your investment into account, meaning your down payment could be invested profitably elsewhere— you can't factor in only the cost of the mortgage. A little while ago, there would have been few such opportunities, but the downturn in housing has brought some property prices to levels that allow you to earn a positive return. Do take into account the stability of the rental income in the area you are looking to buy.

A different type of diversification is agricultural land or forest. Jim Rogers, creator of the Rogers International Commodity Index and frequent commentator in the business media, has said we should all learn how to drive a tractor. In the short run, I agree with him—farmers need credit to buy their seeds, and credit is likely to remain tight. However, supply can be increased in agricultural commodities and in industrial commodities. Weather is also a major factor in agriculture. Indeed, commodity derivative markets were created to allow farmers to manage their risks. Still, natural resources are scarce; investing in farm land or forest would be a unique diversification for many. The market for investment in agricultural commodities is young and rapidly changing. Keep your eyes open for new ETFs and REITs, and as always, try to understand how these investments work—whether they emphasize purchases of the actual commodity, the producers of farm products, or the land itself.

Diversification into Alternative Investments

To grasp the use of "alternative" investments such as hedge funds or commodities, it helps to look at what other investors with a very long-term investment horizon, such as pension funds and university endowments, do. Many have diversified into such investments over the past decade. In particular, so-called *market neutral* strategies have been popular, sometimes encompassing about a third of the asset allocation of institutional portfolios.

Market neutral refers to an investment strategy—often pursued by hedge funds—in which long positions in stocks are offset with short positions. The manager ought to buy securities within the same industry, going long on what he or she thinks will be the winner and going short on those that may underperform. The goal is to have a portfolio that is generally uncorrelated with the markets but is profitable if the investment decisions are correct. Such strategies are not suitable for most investors, because they are not without risk: It's quite possible to lose money on both the long and the short positions. Indeed, I don't want to encourage anyone to buy a hedge fund. But what I like to highlight is that the most sophisticated investors are struggling with the same question: How do you generate new income streams through investments that are not correlated with your standard portfolio allocation?

In recent years, some alternative investment strategies have reached the mutual fund space. Mutual funds generally use less leverage than hedge funds, if any, and are more highly regulated. Personally, I believe that alternative investment mutual funds should learn how to avoid using leverage on a "net" basis. What that means is that any leveraged position should be offset with something appropriate; I don't consider a fund market neutral when, for example, it offsets a position in gold by shorting silver—silver is notoriously more volatile than gold (and gold is volatile enough on its own) and subject to different dynamics. These mutual funds often have the word "absolute" as part of their fund name, allowing you to search for them; usually, they can be found in alternative investment categories in mutual fund databases. I cannot endorse any one of them (by regulation), but if you do consider them, make sure you understand what the fund does and that you understand the risks involved.

Some absolute return funds invest in stocks; some in commodities; others in currencies. Some are mostly black boxes, others communicate very clearly what they do. If you don't understand the investment process, stay away from the fund. The currency space is particularly interesting, because there are so many participants in the markets that are not profit seekers: many corporations hedge their currency risk to reduce their risk of doing business, not to enhance profits. Similarly, tourists are not profit seekers. As a result, some rather basic strategies may be profitable; a similar strategy applied in the equity space would not be profitable, because equity markets are generally more efficient and transaction costs are higher. In practice, many foreign exchange traders apply substantial leverage, but that's by choice, not necessity. Again, I would discourage the use of leverage in any alternative investment strategies unless you are a professional who fully understands the risks involved.

Another alternative investment area is the commodity space. As with other alternative investments, the dynamics are often poorly understood. You typically have the choice of buying the commodity or corporations involved in the value chain of commodity production, processing, delivery, or servicing. Nowadays, you can buy ETFs that track commodities; before, you could only buy derivatives. But generally, the ETFs are simply a wrapper to buy the derivatives. Examine any commodity ETF closely and understand what they are doing. Some are not ETFs, but ETNs—exchange-traded notes that are basically a promise by a financial institution to track an underlying index. But be careful—if you don't trust the financial institution's creditworthiness, you may not trust their ETN, either. Commodity ETFs in particular tend to have difficulty tracking their underlying indices.

Note that this is not an endorsement to buy commodity ETFs or invest in a hedge fund. My goal is to encourage you to have an open mind about ways to diversify that go beyond what you may have traditionally done. But especially with less traditional investments, make sure you talk to your broker or investment adviser to fully understand the risks and dynamics involved.

Traditionally, the general public invested in equity securities (or mutual funds investing in these securities) in the commodity space. This may provide some diversification, but for better or worse, the dynamics are different from investing more directly in the commodities. You can have a commodity rally while the shares of your oil producer barely budge or even decline.

Profit Opportunities in an Uncertain World

In this section, I will address specific investing opportunities I see as timely and prescient in the more volatile world in which we find ourselves today. Based on what I consider the likely scenarios for the world to evolve, you may want to prepare for outcomes not covered by your portfolio already. As we enter a possibly ever more volatile world, cash may lose its function as a store of value, leading not just to challenges, but also opportunities.

Remember, those who lose the least are the winners in a bear market. We spent Chapter 7 discussing crisis investing and possible panic trades. Now, the discussion shifts—a little—from the defensive to the offensive.

Also remember that the Fed can print money, but not wealth. While everyone seems to hope that things will work out all right, hope is not a strategy. The prudent investor aligns his portfolio with areas in which wealth, not just money, is being created.

Additionally, it is important to remember that policy change is policy change, and the scenarios can change quickly as a result. Assume, for example, that the Fed sticks to its promise to fight inflation if and when it comes. It will throw some of the scenarios discussed here off track. Remain vigilant and prepare for different scenarios; adjust as new scenarios become more likely.

Profit Opportunity—Reflation Investing

As I discussed in Part I of this book, I believe that all the money the government is spending is highly inefficient; it may "stick" at

A New Contract with America

Republicans have decided they want nothing to do with the economic stimulus; they say government spending is out of control. Democrats say Republicans are hypocrites, as they were reckless with the spending in the preceding administration; and Democrats have a point. But let Republicans preach a message of fiscal conservatism for two or four years. Two things could happen: the public outrage at fiscal irresponsibility could swing the pendulum back to Republicans; and secondly, fiscal conservatives in the Republican party could come back to life and Republicans could believe their own preaching. I'm not trying to be political, but point out how easily dynamics could change. The public is very much fed up with all the bailouts.

While "change" has come, the political landscape may change again—consider the implications for your investments.

some point, but much more money will need to be spent than policymakers anticipate. That's because some policies are contradictory (subsidizing homeowners while proposing to phase out the interest rate deductibility of mortgages); many policies replace rather than supplement private sector activity (the Fed can offer loans, but the loans crowd out rather than stimulate private sector activity); removing failure as an option makes any negotiation more expensive (your counterparty will be less likely to settle for cents on the dollar); and the cost of financing all these programs may negate some of the stimulative effects.

In October 2008, there was a serious threat of a disorderly collapse of the financial system. The fear and uncertainty around asset values and the tangle of derivative contracts brought banks to discontinue transactions with the general public and among themselves; it was the beginning of a massive deleveraging of over-leveraged banks and financial institutions.

Governments around the world rushed to guarantee the banking system. According to Fed Chairman Bernanke, the guarantee of the banking system was one of two important steps taken during the Roosevelt administration to get out of the Great Depression. The second step, according to Bernanke, was to devalue the dollar by going off the gold standard. Devaluing the currency allows prices to float higher, bailing out those with debt, and it stimulates the economy through more competitive exports. We have seen the guarantee of the banking system, but it remains to be seen how effective Bernanke will be in pushing down the value of the dollar in an effort to spur growth. It is not for the lack of trying: the printing of money is the most obvious tactic.

Some of that liquidity could be "mopped up" by reversing the transaction later on, but the Fed also bought longer-term agency securities (those of Fannie Mae and Freddie Mac) in an effort to drive down mortgage interest rates, thus signaling that at least some of the liquidity flood is more permanent. The Fed has ramped up purchases of Treasury securities, bidding up the prices and driving down the yields on those securities. The result is that foreigners, seeing lower yields on those Treasury securities, are less likely to buy them in the future; the prospect of a fall in the dollar further may discourage them from doing so, but foreigners may simply not be able to prop up the dollar: As there is less trade, there are fewer dollars to recycle; and other countries need the money at home to finance their own domestic stimulus programs.

I believe that at least in the near term the United States will lead the way in terms of trying to reflate the economy. Germany in particular had rebuffed efforts by the U.S. administration to commit to spending 2 percent of GDP on a stimulus plan, declaring that markets needed confidence, not spending. Now, to be sure, the export-driven economies all welcomed spending packages, but were content to rely on the United States to do much of the heavy lifting. After all, in their eyes the problems started in the United States. In addition, arguments like this were heard: If the United States does not want GM to fail, why should Germany provide capital to Opel, a large employer and subsidiary of GM in Germany—especially since GM has raided the cash from profitable foreign subsidiaries? As of early 2009, it looked like the United States was trying to bail out the entire world.

What did this all mean for investors and currencies in particular? A lot of money was being spent, and a good deal of it not very efficiently—it was either being hoarded by nervous banks or supporting financial institutions and legacy companies with broken business models. As a result, at the time we did not foresee a quick recovery in lending, earnings, or hiring. But all this money being printed, where would it go? Here is my analysis, provided as an example of the kind of analysis a wealth sustainer would do; please be aware that the world could look very different by the time you read this book. While I preach long-term planning, being able to revise one's outlook is also important. In an environment where trillions are being spent and policies can change from one day to the next, one has to be prepared for a new surprise every day. Incidentally, that is one of the reasons why so much money has to be spent: bad policy is often better than uncertainty of policies.

Export-Oriented Economies

It would have been premature to conclude that as the world reflated, export-oriented economies would benefit the most. The main reasons were continued difficult access to credit and changing consumer attitudes. If nothing else, the almost $3 trillion in debt raised by the U.S. government in 2008 is money not available to weaker sovereign countries, not to mention most of the private sector in the United States and abroad. It was also clear that a revival in consumer spending was nowhere in sight, as consumers lost income and readjusted their risk appraisals to become big savers. As a result, currencies and securities of weaker countries in Eastern Europe, Asia, and Latin America haven't been as appealing as might have been expected.

Gold and Commodities

Not surprisingly, gold was and still is the most promising long-term beneficiary of these trends. Because industrial activity was likely to lag in the envisioned "recovery," gold, a precious metal with low industrial use, is the purest barometer of the money being printed. As currencies lose their core function as a store of value, investors are scrambling to find a replacement. While central banks are taking a more diversified approach to cash, gold will never go to zero and will always be a store of value. Having said that, before you move all your money into gold, look at the volatility of the price of gold in the 1970s; unless you have experienced such volatility, you may not know just how large a position you can take while still being able to sleep at night. And while I personally like gold as a reflation play in the current environment and in the environment I currently foresee, be aware that some money may be flowing to riskier assets if the world successfully reflates.

The money may then slowly move toward commodities, as the world stimulates production at any cost.

A Diversified Approach to Cash

In that process, and for those who don't want to touch commodities because they are too volatile, commodity-oriented currencies may also benefit. The Australian dollar is an interesting reflation play, because the Australian economy is highly sensitive to the price of commodities. Australia is also a large exporter of commodities to China, which is good because China is likely a long-term benefactor of global economic shifts and the one country that could afford its stimulus plan. Australia is in much better fiscal shape than the United States, although it also has a high current account deficit. That current account deficit worked against the Australian dollar earlier when commodity prices imploded, but could also bring a more pronounced upward move in the Australian dollar as the world reflates. I also like Australia's smaller neighbor New Zealand, especially because the government there has a much more hands-off approach to the global crisis; as a result, similar to Australia, the New Zealand dollar was harder hit during the downturn (their current account deficit was rather severe), but may benefit at an above average rate in a reflationary phase.

The Canadian dollar may also benefit from the reflation trend. There is one caveat: Canada's economy is closely tied to the U.S. economy, and that may cause problems. To date, however, Canada has shown restraint in its aid to the banking sector and fiscal restraint in general. The commodity-oriented economy should benefit from reflation in general; cycles will occur but will move in tandem with the United States. It makes sense that the Canadian dollar would appreciate over time (as it did to par in 2008, only to fall off again as the U.S. dollar gained ground as a safe reserve at the height of the downturn). Those interested in the Canadian dollar should watch the news carefully, as the Bank of Canada has shown a willingness to print money, although not at the same scale as the United States.

Canada may also benefit from a dangerous trend in 2009 in which it almost seemed that any profitable business will be taxed in the United States. Many businesses in the oil sector, for example, can relocate a good portion of their profits to Canada without too much difficulty should tax policy in the United States become too restrictive or unpredictable. It's not just tax policy: The political climate has turned more hostile toward Fortune 500 companies; Canada may be among the beneficiaries of this trend, as well as other more business-friendly countries in the world—Singapore, for example.

If you are wondering why I keep talking about currencies and gold, it is because I am reluctant to embrace a long-term recovery in equities when policies do not support a sustainable recovery. There are certainly opportunities that a traditional investment portfolio would be able to take advantage of, but the one area where there is clarity is the Fed's willingness to print money. In such an environment, I do believe it is prudent to look at cash in other currencies, copying what central banks do—take a diversified approach to something as mundane as cash.

Profit Opportunity—Chinese Yuan

In early 2009 it appeared that China could well be the winner in Asia and possibly the world.

The Chinese yuan, as of early 2009, is restricted to floating in a narrow band and subject to government control. Other Asian countries may engage in competitive devaluation in a desperate attempt to export to the United States. I don't believe China is likely to join, as it would cause a capital flight out of the country. Instead, China may have pursued the most prudent policy of any major country during this crisis. In fairness to other countries, it is a bit easier for China, as they act from a position of strength: China can afford its stimulus because of its massive reserves.

China has shown steady progress in moving toward more open markets. China has allowed its low-end industries—think of toy manufacturers—to fail as these industries move to countries with lower cost bases, such as Vietnam and the Philippines. China has understood and embraced that it must shift its economy toward what I call the higher end of the value chain; it is uniquely positioned to take advantage of what may be the next outsourcing trend. Think about it from the U.S. perspective: To increase productivity, more outsourcing may need to take place; but just about everything has been outsourced already. In this environment, ever more complex processes will be outsourced. China is the only country that has the capacity, management know-how, stability of government, and regulation to absorb these.

When you cater to more value-added goods, you have more pricing power (the Europeans have long positioned themselves accordingly) and can absorb a stronger currency more easily. At the same time, the artificially weak yuan has required the government to have otherwise highly restrictive policies to avoid an unstable inflationary breakout domestically. A stronger yuan would allow the government to remove these "sterilizations," as they are called, and allow for healthier domestic market dynamics.

China is highly dependent on importing commodities from abroad. Indeed, China has been an aggressive buyer of not just U.S. Treasuries, but of resources around the globe. China has been thinking strategically as it manages its huge population.

China's economy is still a third of the U.S. economy and cannot possibly be the one leading the United States out of recession. For China, it is cheaper to stimulate its domestic economy; this has been done primarily through infrastructure spending. These are important investments and more can be put in place easily as there are very long-term plans that can be ramped up.

To help create a more balanced world economy, China would be wise to strengthen its middle class. In my humble opinion, the best way for China to achieve this is to give its middle class a vision. Many Chinese think their livelihood is dependent on the U.S. economy. Already, Europe is the larger trading partner. But what it takes is an unleashing of an entrepreneurial class to service the domestic economy. Allowing the currency to appreciate would add substantial purchasing power and help in that process.

China has been moving toward a free-floating exchange rate, but it does so at its own pace—rightfully so, as companies must learn to deal with floating rates. If you talk to Chinese businesspeople, most will tell you they like fixed exchange rates, as they make it far easier to plan. China has been working aggressively, introducing regulatory bodies and a domestic marketplace, to be prepared for the change. In late 2008, China started allowing trade in the yuan with various neighboring countries, a list that was expanded in early 2009.

Finally, China has taken an active role in the public debate of its holdings of U.S. debt. The Chinese are furious that they should accept blame for the credit crisis—as if it was their fault that they financed the United States' fiscal irresponsibility. China has also grown increasingly concerned about the value of their holdings of U.S. debt, especially in light of Fed policies that may weaken the dollar. China has suggested the introduction of a new "world currency" based on a basket of currencies. While I believe the idea is not realistic, China can implement this world currency on its own by diversifying its own reserve holdings to a basket of currencies. It has done so, but is likely to do so more actively and aggressively in the future.

There's also a very practical reason why the yuan should appreciate: There is less trade with the United States (i.e., fewer dollars to buy); and China needs the money domestically. Add to that policies in the United States that discourage the Chinese from buying U.S. Treasuries (when the Fed buys Treasury Bonds, it raises prices artificially, making them unattractive to rational buyers, including foreign buyers).

China has many challenges ahead, but may be the country best positioned to come out of this crisis. I sincerely hope that China will take the opportunity to introduce structural changes, as otherwise—in a best-case scenario—in 10 years we may yet again face a global crisis, except that China may not have more than a trillion in reserves to manage it.

When to Sell

Warren Buffett's favorite holding period is "forever." Whatever your investment horizon, selling a security is as important a decision as buying it. What is most important is that you have a plan. In my view, a key ingredient of your plan should be a periodic evaluation as to whether the reasons you acquired the security in the first place still apply. In other words, take a look at each security in your portfolio— *would you still buy it today? If not, it's a candidate to sell.*

- If you bought the stock of a firm because you love its products— are the products still great? And more importantly, do you trust the firm to come up with new, great products?
- If you bought the stock because of the dividends paid, can you expect the dividend policy to be consistent?

Buying a debt security is a bit different: If you buy a debt security and hold it to maturity, you will be paid the face value of the security plus interest as long as the company stays solvent. If you sell the security before maturity, you are subject to pricing risks. Ideally, you should decide ahead of time whether you are willing to stick with a debt security even if the interest rate environment changes or if there is a risk that the credit quality of the firm changes. As we have all seen, relying on the rating agencies to do the homework for you may not work. In a bond fund, the fund never "matures" and, as a result, you always have some interest risk—that is, the risk that the value of your portfolio will go down if interest rates go up (because any debt security with a fixed coupon will be less attractive when interest rates go up; any buyer from you will demand a higher yield, offering you a lower price).

Some apply stop losses or realize gains systematically as prices go up. There are advantages and disadvantages to any approach to selling securities. Generally speaking, most investors are better off making long-term decisions, while remaining vigilant. Importantly, don't let the pundits tell you when to buy or sell. Make up your own mind.

How to Invest in a Boom

Finally, as Chapter 7 covered crisis investing and gave some guidance for investing in a bust, this chapter, aimed at finding investment opportunity, offers ways to potentially profit during the boom in volatile times.

It is not easy to identify the start of a boom. There can be many false starts. It's human nature to always hope that things turn for the better—luckily so. Borrowing from Richard Russell, who has studied the markets longer than anyone else alive I know (see a discussion of Richard Russell in Chapter 6), a bear market bottom exhibits true value. Value means low P/E ratios, high yields, with companies trading below book value. Sentiment is horrible in a bottom and quite likely not announced on CNBC.

When a boom has progressed for a while, it may be easier to recognize. People feel wealthier and continue to put their wealth into the markets—into almost anything—and government credit policy usually provides a steady tailwind in that direction. But those are the times when you ought to start being careful again, when people think of risk only as the upside potential.

During booms, and especially stock market booms, there is a recognizable and repeatable pattern of long, steady "up" periods followed by short and typically mild pullbacks. Some of these pullbacks—the 10 percent variety—are termed *corrections*, while a 20 percent pullback is considered a bear market. There were no clichéd terms for anything larger than that (like 50 percent), and many investors have been duped by the financial media and "experts" into thinking the 10 percent correction was almost automatically just that. Interestingly, the 10 percent paradigm works for a while because investors take the signal and buy at the moment the 10 percent correction level has been reached. Of course, this "relief" was only technical in nature, a short-term play. When the fundamental tide really washed out in 2008, it took these technical players out to sea repeatedly as they continued to claim it "must be over." Markets don't repeat themselves too often, for the supposedly smart money gradually turns into dumb money while the true smart money moves elsewhere.

Because it is easier said than done to recognize the early phases of a boom, I suggest we apply the same principles on boom investing as for bust investing, except that it is fine to increase one's risk profile a tad when the future looks brighter. The key is not to get carried away:

- *Diversify your income stream.* Same principle, boom or bust.
- *Take on more risk—but only if you feel comfortable.* In a true boom situation, it could make sense to take advantage of the rising asset price opportunity. Sustaining wealth doesn't just mean staying on the defensive all the time; it means capitalizing on opportunity when it arises and banking that opportunity for the future. So, from time to time, it makes sense to take on some additional risk, when other bases are covered and when the opportunity is worth the risk. The emphasis is on "when other bases are covered"—you take risks when you can afford to.
- *Don't expect to find the top.* Hanging on too long is one of the most common failings of the typical investor. It's a fun ride, and investors want to stay on as long as possible. They're confident that when it's time to get off, they'll know. Many competent investors have ridden it all the way back to the bottom—and worse—with this sort of thinking.
- *Take some money off the table.* The predominant principle to keep a security must be that the reason you purchased a security is still valid. If that's the case, ensure that the overall risk profile of your portfolio is not jeopardized if your winners take too big a portion. If you get nervous about whether your

security can maintain the heights, you likely should trim your position. For securities that don't pay a dividend, remember, until you have sold it, you only have a paper profit, which can vanish rather quickly.

- *Continue to invest what you can afford to lose.* Even in a boom, this mantra still holds true. The "what you can afford to lose" part may change, but it's still important, and you must be realistic about what that amount is.

Toward a Sustainable Wealth Investing Model

Chapters 7 and 8 were designed to give background and build the thought processes of sustainable wealth investing. Chapter 9 captures the thinking, rounds out the framework, and proposes habits appropriate for sustainable wealth investing.

CHAPTER 9

Sustainable Investing

The market can be irrational a lot longer than you can stay solvent.
—John Maynard Keynes

Earn it, keep it, grow it, reach goals, sleep at night, leave a legacy. Six pillars of sustainable wealth—all of which have become more of a challenge as the global economic environment has become more unpredictable and volatile.

What I've presented so far is tilted toward understanding the global economic environment, interpreting its signals, and developing the proper perspective to deal with it. You'll note that I haven't provided worksheets to manage expenses, save, or invest. Those details will largely come of your own design to meet the needs of your own situation.

The important message of *Sustainable Wealth* is to comprehend the greater context, to understand *why* sustainable wealth is important, and to develop a healthy appreciation for the downside if you don't get it right. My goal is to allow you to put your investments into context, to encourage you not to be satisfied with standard textbook diversification, and to always challenge your assumptions to keep you on your toes and be prepared.

That said, I do think it's important to put investment technique in the context of a sustainable wealth investment approach—not to dissect financial statements or technical stock price moves, but with enough detail to give an investing approach and philosophy from which you can develop your specific techniques from other resources and from experience. I call this approach *sustainable investing,* and the idea is as much about applying prudence and discipline as it is about specific analytic technique.

As I move forward, I will discuss how I have applied the sustainable wealth lifestyle to my own investment decisions, including my college savings program, and the choices I have made to manage in times of heightened financial uncertainty. I will also discuss how I expanded my business without jeopardizing my saving priorities.

The Power of Compounding

Simply stated, the choices you make about spending, and then again about investing, will, especially over time, define your path to sustainable wealth. Obviously, if you earn more than you spend, and do it over time, you'll come out ahead. If you're able to invest it well, your wealth will build and become truly sustainable.

The contrast between successful investing and unsuccessful "debtorship" is sharp, and it is magnified in time by the power of compounding. It's important to internalize this basic principle: Values compound through the sequential payment of returns on returns; the nest egg grows at an accelerating rate. But the flip side is also important: When you become a debtor, interest costs and other fees cause your net worth to "compound" in the wrong direction; worse, because you typically pay a high interest rate on your debt, the headwind created by negative compounding is poison to your ambition to create sustainable wealth. Here is an excerpt of how Richard Russell describes the power of compounding:

> Compounding is the royal road to riches. Compounding is the safe road, the sure road, and fortunately, anybody can do it. To compound successfully you need the following: *perseverance* in order to keep you firmly on the savings path. You need *intelligence* in order to understand what you are doing and why. And you need a *knowledge* of the mathematics tables in order to comprehend the amazing rewards that will come to you if you faithfully follow the compounding road. And, of course, you need *time,* time to allow the power of compounding to work for you. Remember, compounding *only works through time.*

But there are two catches in the compounding process. The first is obvious—compounding may involve sacrifice (you can't spend it and still save it). Second, compounding is boring—b-o-r-i-n-g. Or I should say it's boring until (after seven or eight years) the money starts to pour in. Then, believe me, compounding becomes very interesting. In fact, it becomes downright fascinating!

For Russell's full discussion, see "Rich Man Poor Man—The Power of Compounding" at www.dowtheoryletters.com.

As obvious as compounding may seem, it hasn't been widely internalized by many individuals in real life. First, the infatuation with consumption and inexpensive debt tempts many toward negative compounding. Second, the path upward isn't so stable and predictable—there are many bumps and crises along the way against which you'll need to play defense.

Compounding Savings Add Up

Compounding, of course, pays returns on reinvested returns, and the longer these returns are left on the table, the more powerful the effect. The basic formula is (present value $(1 + i)^n$), where i is the rate of return and n is the number of periods—years—the sum is left on the table. It's not hard to see that since n is an exponent, the power builds rapidly as n gets larger. A sum of $5,000 invested at 6 percent for 10 years grows to $8,954, not bad but not terribly sexy, either. But that same sum left for another 10 years—20 total—grows to $16,035, and another 10 years—30 years total—reaches $28,717, almost a sixfold increase. Now, if you deposit $5,000 *each year*, a normal IRA contribution, it will grow to $395,290 in 30 years. And if you deposit $15,000 a year and get a company match in a 401(k) plan—you'll retire a millionaire. That, of course, assumes steady 6 percent returns, and that assumption must be handled with care. Still, there could hardly be a more fundamental building block to sustainable wealth than compounding.

If you are scared of the formula, do a search on "compounding calculator" and select one of the sites that does the math for you based on simple inputs.

Compounding Debt and Inflation Destroy Wealth

Compounding can be "man's best friend"—when it's lined up on your side, that is, and we're discussing returns on your investments. But what if you reverse the deal? That is, what happens when you have debt and someone else is profiting from the compounding on their investment in you? Consider the numbers at today's credit card interest rates, which are often 18 percent or higher. Compounded at a monthly rate of 1.5 percent, a single $5,000 debt would become $29,847 in 10 years and a whopping $178,164 in 20 years if you didn't pay any of it off in the meantime. Or, if you went just $100 each month into debt—$1,200 a year—at these interest rates, again with no pay-off, you'd be $33,128 in debt in 10 years and $230,885 in debt after 20 years. The power of compounding can and does work against you. Don't count on the minimum payments to bail you out, even if they will lower your total cost just a bit from the example shown.

Similarly—and perhaps more dangerously—the power of compounding can work against you in the form of inflation, too. A nest egg will lose half of its purchasing power in just 10 years at an inflation rate of 7 percent—roughly the average experienced in the 1970s.

Now, should you correctly choose the sustainable wealth route, it's critically important to avoid becoming complacent about the "shape" of that route. There are bumps along the way—not only for the entire economy, but also for every asset class and every individual investment. Recent history has shown that you may not even be able to rely on your personal residence as a store of growing wealth; that's why it is important that you try to own your home free and clear. Your home is truly a store of value, and you can worry less about the short-term fluctuations in real estate prices.

While I'm a big fan of compounded growth, I must caution that while it is easy to run the numbers on a financial calculator, it is considerably harder to bring in the steady 5 or 6 or 8 percent returns, with no pullback, to make it happen in reality. As such, compounding and steady returns remain an objective, but by no means a given. I find many investors get too caught up in and, frankly, complacent with a steady compounded wealth track, and to their detriment, they disregard factors that derail the compounding train.

Investors must be aware of the pitfalls inherent in the steady-compounding model. One is the tendency to overestimate the safety of underlying assets and their returns. Sure, it seems like a bond paying 8 percent every year is a sure ticket to long-term financial freedom. But what about the credit, or default, risk? And if you can take that away, perhaps by buying Treasuries, great, but now what happens to your 8 percent return? Beyond that, what about the effects of inflation? Even this supposedly safe asset either (1) isn't so safe or (2) is incapable of producing the kinds of returns really necessary to unleash the power of compounding.

Second is the failure to pick investments that actually pay cash returns. Cash on hand is what counts; paper profits can disappear quickly in the next bust. So the need for solid and steady real returns naturally conflicts with the idea of leaving money on the table to compound. If you allow successful investments to grow very large, you must make sure that you don't become too dependent on that investment; if you cannot afford to let that investment become a disproportionally large share of your investment portfolio (i.e., to absorb the risk if that investment were to turn sour), you should consider trimming it down. Take cash returns and reinvest them effectively, so as to preserve the compounding effect. Such reinvestment is best done with a cost-averaging approach—that is, one in which small but steady amounts are invested regularly. It's the opposite of trying to time the market.

Third, today's relatively low investment returns, driven in part by Fed policies to reduce interest rates, have made it very difficult to invest at rates of return that truly unlock compounding power without taking excessive risks. The desperate search for returns necessary to retire is partially to blame for the crisis in the first place. It leads many unwary investors to take such risks—to invest in hedge funds and risky specialty securities—to try to beef up those returns. Compounding may be magic at 6 or 8 percent, but when it entails a risk of losing 50 percent it must be regarded with great care. When returns are low, do not resort to irresponsible measures. Think of Tiger Woods: What makes him the best golfer in the world is his discipline and consistency. By making fewer mistakes, yet taking no unreasonable risks, he consistently comes out ahead.

So most of us mortals are faced with a choice of volatile assets or returns so low that compounding can't create sustainable wealth.

A yield of less than 3 percent on 10-year Treasury bonds, recently in place for longer-term Treasuries (down to near zero for shorter terms), simply won't create sustainable wealth, especially when the inflation rate exceeds that. During periods of heightened uncertainty and low returns, it is okay to focus on capital preservation rather than chasing the first glimmer of hope. Treasuries may not be the path to sustainable wealth, but short-term Treasury bills are a good parking space to use while waiting for the dust to settle. If nothing else, you'll be able to sleep at night. Always remember that return *of* capital is more important than return *on* capital. That said, as a prudent investor, your job is to keep the compounding train on its tracks.

Doing Investing Right

There are many ways to make (and lose) money in the markets. Some investors pick stocks based on a bottom-up analysis, analyzing the fundamentals of firms. Others apply a macro approach, identifying trends. Still others apply technical analysis, the often-quantitative analysis of specific price movements and trends. Or some know a particular industry very well. Like Warren Buffett, you don't have to participate in every trend in every market. Focus on what you are comfortable with. Even if you can buy an entire country with the click of a button, don't do it unless you understand what you are buying and, more importantly, *why* you are buying. The following three rules should be kept in the background and continuously applied to your investing practice:

Keep the Discipline

Discipline does not mean stubbornness. If the facts change, it's important to re-evaluate your investments. Always remember why you bought a security—if the reasons you bought the security still apply, don't be shaken by cross currents. If you veer from your investment strategy, you will chase market trends, buy at the top, and sell out at the bottom. It is okay to listen to experts and to gather information, but remember that you are the pilot; you make the investment decisions. The same applies if you work with an investment adviser or broker: Evaluate him or her based on the agreed guidelines; periodically, review whether the guidelines are still appropriate, given the changes in your life and the changes in the markets or economy.

Match Investments to Specific Financial Needs

I strongly believe in separately tracking the largest of your declared financial objectives, for instance, college for your kids or a down payment for a house. You don't need to carry these in separate accounts, but I encourage you to do so if it helps you manage them. There are three very important reasons for this. First, this style allows you to match the returns and the risk profile of the investments to the size and timing of the objective. Second, it gives you a clear understanding of where you are with respect to achieving the objective. Third, with this information, you can make specific adjustments to your savings plan, your investment plan, or the objective itself to maintain the objective if investment performance doesn't meet expectations.

One important point before proceeding—this approach makes the most sense for larger and longer-term objectives; I don't advise setting up a separate investment account to buy this year's holiday gifts or that antique armoire you've had your eye on—that's too much detail and you won't be able to invest efficiently. These separate investment pools should be created for objectives in the low- to mid-five-figures and more than five years out. Some think this separation has already been done for your retirement investments, with separate IRA and 401(k) plans; however, please note that your 401(k) or IRA is simply one retirement savings tool; you cannot rely on it being sufficient. Many 401(k) plans don't offer you as broad an investment range as you deserve (in fact, you should lobby the trustees of the plan if you would like to invest in something not offered). Tax considerations, including tax-deferred accounts, should not be your primary consideration for investment decisions. Consider using retirement accounts extensively, but use them as tools.

You also want to match the investment horizon with your obligations. If you need the money within one to two years, you should not put the money into very risky investments. Conversely, if you want to pay your mortgage down over 15 years, plan accordingly and do not be dependent on favorable market conditions to refinance at the end of the term. The same rules apply for individuals and companies alike. Too many corporations relied on short-term credit to finance long-term obligations. If financing dries up, you can be out of business in no time. The only exception to deviate from this is when you can afford to. If you can pay down your loan in an emergency and are not at the mercy of banks, then, by all means, negotiate what is most appealing to you.

Manage Your Risk

Risk is the most overlooked factor in finances and investing, especially in boom times. When many of us invest, we have a natural tendency to support our own choices and look the other way when it comes to risk. We wish to hide behind "that can never happen;" but really, it's another form of complacency. We start to believe in the 10 percent correction "rule." We start to believe that no AAA-rated company, no company with a big Wall Street brand and Manhattan skyscraper, could ever fail. We ignore the black swans, or blame them on someone else; we fail to learn our lessons and leave ourselves vulnerable to repeating our mistakes.

Investing in anything that provides a return, whether a stock, a rental property, or even a business you start, requires a levelheaded balancing of rewards against potential risks. Interestingly, as entrepreneurs, many people are so worried about the entrepreneurial

No Free Lunch

When market returns are 2 or 3 percent, sometimes lower, sometimes negative as we experienced in the recent crisis, how can anyone achieve the 6 to 8 percent returns so important to achieve favorable long-term compounding? Unfortunately, one answer for many hapless victims was to trust Bernard Madoff, but that obviously wasn't a very good answer, and the 8 to 12 percent returns he promised and apparently delivered turned out to be a giant Ponzi scheme. Outside of outright Ponzi schemes, such returns are either achieved through buying assets with excessive inherent risk, or they're done with leverage, that is, taking your $1,000 and borrowing $4,000 more to build a portfolio. If that portfolio goes south, you know what happens to your $1,000, because that $4,000 obligation will still remain. As the saying goes, if it sounds too good to be true, then it probably is. Only a crisis can teach you: Return *of* capital is more important than return *on* capital.

risk of losing everything that they fail to make the most of their business; they fail to invest enough into it for fear of loss. I've seen those same people buy a stock or bond loaded with risk—and ignore that risk completely. If it yields more than Treasuries, it is risky. A money market fund, commercial paper, auction rate securities—the financial crisis showed that there is no such thing a safe asset, and that you may want to take a diversified approach even to cash.

Risk isn't inherently bad, as it also provides opportunity, but always be aware that risk works not only to the upside, but potentially also to the downside. I write a lot that you should only put at risk what you can afford to lose. Depending on the economy, the markets, and your personal situation, that amount may vary. To illustrate this point, let me walk you through personal investment decisions I have made in recent years. Your personal situation will, without a doubt, vary. However, I do like to show you a real-life example of how risk management may be applied in the context of personal priorities and constraints.

A Golden College Savings Plan

My wife, Hanna, and I decided long ago that a top priority for us would be to be able to give our children the opportunity to go to a top college of their choice, should they be smart enough to be admitted. The plan discussed here can be applied to any type of savings objective for which the total amount to be saved is a moving target. In 2003, when we formalized the plan, we had three children; now we have four. Given the high and rising cost of education, it may seem like a daunting task to achieve this objective.

Most that do plan ahead would likely consider a so-called 529 college savings plan to achieve their purpose. However, most 529 plans have a heavy emphasis on stocks. Nothing wrong with that if you believe stocks will go up over your investment horizon, but at the time, I was a traditional investment adviser with plenty of exposure to stocks. Our feeling was that investing through a 529 plan would not provide us with the type of diversification we were looking for. Obviously, there are 529 plans that do not invest in stocks; some invest in stocks but also provide a downside protection. But by the time I was done reviewing 529 plans, I thought they were too much about the conventional wisdom of saving taxes and not enough about our needs. And although 529 plans do offer significant tax benefits,

I firmly believe that tax considerations should not be the primary driver in any investment decision.

Back in 2003, we contemplated the hypothetical question: If you had to choose one asset class over the next 10 or 20 years, which one do you think would perform better than many others? We picked gold. The trends that we see unfolding these days were already in the making years ago. It was our view that in the absence of some miraculous reform of entitlement programs such as Social Security, odds would be high that policymakers would nominally keep their promises, but erode the purchasing power of the dollar. There were numerous other factors, many of which are discussed in this book, that encouraged us to use gold as the basis of our college savings plan. I do not consider myself a gold bug—I like gold because I believe long-term dynamics favor gold; but if those dynamics were to change, I would be prepared to change my strategy.

You may say: "Gold isn't very diversified, is it?" It may not be, but I would like to point out that one has to see any investment in the context of one's total investment allocation, and—at least in those days—I had significant stock market exposure. But more importantly, I would like to restate what I said earlier: There are many ways to invest—what is relevant is that you apply discipline.

Here is how our college savings plan was, and still is, designed:

- *Calculate total cost of education.* You take the total cost of college tuition, including room and board, and multiply it by four to get the total cost of education for one child. That's $50,560 (gulp!) for one year for Brown University, the alma mater of both my wife and I. At the current rate, it costs $202,240 to pay for a four-year Ivy League education for one child.
- *Calculate the number of years left until your child would normally graduate from college.* If you start when your child is one year old, you have to put $10,112 aside every year to allow your child to graduate debt-free. You don't have to be a math genius to realize that you had better start this program quickly, as the amounts you need to save each year are rather staggering. Of course, you can always be lucky and have a smart kid who gets a scholarship. But don't count on financial aid—you might just be one of those unfortunate ones too rich to qualify, but too poor to afford the payments. Your child can also supplement the income while studying. For example, my wife worked 20 hours a week during college; she

paid for her education with grants and loans. She paid back all her college loans—and they were substantial—within two years of graduating, by minimizing the rent she paid for her own housing and living an extremely frugal life. Tuition in those days was expensive, but not as extreme as it is today.

Why do I use the current cost, not an estimate of the future? After all, even if some say that the cost of college education may be one of the last bubbles to burst, the cost has been rising far in excess of the rate of inflation. Here's the deal: You invest this money in whatever way you have decided on. Let it be the 529 plan if that's what you choose. A year from now, the money you have put aside will have changed in value—hopefully, but not necessarily, it will have appreciated. But similarly, the cost of education will have changed—it will likely have gone up. You start over with your calculation, except that you deduct what you have already saved from the grand total that you need to save. You divide that by the number of years left until your child is likely to graduate from college. By making this adjustment on a yearly basis, you do not need to make difficult guesses about inflation or the cost of education in the future.

- *Work it like a pension plan.* As you get closer to college, if you have invested profitably, your annual contributions may be lowered; otherwise, you need to make up for the shortfall by increasing your contributions.
- *Repeat the exercise for each child.* You'll likely want a spreadsheet to help you keep track of the cost. You may also want to pinch yourself once in a while to assure yourself that these costs are real and that you not dreaming!

"How lucky for us that the cost of college education has been going down since we started the program," I have said at times when explaining our family's plan. Then I add, importantly, " . . . when measured in the price of gold." From 2003–2005, when gold was at about $400 a troy ounce, the cost for a one-year college education for one child was about 100 troy ounces. In 2006, as gold rose to $600 an ounce, the cost fell to about 72 ounces; in 2007, with gold at around $700, it fell to 66 ounces; and at the end of 2008, with gold rising to about $900 an ounce, a one-year education cost about 56 troy ounces.

As you can imagine, even with a tailwind of rising gold prices, saving for college for four children is quite a commitment.

Every year, we buy the physical gold—bars or coins; we like the idea of our children going to the cashier's window with a laundry basket filled with gold. Actually, the gold would fit in a very small laundry basket; if you have never held a gold bar in your hand, go to your local coin dealer and see whether you can get your hands on one. There's a reason why central banks use them as a store of value: A kilobar (32.15 troy ounces) is smaller than a chocolate bar; at $900 an ounce, it's worth almost $29,000. And no, we do not store the gold in a laundry basket at home—it is stored in secure locations.

A college savings plan based on gold is not for everyone; the price of gold can fall—you have to be willing to make up any short-fall of your investment decision. Again, though, the above principles can be applied whether you use gold or a more diversified portfolio.

Policies Influence Student Loans

You should be aware that college planning is more complicated if you're dependent on financial aid, as many are. The majority of financial aid is granted based on need, and need is a function of income and your accumulated wealth. The "need" calculation typically excludes the value of your home, and of your retirement savings, so if you think you will depend on financial aid, it makes sense to divert more funds to these areas of saving (i.e., pay down your mortgage and, to the extent possible, move money to retirement accounts). These are nuances that a qualified college planner or financial planner can help you address. The best approach is to plan as though you won't *need* financial aid at all, but that may not be realistic for everyone. If you save, and financial aid (especially a scholarship rather than a loan) comes your way, so much the better. Buy the kid a nice car (the money spent may increase your eligibility for a college loan, as it won't show up as part of your assets), or better yet, set up a nice retirement plan for the kid. Any way you do it, coverage of college costs is one of the best legacies you can leave your children.

In general, I discourage making investment decisions based on taxes or regulations. But sometimes the incentives are overwhelming; at times, a lot of money can be saved by working with the system.

Taking Risks Without Jeopardizing Sustainable Wealth

Even with a college savings plan, other life commitments continue. In 2004, I decided that my firm should enter the mutual fund business. You may or may not be aware that launching and running a mutual fund is a high fixed-cost business; typically, mutual fund management companies also cap the expenses of new funds, thus taking on costs to keep the fund's fee structure competitive. Indeed, most would advise you against it, as the odds of succeeding are low—after all, why on Earth should anyone buy your fund when they can choose from about 8,000 other funds? We decided it was the right direction for our business to take, but substantial capital would be required.

We did not seriously consider taking on debt to launch our first mutual fund; it would have made running the firm too stressful. Instead, we bolstered the capital of the firm by liquidating savings—including a small condominium in southern California, as we thought the market was overheated. We did not sell at the top of the market; we sold because we believed investing in our own business was a more prudent use of the money. To increase the return of our investment, we rolled up our sleeves to do a good part of the renovation necessary to get the condo in shape ourselves. If you need to have a new kitchen installed in your home, or need a hardwood floor, my wife and I know both IKEA (great value for kitchens) and Home Depot (for flooring) inside and out. Upgrading electric outlets? No problem. It's a great teambuilding exercise, too, to renovate your own home, especially if you have kids running around, all trying to be helpful (to varying degrees and with varying endurance).

We also kept our personal expenses low—staying with relatives for vacation rather than spending the money on expensive hotels. Even these days, as our cash flow could allow spending money on a more elaborate vacation, we look at what are said to be attractive packages for families, but we simply shake our heads how one can spend so much money on vacation. We prefer two- to three-night stays at the most when we do go to a hotel while not traveling too far; while cost is a factor, we also prefer it that way, as managing a large family in a hotel can be a lot of work, too.

We set a clear budget of how much cash we could burn before the management firm would turn cash-flow positive.

Many business owners forget to pay themselves. They are so absorbed with growing their business that they do not draw a salary, do not put money aside to sustain wealth. There may be a phase when that is appropriate, but it should always be for the short term only. We applied another principle: no matter how painful, continue contributing to the college savings plan. And that's the key message here: *Take prudent risks when you feel strongly about an opportunity, but do not jeopardize your long-term saving priorities.*

It turned out that we achieved our cash flow goals ahead of schedule; in retrospect, we firmly believe we made the right choices. But even if we hadn't, we had ensured that the risks we took would not jeopardize our college savings plan.

Streamline Your Income Streams

In my firm, we also had a "legacy business"—a separate account advisory business as well as a couple of small hedge funds. While we were profitable, our business model wasn't particularly scalable, meaning it wasn't easy to grow. We faced the same challenges many advisory firms face today: Margins are slowly decreasing as regulations increase. Our situation was exacerbated by the fact that we had turned more conservative and were managing more cash, including international cash, where fees are typically lower. While our challenges were unique to our business, many businesses in other industries, large and small, also worry about margins and scalability.

As the mutual fund business was growing, we started to phase out the legacy business to be able to focus on where we thought the growth in our firm would be. But it's not a good idea to give up your old income streams before you have secured new ones. It took until the spring of 2008 to transform our business into an exclusive mutual fund management firm. At the end, we were mostly managing cash for investors, as we did not like the price of most securities—we should have charged clients a lot for keeping their money in cash, but instead sent the money home.

This streamlining of our business has allowed us to be more focused. While I advocate creating multiple income streams, there is a risk that the administration will eat up all of your time. Periodically, you need to trim back and focus on your strengths. While I provide an example from running a business, the same can apply for you as an employee; or as an employee and a business owner; and the same also applies to an investment portfolio. There is a time to build complexity in your life, but you also need to simplify to have the capacity to tackle new ventures. Like writing a book, for instance.

Active Risk Management in the Face of Uncertainty

Part of the reason we insisted on contributing to our college savings plan was that I was concerned about a potential bursting of a credit bubble long before most realized the possibility. No matter what, we wanted to continue contributing to the plan.

In my life, there was another variable I could control. Back in 1997, my wife and I purchased an investment property (by now you know we can renovate a kitchen—the story of renovating this property is unfortunately beyond the scope of the book, but it was also very much hands-on). Our mortgage on the property was to be refinanced in 2007. Our cash flow was already tight from saving for college and investing money into our new venture. But we decided that we must reduce the mortgage to prepare, in case of a credit crisis or in case our business didn't perform as expected.

While paying down a significant portion of the mortgage caused short-term pain, it improved our cash flow; our business was also doing well. It was just in time, as the credit crisis was looming around the corner. In previous chapters, we discussed how to prepare for a crisis. The lesson, again: The preparation does not start the day the crisis hits, but is a long-term process of reducing your risks—be that your portfolio or other ventures in which you may be engaged.

Fast-forward to September 2008. The world's financial system was in crisis, threatening to implode. I trusted little if anything, not even money market funds. But wait: What if the world financial system did indeed implode? Sure, the government might ride to the rescue, but would they succeed? As I have said—hope is not a strategy. Our decision was that we must secure our top priority—the college education. To the extent that we could, we increased the funding for our college saving plan; because our business had been doing well and we had taken decisions earlier to improve our cash flow in our investment property as well, we were able to commit a substantial amount. You may argue that had there truly been an implosion of the financial system, the cost of college tuition may have also come down. You can always find an excuse not to make the tough choices. We decided it was the prudent thing to do. Note, by the way, one advantage of either a 529 savings plan or a physical gold savings plan—over, say, simply buying stocks in your ordinary brokerage account—is that you are discouraged from reversing your choices (i.e., pulling your money back out from the plan).

Sacrifices to Sustain Wealth: A Matter of Risk

In the process of all this, we made a sacrifice many others would not have chosen: We rent, rather than own, our home. We moved to the San Francisco Bay area in early 2001. The value of homes has gone up quite a bit since then, even taking the steep decline into account after the housing bubble started to burst. But for most people, owning a home should primarily be a risk-based decision: can you afford to have the mortgage? Buying a home is not only the largest financial decision most make, it is also the most leveraged one.

The fact that we thought homes were too expensive compared to renting was one factor that influenced our decision. But the primary decision factor is one of risk evaluation: It is not prudent to load yourself up with a mortgage when you expand your business and expect credit conditions to tighten. Fast-forward to 2009 and the situation is different: Our cash flow now allows us to take the risk of buying a home; we can afford the risk.

Now it becomes a valuation question. I happen to believe that the housing markets of interest to us may not bottom out for a while. We have locked ourselves into a rental contract for now—to resist the temptation to buy a home! If we buy one, I don't expect to buy at the bottom, although it would certainly be nice. The key factors will be whether we can afford to buy a home and whether we can afford it even if the property prices fall further.

You may have noticed that I discussed reducing personal expenses earlier, but only list renting versus buying as a sacrifice. That's because I never considered eating out less as a real sacrifice; it's wonderful to have family dinners at home be the norm. However, when you rent a house where the landlord can terminate the lease on short notice or contracts rarely last longer than a year, it may make your life seem less settled. There's more to a house than its cost; it provides roots to your family. From that perspective, postponing a house purchase decision to reduce risk, to me in any case, is a sacrifice; spending time with the family at home rather than at Club Med is prudent saving.

I have tried to give you a personal flavor of sustainable investing. But the scenarios described here can be applied to many other situations. Let us now return to the general concepts of sustainable investing.

Purpose-Driven Investing

If you take a sufficiently broad, candid, and long-term view, by now it should be clear that the sustainable wealth model holds that *no* investment is safe, in good times or bad. Prudent sustainable wealth management requires a clear understanding of all risks to each investment and to a broader portfolio. This is true whether in crisis times or not, but becomes even more true when a crisis hits.

I practice an engaged investing style. That doesn't mean I trade my positions on a daily basis; in fact, I do quite the opposite. My active style, of course, starts with staying in tune with what is happening in the world. By the way, one reason I live in California rather than New York, despite being in the investment business, is because it allows me to keep a little distance. Day traders are glued to the screen all day. Unless you are a day trader, however, you are better off with a more analytical approach to investing; for that, try not to be pulled into the frenzy, an opportunity too good to be true, or a panic. You should already be positioned.

Without getting into the particulars of evaluating specific investments, consider the following principles, summarized as follows and detailed in the rest of this section:

- Invest only what you can afford to lose
- Don't let taxes make your investing decisions
- Re-evaluate, adjust, and rebalance at least each year

These principles apply in all markets and all parts of the business cycle, and are further described as follows:

Invest What You Can Afford to Lose

This is one of the most important principles in all of sustainable wealth management.

This principle is not unheard of in the common language of life; people quite often talk about "gambling only what they can afford to lose." The more obvious difficulties people have with this principle are determining what "afford to lose" really means, and having the discipline to actually restrict losses to that amount once chance takes its course. There is one more point, often forgotten by many: The amount you can afford to lose changes when markets change or crises hit. If you lose 20 percent of your overall net worth, does the amount you can afford to lose stay the same? No, not at all. The amount you can afford to lose is dynamic and depends not only on objective results and changes in your wealth, but also on more abstract changes in your job situation or even the economy as a whole. In a crisis, the amount you can afford to lose normally would decline. You should thus avoid the temptation to "ride it out" that so many of us fall into during a crisis.

Further, the concept of investing what you can afford to lose has a longer-term element—that is, are you capable of working to make up any losses, and if so, for how long? Another way to look at it is that what you can afford to lose is greater if you have a long time to replace it; that is, you're young and just starting out in your career. Therefore, younger people can take risks. In some instances, some older people can, too, because while their earning power is diminished, the length of time they need to be self-sufficient also declines, so their *needs* are less.

The afford-to-lose equation is all about what you need, what you have, and what you can produce.

Don't Let Taxes Make Your Investing Decisions

I see too many people making investment decisions based on tax consequences. Taxes are a fact of life, and the reluctance to sell a

Longevity

At the time of this writing, I just received news that a 96-year old friend had passed away; he was a fighter and wanted to live to be 100. Just because he could have afforded to lose some money, it didn't make him a gambler. If you have lived according to a sustainable wealth lifestyle your whole life long, you are not about to give up on your savings, but are likely to enjoy life and work on leaving behind a legacy. That's in stark contrast to those who believe they have used their savings efficiently if by the time they pass away their net worth is exactly zero.

security and pay a capital gain on the sale is understandable. That said, if it's time to sell the security, it's time to sell the security; you'll probably pay tax on it sooner or later anyway. Many, many people lose their heads trying to save a 10 or 20 percent tax.

Likewise, some are inclined to invest in the wrong vehicle just for tax reasons. I already discussed the so-called 529 college savings plans, which offer tax-free withdrawals of any earned returns (the original principal contributed is done with after-tax dollars). If returns are strong and steady, such tax-free returns are nice, for the compounding effect is allowed to expand to its full girth. That said, today's 529 plans are very restrictive in terms of the kinds of investments they offer—usually a mix of stock funds, bond funds, and stock index funds. These investments tend to be fairly volatile in times of crisis; in addition, fees are high enough to put a dent into returns. So for my college savings plan, I have eschewed 529 plans in favor of gold; while I must pay taxes on gains in gold, I find that prospect less risky than enduring a possible decline in stocks, especially with the time-sensitive nature of a college education. I can wait to buy a house, but making my daughters and son wait for better market conditions to go to college is not in the cards.

All in all, I don't wish to discount the value of good tax planning—it can save a bundle over time. I'm just saying don't let tax considerations play too much of a role in investing decisions. I have seen too many people choose tax savings vehicles simply because of the tax "benefit." The wrong investment chosen for the right tax reasons is still the wrong investment. I live in California, despite high taxes, because of the entrepreneurial spirit in Silicon Valley (I sometimes joke that only optimists live here, because anyone who has lost their job cannot afford to stay), a dynamic environment that fosters risk taking and a focus on scalable business models. With hard work, it is possible to make a good living in California. Would I rather pay lower taxes? Certainly. Would I be able to pursue my career elsewhere? Possibly, but it takes more than low taxes to succeed.

What about moving offshore? It's always an option, but the grass may always appear greener on the other side. I have worked in other countries and have settled in the United States because it is still the fairest playing field for entrepreneurs. We may complain about regulations, but at least there is clarity on most regulations—in other countries, you are easily dependent on the mood of a bureaucrat as to whether a license is granted to you or not; and you don't need to go to Asia or Latin America to encounter this—living and working in Europe for many years very much encouraged me to relocate to the United States.

Uncertainties in taxes and regulations primarily increase the barrier to entry. Large enterprises can manage them, but small businesses may never come into existence. That's bad for the health of the economy; small enterprises must be allowed to challenge the establishment. Subsidies of any form, either directly through bailouts or indirectly through barriers to entry, are poison to an economy.

I know how precious the values of the relatively free U.S. economy are. They are worth fighting for and cannot be taken for granted. I do my part in speaking up when I see these values jeopardized and encourage everyone to do the same.

Re-evaluate, Adjust, and Rebalance Each Year

Markets change, policies change, businesses go through structural change—change, change, change.

While I appreciate the power of compounding and what it can do for you, I believe that your investments should be thoroughly reviewed—almost as if you're starting over—at least each year. Once you buy a security, or a house, you are tempted to find every reason in the world that it must be a good investment, or you only want to sell it once you have recouped your losses. What happened yesterday is water under the bridge. Have the courage to be critical of your own choices. But make your decisions based on reason, not based on the opinion of pundits.

You need to appraise each investment and your entire portfolio for changes in risk as well as changes in your own situation or needs. Has college tuition gone up more than expected? Need to invest more in your college plan. Has your job become more risky? Need to turn down the risk on your emergency fund. Did your home down payment fund shrink this year? Need to add more to the fund, or scale down your expectations for the size of the home.

Sustainable Investing and the Sustainable Wealth Lifestyle

As we've seen in this chapter, unless you're born with a silver spoon or inherit one along the way, you're on your own. You will have to make tough choices to create and sustain wealth. Sustainable wealth isn't just about the creation of wealth; you'll have to build and sustain the savings you earn into sustainable wealth. It's an active, not a passive, process, and it means making a lot of important tradeoff decisions along the way. If you make these decisions with clear priorities and a level head, you'll come out ahead in the long run.

CHAPTER 10

The Pursuit of Sustainable Wealth and Happiness

Make all you can, save all you can, give all you can.

—John Wesley

By now, it should be quite clear that we live in a volatile world of debt and consumption. If anything, the complexity of this world is likely to increase. You have learned and hopefully have embraced some sound philosophy and practical points about how to cope with your finances to achieve financial security.

I hope by now you've built the foundation of a thought process whereby you can consciously and subconsciously approach the world and your own finances to make the most prudent and most effective decisions for the long term, where your long-term rewards transcend short-term needs, where you build wealth slowly and steadily without taking excessive risks.

Wealth is a relative concept. There are millionaires who struggle to make ends meet; and there are those of very modest means who have all they need. In some cultures, a middle-class family may have a cook and a driver; in the United States, even the wealthy may clean their own toilets. The Declaration of Independence lists "the pursuit of happiness" as an unalienable right. Wealth can't buy happiness. However, debt may prevent the pursuit of happiness. Satisfaction and happiness are *more easily* achieved with financial security, achievement of specific life goals, and by leaving a long-term legacy to your loved ones and the greater world you're part of. What we've covered in this book is the means to achieve sustainable wealth.

Some may say, "Let's do it like our grandparents did it, and build wealth the old-fashioned way." There's some truth to this when it comes to consumption; the lessons learned during the Great Depression have been forgotten by too many. Our generation has not experienced tough times; we have always been able to pull ourselves out of problems with government help. But governments cannot generate wealth; governments can only print money. The U.S. economy is the most flexible in the world—it can adjust. At times, these adjustments are painful. But they also provide opportunity. In *Sustainable Wealth*, I have attempted to show you how to identify major trends as the world adjusts, despite government efforts to the contrary. Other countries have shown what happens when you prevent this adjustment process: It reduces the overall standard of living. Former British Prime Minister Margaret Thatcher put it bluntly when she said: "The problem with socialism is that you eventually run out of other people's money."

You Cannot Depreciate Your Way to Prosperity

There are many who think that rebuilding after destruction is a path to economic prosperity. Buildings decay, or are knocked down by the forces of nature as in the 2009 earthquakes in Italy, and everyone gets excited because of the rebuilding that is to follow; does such rebuilding produce prosperity? Do wars produce prosperity? I would like to caution: GDP is "gross" domestic product and does not make deductions for destruction; it also doesn't take debt into account.

When Fed Chairman Bernanke says going off the gold standard during the Great Depression boosted economic growth and, in Bernanke's words, "alleviated the hardship on the people," the argument is along the same lines: If you take away a portion of what people own, of course they have an incentive to work hard to regain their standard of living. But they lost part of what they own, so are they prosperous?

The question is whether destruction—either through natural disaster, war, or currency devaluations—truly increases prosperity. You cannot depreciate yourself into prosperity. This applies to individuals and especially to nations. It doesn't work.

The Rewards of Living Within Your Means

Let me contrast some attributes of *sustainable* wealth with what may the opposite, *unsustainable excess.*

Sustainable wealth: Build a nest egg; have time for your spouse, children, grandchildren, and friends. Be able to quit your job to change careers, start a business, take some time off, recharge your batteries, do something special with your life. Be able to afford something fun or different or exciting without worrying about it.

Unsustainable excess: Tied down to your job, fearful you'll lose it, work to pay off your debts, dread your monthly bills, can't afford a vacation. I owe, I owe, so off to work I go.

I've been talking about sleeping at night, achieving goals, building a legacy. Those are all good things, no doubt. But the concept of sustainable wealth becomes clearer and more vivid when you observe or experience its liberating effects. With sustainable wealth—without debt—you can't be *forced* to work, you are *free* to work. Think about it. The difference between the two choices is enormous.

There can be no clearer illustration of the benefits of sustainable wealth than to observe the experiences of real people who have not only talked the talk but walked the walk. It's truly enlightening. These are not people who made it big and cashed in on the dot.com or some other boom. They succeeded by working hard; living within their means; and prudently managing their incomes, their wealth, and their lifestyles. I have three examples; what's extraordinary about them is that they are so ordinary—you, too, can achieve sustainable wealth.

Success, One Customer at a Time

The first, and it may or may not come as a surprise, is my hairdresser. She emigrated from Ukraine 20 years ago; her husband started as a janitor and is now a machinist. She hardly makes a doctor's or lawyer's or executive's salary. Yet by living within her means and consistently saving, she was able to pay for her son's undergraduate education, then law school at the University of California at Berkeley. Her son had received a modest grant as a result of his good grades, but the overwhelming majority was paid for by Mom. Now her son works as an attorney and makes more than his mom ever did. Let's hope he'll follow in her footsteps and use his savings wisely.

This couple did buy a home, but kept it modest enough that they have been able to pay most if it off by now.

While she lives modestly, she does enjoy life and indulges in a little luxury once in a while. She had been saving for a new car; last year, she purchased a new BMW. She had her son pick it up at the factory in Munich, Germany. As you might imagine, the experience was a treat for both mom and son. She stayed in California to generate income, one head at a time.

She loves talking about her Beemer. Except that one time when she got a ticket. . . .

A Second Career by Choice

Another colleague of mine left the corporate world at age 44 to embark on a much more fulfilling career as a financial author and columnist. His income was about $90,000 a year with benefits, and it was a hard deal to walk away from. But he had pretty much had it with the ways of the corporate world, and knew he needed a change after 21 years.

But was that a snap decision? Hardly. He made the most of every savings opportunity, refinanced into a 10-year mortgage, maximized his 401(k) plan and match, added more through automatic payroll deductions into savings and a stock purchase plan. At one point, he was saving close to 50 percent of his gross income. He always kept his standard of living modest; in fact, he still drives the same 17-year-old car he bought during his working days—saving considerable sales tax and depreciation over buying and owning multiple cars for a typical 6- to 8-year period each.

When the time was right, he paid off the small remaining balance on his house, took a buyout deal, and started out as a writer. He never made as much as a writer as he did at the company, and he had to write checks each month for health insurance, too. But the freedom and self-actualization he feels when he sees his books on the shelf makes up for it. "There's no way I could have done this without paying off my home first," he advises.

It's a great example of the flexibility one can enjoy in life by following the principles of sustainable wealth.

Compounding Works!

Manny Maciel emigrated from the Azores to the United States and became a naturalized citizen in 1948. He held odd jobs, eventually becoming the owner of a fuel concession and later a modest restaurant at the small Sonoma County Airport. His business—Sonoma Aviation Fuel Services—was known simply as "Manny's."

According to Dave Hirschmann's account, published in the Aircraft Owners and Pilots Association (AOPA) *Pilot* magazine, Manny didn't live rich. He drove an old Buick and, later, a 1965 Ford Mustang. Later, he owned a Piper Comanche (a four-seat, single-engine piston aircraft), which he leased back to a local flight school. Manny worked hard and did most of the dirty jobs himself. Eventually, he became a savvy long-term investor, buying some nearby rental properties. But he kept his long-term goals for the business in mind by keeping enough aside to reinvest in his business, eventually growing it to 20 employees as wine country traffic in the area increased. Finally, he sold the company in 2001—and bought the restaurant, after 54 years of working in and around the airport. He managed it almost until he died at the age of 88.

He left most of his estate—which exceeded $5 million—to charities supporting aviation research, the AOPA Air Safety Foundation, and two other organizations. Members of the nearby elite retreat known as the Bohemian Club knew Manny from flying in and out of his airport, but few guessed him to be a multimillionaire.

Sustainable Work-Life Balance

For Uncle Scrooge McDuck, the frugal Disney character, financial success may be the only goal in life. But financial success is of little value if you can't live to enjoy it. Many wish that they could spend more time with their spouse, significant other, children, or friends. Generally, there is a phase in your life during which you work the hardest, so that you can reap the fruits of your labor later. But is the cost worth it if you never see your loved ones? Families fall apart and some parents can no longer communicate with their children because they can't spend enough time with them.

If you have the discipline to achieve financial security by applying the philosophy outlined in this book, you should have the discipline to apply similar standards to your life. After all, work is a means to an end, not the end in itself. For many hardworking people, there are no easy answers on how to address all the complexities of life. Sometimes a disease or handicap of a loved one influences your choices. But even if everyone you know around you appears as if they don't need you, you need them. Building and fostering a network of friends is extremely important.

It is beyond the scope of this book to present you with answers to these challenges. But let me give you a little insight into how I try to strike a work-life balance while working 50 hours a week, often more. Being a workaholic does not mean you can't take time. While everyone has to find their own path, my typical day is as follows:

- 4:45 A.M. wake up
- 5:30 A.M. at work
- 7:00 A.M. go home to prepare kids' lunches (4 kids), help get them ready for school, have breakfast
- 8:00 A.M. back at work
- 4:30 P.M. return home for family activities
- 9:00 P.M. bedtime

I work 10-hour days, but am able to see my kids for breakfast and dinner. I choose to live close to work (a 15-minute commute) and choose to spend some time with the family in the afternoon. I try not to work weekends and try not to work in the evenings; I generally don't take late dinner invitations on weekdays and can't spend a weeknight at concerts. But this schedule allows me to work hard while pursuing a quality of life that works for me. Everyone has a different situation, but you are in charge of your destiny. Many of my friends tell me that they have to work till 8:00 P.M. because their colleagues do, too. Some variables are difficult to control, but you choose the career you pursue, you choose where you live, and you make choices almost every day that affect your work-life balance.

Sustainable Health

To round up the work-life balance, your health is an integral part. What good is sustainable wealth if you have a heart attack at age 50? This book won't prescribe a fitness program, but do take this area very seriously. Most of us adopt a sedentary lifestyle after we graduate from college. Over the years, we add pound after pound; obesity has become an epidemic. Obesity leads to cardiovascular disease.

A healthy diet is something you should seriously consider if you want to reap the benefits of what you have worked so hard for. You do regular maintenance on your car and feed it with appropriate oil and fuel. It's a bad idea to treat your car better than your body.

Good eating is one part. Exercise is another. If you have a family, try to exercise with your kids to instill good habits. My entire family takes karate lessons—the parents participate, don't just watch. Back in 1996, I also picked up running. I'm not a gym person; I love being outdoors. Running isn't for everyone, although you can start at any age and only need a pair of running shoes. Running is part of my regimen mostly because it is the simplest to do—you can start at your doorstep. I have run the Big Sur Marathon (among others) twice: it is 26.2 miles of the most beautiful coastline in the world, winding up and down the hills along Highway 1 between Big Sur and Monterey in California. As you can see, I have a tendency to go overboard in many things I do. There's certainly no need to run marathons to stay fit. Regular walking at an elevated pace already helps a great deal of people stay in shape. Some take the stairs instead of the elevator if they live or work in a high-rise. But be committed to exercise and do it regularly; if you can incorporate it into your daily routine by leaving the car behind once in a while, you also do something for the environment.

Sustainable Entrepreneurship

In Chapter 9, I discussed taking prudent risks, including keeping your priorities focused if you decide to start your own business. But when is the time right? The answer differs for everyone. Some of the world's most successful companies have been started by men and women in their 60s. At that age, you have made plenty of mistakes elsewhere to learn from; you have seen teams in action. With age comes wisdom—and possibly the benefit of being able to assess the opportunities and risks of a prospect more realistically.

Especially in Silicon Valley, where I live, many successful firms were started by high school or college dropouts. There is something both groups have in common: They quite likely can afford to take the risks of entrepreneurship. When you are in your 60s and have lived according to sustainable wealth principles, odds are that you can afford to take the risk of starting a venture—your kids may be off to college, and you may have paid down a good portion, if not all, of your mortgage. Conversely, when you don't have a family yet, what do you have to lose? No spouse, no children you have to worry about? If you fail with your business idea, well, you either come up with another one or you get a job. As a youngster, you usually don't mind a low-budget lifestyle, as you are used to it anyway.

While I am no high school dropout, I did drop out of a Ph.D. program to pursue my business. My future wife and I had gotten engaged a few months before I started my business, but we did not have any children. I followed my wife where her jobs took her for a few years, arguing that I could work from anywhere. It was a choice that slowed the ramping-up of the business, as it is always easier in theory than in practice to work from anywhere, but it was a work-life balance choice I never regretted.

If you are out of a job and there is no new job available, setting up your own business might be a blessing: the downside risk is limited because you don't have an income to lose. Be realistic, though, and go back into the workforce if your business falters and you have a shot at finding a job.

What about the rest? If you don't have anyone dependent on you, the same idea applies. But what if you are 40 years old and have two kids and need to save for college? What if your spouse's income may not be able to cover the shortfall in family income in the startup phase of your firm? Successful businesses have been launched by men and women, no matter what age group or life situation they are in. The key, however, is that you must make a more conscious judgment as to whether you can keep your priorities if you start your business. If you have dependents, you bear a responsibility that goes beyond yourself. By all means, pursue your dreams, but be realistic and make the tough decisions to keep your priorities intact.

Leaving a Legacy: Sustainable Giving

I've commented continuously in this book about the importance of leaving a legacy for your family to help ensure they have sustainable wealth long after you're gone. But that's only part of the story. In the United States, looking after weaker links in society is, to a great extent, left to the private sector. We have a flexible society, but there are those who fall through the cracks. I discussed early in the book that some policies pursued widen the income gap. To the extent any one of us can, we should all give back to the society of which we're part. From my perspective, it doesn't matter which cause or what kind of organization you give back to, nor in what form (whether money, talent, work, or knowledge) you give. But giving back makes you a more complete person and leaves an imprint that will last long beyond your mortal years. It's important.

Just as your sustainable wealth is best created and managed with focus and a plan, it also makes sense to me to apply similar focus to your charitable giving. At minimum, you should follow four steps:

1. *Make up your mind* to leave a charitable legacy. Make a family commitment, including what kind of legacy you want to leave to which causes. Those causes can always change over time; the important point is to get the goal out there.
2. *Make a plan* that is similar to, or part of, a purpose-driven financial plan: Set a goal, note constraints, and if the goal is substantial, create an investment base to support that goal.
3. *Execute the plan*; it's obvious, but many people fail to consider the priority of their donor legacy and tend to think of it as an "if and when I have the money or time" basis—and somehow, it never gets done. Not that charity should come before eating or buying clothes for your kids, but if it is part of your plan, you'll feel better if you actually stick with it.
4. *If you deviate from the plan, have a good reason.* Again, don't just consider your causes worthy of any "extra" dollars you might have—try to make it a rigorously followed part of your financial plan, and deviate only if another *major* goal gets in the way.

You don't necessarily have to part with charitable dollars each year to leave a legacy. Warren Buffett famously donated very little as he accumulated his wealth—then gave billions late in life, once they were available. His rationale was to build the gift into something much larger later, and since he was a good investor, he was able to do this. He also felt that any money given should actually be spent at the time by the recipient, not just invested again. The approach works if you have the discipline and the skill to build the investment and keep it intact; but don't let it be an excuse not to give.

I think it's a good idea to have a giving plan and consider making it as a percentage of your income. Tax considerations may influence your giving, but should not be your primary driver. Your primary driver should be whether you can afford to give and whether the causes are worthwhile. Indeed, there's been a trend to give to causes that may not be tax-deductible. Microfinance is a recent example; in 2006, the Nobel Peace Prize was awarded to Muhammad Yunus of Bangladesh, who built a business extending very small (micro) loans to poor people, mostly women, so that they could buy simple tools and supplies to produce goods and make a living.

Finally, please make good giving decisions. Many write checks to charities almost without thought or investigation. They don't check out how effective the charities are or whether they do what they say they do. It's important to think about who needs and uses your donation best. I believe that good charity begins locally, for it helps your community and, since it is close at hand, you'll have a better idea of what is being done with your gift. Local charity makes for a more stable society, reduces crime, and improves the standard of living in your community.

If you can't afford to give money to charity, consider donating your time to help out in the neighborhood or local charity. If you can't give time for that, do take time for your family; and if you don't have time for that, fix your priorities!

Sustaining Wealth Spans Generations

Sustainable wealth doesn't stop with you and your generation. True sustainable wealth outlives you as you pass a culture of sustaining wealth on to the next generation. There are very few families that manage to build wealth and keep it for generations. Taxes and inflation are two factors that work against you. But it is more than that: Just as you can never rest on your laurels, neither can the next generation if you have built an estate you can pass on.

These days, reverse mortgages are advertised on large banners at major financial institutions. Especially for many baby boomers who have lived beyond their means, such tools may be appropriate. However, the terms of reverse mortgages are rarely attractive—often, you would be better off downsizing by selling your home. Also, note that part of taking a reverse mortgage is an insurance that the value of the home will never fall below the value of the mortgage. Such insurance reminds me of financial instruments that may not be worth the paper they are written on in times of crisis; although the government might just have another bailout handy if that industry had serious difficulty.

As you can imagine, I am no friend of reverse mortgages. If you embrace the sustainable wealth lifestyle early enough, your priority should be to leave a legacy, not to squeeze the last cent out of your net worth by the time you pass away.

SustainableWealth.org

The episode with Neil Cavuto is available at www.sustainablewealth. org. Please go to the Web site and subscribe to the blog and newsletter. To stay ahead in a volatile world, the site provides you with timely information to understand your world and your wealth. At sustainablewealth.org, you are invited to submit questions. I look forward to continuing the discussion with you there.

Wisdom comes with age, they say. As we grow older, we become more humble and have a different perspective on living. We need the adventurous spirit that comes with youth. But if we manage to have our children embrace the concept of sustainable wealth, our world may become a more stable place.

What about your children? How do you teach your children about money? You don't need to raise your children to discuss monetary policy at the dinner table when they are 10. My son actually did when he was 11; subsequently, I mentioned to Neil Cavuto on Fox Business that my 11-year-old understood more about monetary policy than some policymakers—that left Cavuto speechless, something that does not happen very often. A few months later, Cavuto came back to the incident and asked me whether I was very stingy with my kids' allowance, to which I responded: "You betcha."

The point here is not that you turn young kids into economists. But you want to give your children an appreciation for the value of money and the importance of wealth. One way of doing that is by giving a rather modest allowance, say $1 per week for an 8-year-old. Most likely, you take care of all required expenses for the child, so the $1 is discretionary spending power. But your child needs to learn that money doesn't grow on trees, and that one needs to save in order to afford something.

Surgeon General's Warning: Sustainable Wealth May Be Addictive

Sustainable wealth may be addictive. On the one hand, once you are on a sustainable wealth path, you are going to reap the benefits of saving and compounding. Even if you have had to make some tough choices to get to this stage, you are likely going to get increased gratification out of your achievements.

On the other hand, however, you may find yourself in a situation where you have achieved more than you ever dreamed of, but still think it is not enough. The "$1 million isn't what it used to be" syndrome may catch up with you. A healthy respect for the dangers of inflation is good at all times and will keep you on your toes. Do not forget that as you increase your wealth, your standard of living and expenses may also go up. That's well deserved, although you should be prepared to throttle your expenses back down if needed. When times become too good, remember the chapter on crisis investing and start trimming back.

Final Thoughts

It's been my goal in *Sustainable Wealth* to empower you to achieve your financial goals by unleashing the shackles of debt, no matter how uncertain the future may be. You have gained in-depth insights and practical advice. At this stage, you have the tools to predict economic booms and busts before they happen, adapt to changing markets, and plan for lasting financial stability.

You can now make your financial decisions in a global context and see how factors ranging from the Federal Reserve and Congress to trends in Asia and Europe influence your financial well-being. I have coached you on how to recognize major economic trends before they happen, and on how to keep the next crisis out of your financial backyard. Using the plans provided, you should feel more comfortable coping with expenses and saving for retirement while building a legacy of wealth, not a mountain of debt.

And you have learned why "staying the course" when governments or markets change the rules may be hazardous to your wealth.

As others struggle to adapt to the new financial landscape, *Sustainable Wealth* has provided you with answers to the tough financial questions we face, and the tools to achieve a financially sustainable lifestyle.

Don't just put this book aside nodding in agreement. Act and embrace the sustainable wealth lifestyle.

Help spread the word on sustainable wealth. Make your next stop *SustainableWealth.org*.

Someday, you'll be glad you did.

Resources

Following are books and reference materials I've employed in *Sustainable Wealth* and use in my daily work. I strongly recommend these sources to help keep up with economic events and their interpretation by experts:

Books

America's Great Depression (Murray N. Rothbard: 5th ed. Ludwig von Mises Institute, 2000)

Manias, Panics, and Crashes: A History of Financial Crises (Charles P. Kindleberger, Robert Aliber, and Robert Solow: Wiley, 2005)

Fooled by Randomness: The Hidden Role of Chance in Life and in the Markets (Nassim Nicholas Taleb: 2nd ed. Random House, 2008)

Tomorrow's Gold: Asia's Age of Discovery (Marc Faber: CLSA Books, 2008)

When Genius Failed: The Rise and Fall of Long-Term Capital Management (Roger Lowenstein: Random House, 2001)

Print and Online Publications

Asia Times (online)

Barron's

Bloomberg

BreakingViews.com

BusinessWeek

The Christian Science Monitor

MarketWatch

The Economist

Financial Times

Forbes

Free Market News Network

The Globe and Mail

Investment News

The New York Times

San Francisco Chronicle

TheStreet.com

USA Today

The Wall Street Journal

Radio

American Public Media's *Marketplace*

BBC

Bloomberg

FinancialSense.com

KCBS, KNX

The Korelin Economics Report

National Public Radio

RTTNews.com

TV

Bloomberg

CNBC

FoxBusiness

PBS's *Nightly Business Report*

Online News Aggregators

321gold.com

CaseyResearch.com

finance.yahoo.com

FinancialSense.com

Kitco.com

Safehaven.com

USAGold.com

24hGold.com

MarketThoughts.com

merkfund.com/money

ResourceInvestor.com

LeMetropoleCafe.com

RealClearMarkets.com

RealClearPolitics.com

The Gold Report (theaureport.com)

Newsletters

Mary Anne Aden and Pamela Aden's *The Aden Forecast*

Marc Faber's *The Gloom Boom & Doom Report*

Richard Russell's *Dow Theory Letters*

Bill Bonner's *The Daily Reckoning*

Bill Fleckenstein's *Daily Rap*

Lance Lewis's *Daily Market Summary*

Merk Insights

SustainableWealth.org

John Mauldin's *Thoughts from the Frontline*

Terry Savage's *The Savage Truth*

About the Author

Axel Merk is an expert on personal finance. Known to put his money where his mouth is, he not only warned about the credit crisis early, but also showed investors how to seek shelter. He is also a recognized leader on macroeconomic trends, hard money, and international investing.

An authority on currencies, Merk is a pioneer in the use of strategic currency investing to seek diversification. A graduate of Brown University, he is President and Chief Investment Officer of Merk Investments, a Palo Alto, California–based mutual fund management company.

His insights and analyses are sought after by investors large and small, from endowments to advisers to individuals. He appears regularly on CNBC, Fox Business, American Public Radio's *Marketplace* on NPR, and is quoted in *The Wall Street Journal, Barron's, Financial Times*, the Associated Press, and Reuters, among many other domestic and international publications.

Merk is a frequent guest speaker at conferences and publishes *MerkInsights* at www.merkfund.com; several prominent Web sites and YouTube also carry or discuss his views. At SustainableWealth.org, he publishes a personal finance blog.

Merk lives with his wife and four children in the San Francisco Bay area and is a private pilot and marathoner.

Index